Praise for *The Cure*

"I found the different first person perspectives developed during the story to be realistic, fascinating and very insightful. I've seen many pieces of *The Cure* throughout my career, but never so logically and forcefully knit together. The book is rich in valuable lessons for managers. I had many flash-backs to real situations I could have handled better with the insights provided here."

—Cullen Murphy, President, National Medical Systems

"The Cure is real. I've used the principles of Enterprise Medicine to create both rapid change and clear alignment, encompassing strategy, work processes and culture."

—Mike Hoopis, President & CEO, WaterPik, Technologies, Inc.

"Most business readers will recognize the problems treated by *The Cure* as very real. The book is a provocative way to get an organization to think practically about how to approach and drive cultural change. *The Cure* portrays the "whats," the "whys" and, most importantly, the "hows" behind achieving effective alignment of a business around its strategy."

—Jeff Ackerberg, Vice President Sales & Marketing, ACCO

"*The Cure* hits close to home. Enterprise Medicine is common sense, but not commonly applied."

—Walter Scott, Director Strategic Planning, Corporate Express

"Enterprise Medicine is powerful. I've lived it in several businesses. The results are rapid and dramatic, yet the principles are strikingly simple."

—Frank Feraco, President, Pentair Tool Group

"I heartily recommend *The Cure*. After thirty-seven years of competing with General Electric, I'm impressed by the way Dan Paul and Jeff Cox have captured GE's secrets-to-success. Having held senior positions in government, education and industry, I believe the principles and practices of Enterprise Medicine can and should be widely applied."

—Tom Murrin, President of Westinghouse Energy & Advanced Technology (Retired)

"*The Cure* ought be called "the journey to common sense." All you have to do is eliminate the fear, share the power, and shake up the politics. It's simple medicine that is surprisingly effective."

—Charlie Whipple, President, Ames Tools

"I could easily identify with a lot of the situations described. The clash of perspectives on common problems across the different characters resonated as very real and as very important to resolve. *The Cure* offers common sense solutions that are often overlooked in large organizations, and shows how they can be implemented."

—Jim Osgood, Vice President, Product Development,
The Coleman Company, Inc.

"*The Cure* contains invaluable advice for anyone embarked on organizational change. I found the book very informative and instructive. Several of the characters and situations were very familiar, which gave the book a strong sense of authenticity."

—Al Barlow, Director Product Management, Porter Cable

"A captivating novel with a diagnosis no executive pursuing cultural transformation in an organization can do without."

—Harold Pinto, President, E-One

"Thought only GE could succeed in creating a large company reformation? *The Cure* tells us that it is possible for every company, and shows us the model. The characters interact realistically and act pragmatically, and as a result we become invested in how these people tackle their challenges and create real solutions."

—Jack Covert, President, CEO Read

"*The Cure* is a good story and a good lesson for any business executive. As I read the book, I reflected on how we had made many of the same mistakes. I kept wishing I had *The Cure* back then."

—Bill Byham, President & CEO, DDI and co-author of *Zapp*

The Cure
Enterprise Medicine for Business
A Novel for Managers

Dan Paul & Jeff Cox

John Wiley & Sons, Inc.

ISBN 047126830-5

Printed in the United States of America

10 9 8 7 6 5 4 3 2 1

To Integrity

Introduction

I came into the business world nearly forty years ago not with an MBA but with an engineering degree. Having studied electrical and mechanical engineering at Iowa State University, I joined one of the then-great icons of corporate America, Westinghouse Electric. What soon struck me in the early days of my career was the obvious disparity between engineering and management. The practice of engineering was ruled by logic and discipline. The practice of management, on the other hand, was commonly driven by psychological factors that seemingly had little to do with business per se. Many times I observed firsthand that real-world management decisions were based not on common sense and a clear understanding of business realities but instead on factors such as corporate politics, protecting the status quo, CYA, and fear. What a waste.

The years went by, and as a manager both at Westinghouse and at another then-well-known icon, Litton Industries, I began to discern dysfunctional patterns in management culture. Over time, I eventually learned that these patterns were common across all types of businesses and industries. But they were not universal.

A major turning point for me as a manager came when I joined General Electric. Here was a company that truly practiced management with a logic and discipline to a degree equivalent to the engineering profession. This was business the way it should be.

At GE, I worked with a man who is, I think, the greatest corporate leader of the past half century: Jack Welch. This was before Jack became chairman of GE, but even then his exceptional talent and drive were apparent to those who worked with him. Ever since then, Jack Welch has been a strong, positive influence on my approach to management, and I personally believe there is no other single executive in modern times who has had the positive impact on the practice of management than him. Jack reshaped GE's already-strong management practices to be even stronger, faster, more agile. The result: GE became the best performing corporation in the world, and he shared with the world how he did it through the management letters of GE's annual reports.

For better or worse, however, I did not stay with GE. Ambition lured me to another famous corporation, Gulf Oil, but with that move I succeeded in going from one of the world's best-managed companies to what seemed like one of the world's worst. What fascinated me was that the caliber of people at both companies was about the same. Just because a corporation was poorly run did not mean that its individual managers lacked intelligence, or superb education and credentials, or leadership capabilities. Indeed, Gulf was probably on a par with GE in terms of raw managerial talent, yet the management functionality and performance of the two companies were worlds apart.

While at Gulf, I was a speaker at many American Management Association and *Business Week* conferences, where I described the patterns I observed across these four corporations and the lessons I learned from them about effective management. Over seven years I spoke to thousands of people from hundreds of companies. These speaking engagements made my convictions even stronger about the dysfunctional patterns because of the nodding heads in the audience and the resounding agreement during discussion afterwards. Clearly, I was on to something that resonated with a broad spectrum of American businesspeople.

Shortly thereafter I started a consulting firm, GMT, with some very bright and experienced partners and gained experience working with a wide range of clients in many different industries. As I expected, I saw these same management dysfunctions I had observed as a corporate manager were commonplace throughout business everywhere.

From all of this, I began to formulate the set of practices that we now call Enterprise Medicine. Basically, Enterprise Medicine is a disciplined, common sense way to dismantle the dysfunctional behaviors afflicting the vast majority of businesses and replace them with healthy management practices that lead to measurable, real-world performance improvements. When I say "the vast majority of businesses" by the way, I am not exaggerating; companies like General Electric with strong management discipline are unfortunately the exception rather than the rule. Great management doesn't just happen; it is created and it flourishes only when the senior managers of the business make it happen. And this is not easy, because most managers have spent their careers in functional silos and have been promoted because they defended their silos well. No one taught them how to lead an enterprise in a fast changing world; there are no universities that teach Enterprise Medicine.

Enterprise Medicine is similar in many ways to Jack Welch's concept of boundaryless management. In fact, boundarylessness is the end result that Enterprise Medicine achieves. However, we have designed Enterprise Medicine to be effective in all kinds of businesses, especially those that don't have a legacy of strong management like GE.

This book, *The Cure,* is about the journey from normal, everyday—and often dysfunctional—management to a boundaryless management culture using the process of Enterprise Medicine. Jeff Cox and I have written the book as a business novel using fictional companies and managers to show how this journey can be accomplished. Let me assure you, that although the story is fiction, everything in it is drawn from actual experience in well-known companies, as I think you will see when you read it. This is a novel, not a fable; it is detailed and realistic.

The story is told through the voices of many different managers, from the regional field sales manager to the company president to the corporate chairman and CEO. Initially, though, we see the situation through the eyes of Jake Foster, who joined the Essential Corporation as vice president of operations after a prolonged illness. What Jake finds is a company that is superficially on a growth track, and seems to have lots of things going for it, but is in fact in disarray. The company president, Rick Riggins, has a vision—a vision that unfortunately is disconnected from market realities and from the true strengths of the company. The VP of sales and marketing, Vince Springer, can't bring himself to let go of yesterday's successes (which are liable to be tomorrow's failures). The head of engineering has built his own secret fiefdom based on ideals like "technical excellence" at the expense of all else. The operations people are more concerned with looking good than executing well. The very organizational structure of the company is traditional and out-moded. The symptoms go on and on, and if you find yourself recognizing some or all of them, trust me, you're not alone.

The central theme is this: How can the manager who wants change, who wants long-term success for the business, make headway in an organization apathetic to the need for real change? How can you get to boundaryless behavior when the entrenched power structure will not allow any significant departure from the status quo? That is what the book is about, taking the journey—not as an individual but as an entire enterprise—from the existing state of affairs to a new culture that enables ongoing success and improvement. *The Cure* shows how it is done, based on the experience of myself and my partners with dozens of well-known clients. We hope you enjoy it, and that you gain a sense of the possibilities if the power of Enterprise Medicine could be brought to bear in your own company.

Dan Paul
January 2003

Harsh facts are friendly.
Robert H. Waterman, Jr.

Essential Corporation
A Borcon Company
Rick Riggins
President

Jane Grimm
Vice President–Finance

Leo Jacobs
Controller

Gordon Villers
Manager–Information Technology (IT)
Mandy Koslowski
Systems Analyst

Vince Springer
Senior Vice President–
Marketing and Sales

Felice Torrance
Director–National Accounts

Tom Wright
Director–Field Sales Force
Charlie Packer
Regional Manager–Field Sales
Ozzie Brown
Regional Manager–Field Sales
Kathy Ambrose
Regional Manager–Field Sales

Nick Corrigan
Director–National Retail Sales
Don DiPrenza
Regional Sales Manager–Retail
Angeline Ramos
Regional Sales Manager–Retail

Xavier Estaban
Director–International Sales

Linda Wong
Director–Marketing

Adam Bernstein
Marketing Manager
Sandra Moss
Product Manager
Patrick Tyler
Product Manager

Karl Porter
Marketing Manager
Vivian Lebeque
Product Manager
Andy Innis
Product Manager

Pamela Cantrell
Vice President–Human Resources

Kevin Lee
HR Manager–Training and Development

Jake Foster
Senior Vice President–Operations

Frank Harlan
Vice President and Director–Engineering

Sterling Grove
Director–Engineering and Design
Tony Natuzzi
Engineering Manager–Product Design
Hank Urban
Engineering Manager–Process Design
Brenda Pearl
Engineering Manager–Estimates and Pricing

Will Younger
Director–Advanced Systems Engineering

Rahzi Kotsami
Director–Research and Development

Mike Zarelli
Director–Manufacturing
Diane Sullivan
Manufacturing Manager–Logandale Plant
Bill Albrecht
Manufacturing Manager–Kenosha Plant

Heidi Jordan
QC Manager

Larry Oletta
Director–Material Resources
Wendy Orman
Manager–Purchasing
Chris Finnegan
Manager–Distribution
Eric Tillwell
Manager–Production Scheduling

SYMPTOMS

1

Jake Foster
Senior Vice President–Operations

The Louisville Slugger into the face, as far as I'm concerned, was the dinner with Bud Smoot. Bud was CEO and founder of Southeast Supply, a major distributor in our industry and one of the Essential Corporation's larger customers. He sat across the table, stately as a king, with his bright white hair and his diamond-stud cuff links, fingers toying with the tumbler of bourbon over ice on the linen cloth, listening to our grand promises for the future and our sorry excuses for the past.

When we had finished, Bud leaned back and in his glorious Georgian drawl told us, "W-e-l-l . . . that's all fine and good, but the plain fact is that you boys cain't even ship on time. Why should we continue to do business with a company that cain't even get us the product when we need it?"

And Rick Riggins, our fearless leader, our president, who has seldom in my experience been at a loss for words, just sat there and said nothing.

"I mean," said Bud, "I was under the impression that we had these nice little dinners so we all could iron things out and get things done. But they ain't gettin' done. I heard you say six or seven months ago pretty much word for word the same things you just said tonight. And the only thing that's changed, that I can see, is you brought in this handsome, young fella across the table."

He was referring to me, though I was neither handsome nor young. I was relatively new, however. I had been with Essential only a few months, and this was my introduction to Bud. My special introduction.

"Now, here we have you, Rick Riggins, the president; and you, Vince Springer, the vice president of sales—sales *and* marketing, as I recall; and your fine salesman, Charlie Packer, who is one of the dwindling number of positives as to why Essential remains a vendor for Southeast; and *you* . . . I am sorry, I forget your name."

"Jake Foster," I told him.

"Yes, Mr. Foster, who is . . ."

"Senior vice president of operations."

"Well, whatever. And I mean you no disrespect, Mr. Foster. My point, in any case, is that with all this authority here at this table, with all this managerial *talent,* why is it that we cain't get a few problems solved? If y'all cain't make it happen inside your own company, then *who* can?"

From our side, silence.

"Don't all speak at once, but that *was* a question and I *would* like an answer," Bud concluded, raising his bourbon to his lips.

I glanced at Rick to see if he was going to take the point, but he was looking, frowning directly at me. I cleared my throat.

"Bud, let's sort this out. Because I—in fact, all of us—really want to understand your point of view. Let's start with the delayed shipments. Now, we are aware there have been some problems in the past—"

"Some?"

"Well, a few."

"I do not mean to contradict you, Mr. Foster, but I would hardly call it 'a few,'" retorted Bud. He turned to the woman next to him. "Gloria, what was that figure you quoted me the other day?"

Gloria Kass was the sixth person at the dinner. She was Southeast's vice president of purchasing. "Mr. Foster, we've been tracking all of our vendors, and statistics show we receive Essential's shipments late more often than we get them on time."

"All right, perhaps I misspoke," I admitted. "That certainly seems like more than a few. However . . ."

The waiter began serving at that moment and set plates in front of first Gloria, then Bud. I paused, welcoming the interruption to collect my thoughts and to glance at my comrades from Essential. There was Charlie, a heavyset guy, who was looking very nervous. I don't blame him; the Southeast account was serious money, and I'm sure he was worried about that business going away. Next to him was Vince, who was calm, but serious. Vince was your basic clean-cut, square-visaged salesman who had risen from the ranks to his current executive post. At age 57, he was a few years older than I was, and his formerly sandy hair was highlighted with silver.

Then there was Rick Riggins, my boss. Rick was quite fit and tall, and even at 55 had a full head of jet-black hair. Depending on the lighting and his mood, his looks could range between princely handsome and storm-trooper ugly. But right at that particular moment, he was neither; he just seemed shell-shocked. Whenever he looked at me, it was as if he was saying, *you'd better not let me down, Jake.*

So I continued. "As I said, we do acknowledge there have been late shipments in the past, but we are working to improve that. Gloria, you say you've been tracking vendors' performances. Do you happen to recall an approximate percentage of on-time to late deliveries?"

"I can give you exact percentages," said Gloria. "Fifty-two percent of all orders placed with Essential arrive at our facilities after the date promised."

"Hey," cried Charlie, "that means we're almost batting five hundred! Right?"

Charlie just was trying to lighten the mood, bless him, but the cold stares from around the table iced the smile on his face, and he went back to being nervous.

"Furthermore," Gloria went on, "of those orders arriving late, more than forty percent are over a week late. About twelve percent are more than three weeks late."

I had by now taken out my pocket organizer from my suit jacket and was jotting down the metrics as Gloria rattled them off.

"And frankly," she said, "I must tell you I am a bit underwhelmed that you, the supplier, are not tracking these data on your own."

"Um, well, as a matter of fact, we are beefing up those systems now," I said. (Which was stretching it; I had talked to the IT people, but it seemed to be taking forever for them to do anything.) "But let me ask you a few questions. What impact is this really having on your business? Are you consistently out-of-stock on certain units? If that's the case, could it be that the safety stocks are set too low? Or perhaps that the lead times need to be increased?"

Bud began shaking his head. "Let me explain something. I will concede that if we stuffed our warehouses full of inventory, this would be less of a problem. But we're not going to do that. As Vince and Rick may well recall, we at Southeast have had our inventory troubles in the past. We have no intention of going back to those times. Southeast today is a lean company, and we strive to keep our inventory low and our turns very high. Our other vendors have been willing and able to cooperate with us. So why can't Essential? No, we are not going back to the high inventories of the past. We *will not* go backwards for the sake of you or any other supplier."

"Of course not," I said. "I'd never suggest that."

"We feel our inventories are where they should be," said Gloria. "But in any case, you're the one who tells us the dates. We're not dictating to you so much as you're dictating to us. Yet still you can't deliver. And another thing, given that it's practically a coin toss whether the product will show up when we need it, we *do* apply a certain fudge factor. But even then it's a crapshoot as to when it's actually going to show up."

They kind of had us by the you-know-whats. Or, I should say, they had me.

"Well, first of all, I do apologize for the aggravation," I said. "However, let me ask you one more thing: How old are the data that you're working with? Because I know there was a problem in the past, but we honestly have been—I've been—trying to do better. And the last I checked on this, it seemed that things had improved somewhat."

"Well . . . marginally perhaps. But if the problem had been fixed, we wouldn't be talking about it. As a case in point, even as we sit here now, our distribution center is waiting on a shipment of AZ-150s. It was supposed to have reached us two weeks ago. My people have been bugging Charlie, and Charlie has been calling Production . . ."

I felt the slightest tap on my sleeve. Charlie was leaning across the table, timidly handing me some computer-printed order forms.

"This is what she's talking about," he mumbled to me.

"Anyway, your plant supposedly swore up and down that the order would ship yesterday afternoon," said Gloria. "Which means, it should have arrived today. But as of forty-five minutes ago, the whole order was missing in action."

"What? What do you mean, 'missing in action'?"

"You tell him, Charlie."

"Well, see, I called," said Charlie, talking just to me now, his voice barely above a whisper. "I thought this might come up tonight, so all day long I was checking on it. Southeast hadn't received it, though they should have. So I called our people, and it turns out the Logandale plant says the order shipped. But then I tried the trucking company, and the dispatcher said they don't have it."

"How can that be?"

Charlie shrugged.

"This doesn't make a lot of sense."

"I know," said Charlie.

"We have a good bar-code tracking system. If the system says it shipped . . . how could they just lose a million-dollar order?"

"Million and a half," said Vince as he sliced his steak.

Except for Charlie and me, all the others at the table had picked up their forks and were eating. Rick, as a distraction I suppose, was asking Bud about his golf game. But really they were all eyeing me.

"All right." With a sigh, I reached for my cell phone. "Let me talk to the plant."

The waiter had set a gorgeous piece of grilled salmon in front of me, but by this point I had lost my appetite. I started to dial, but decided I preferred to handle this in private. So I waved the phone around, like I was having technical difficulties and couldn't get a signal, and I stood up and left the table. Actually, in addition to privacy to sort this out, I wanted a long, deep breath of fresh air.

Because while I didn't doubt how screwed up things were—I knew they were—I also had the sense that Vince Springer had deliberately set me up. I had felt it coming. You see, I wasn't even supposed to be at that dinner. Rick had asked me to come along just the day before. I was sure that Vince had wrangled him into it.

Vince Springer
Senior Vice President–Marketing and Sales

Did I set up Jake Foster to get slammed at dinner by Bud and Gloria? Well . . . I don't know. Yeah, maybe I did. But at that point, I felt it was in everyone's best interest to do that. To have Jake hear straight from the horse's mouth exactly what the problems were.

Jake had not been with Essential for very long, a few months at the most. He'd been coming to senior management meetings at Essential and spouting off all this stuff about teamwork and communication, using buzzwords like "boundaryless" and all that high-minded stuff. He may have believed in it, I don't know. I'm not saying he wasn't sincere. That's not the issue.

Let me put it this way . . . I've been around a while, and I've been through just about every kind of management flavor-of-the-month. I've seen them come and go. What counts with me is what works. Which, from my perspective, is what sells. If putting on a purple zoot suit and singing "Auld Lang Syne" is what will win sales, then hey, that's what I'll do. And that's what I'll make my salespeople do. Whatever it takes. Whatever works.

On the other hand, don't waste my time—or my salespeople's time—with a lot of malarkey about teamwork and empowerment and quality and service and whatever the buzzword of the moment is. We've got better things to do. That was my attitude. Of course, I usually couldn't *say* that, not directly or very often. But that's how I felt.

So Jake joined the company, and he's spoutin' off about communication. About how important it is to work together and communicate. And I'm thinking, *Okay, Jake . . . you want communication? Let me introduce you to Bud Smoot and Gloria Kass. They've got some things to say that I think you ought to hear.* I didn't do it just to make him look bad . . . although, if that's what happened, so be it. That's not my problem.

There are a couple of things you should know about Bud Smoot. First, that countryboy, Georgian drawl is genuine, it's not an act. And, second, Bud can drop that drawl and speak broadcast-quality American English in a New York heartbeat whenever he so chooses. Which is to say whenever it's to his advantage to do so. He's a smart man—shrewd—and he's tough. He built Southeast into what it is today, the largest distributor in the southeastern United States.

Bud Smoot is . . . well, I do consider him to be a friend. Southeast used to be my account when I was at a level equivalent to Charlie's position, and Bud helped me out many a time. If I was having a bad month and needed to make a quota, he'd take a little extra. And I helped him out many a time as well. At one point, when he was overextended, we were practically financing his inventory of AZ. It was different then. There was loyalty.

Of course, Southeast was proportionally a much larger customer in those days. That was before BigBox and others took over the top spots. But Southeast was still up there. Certainly we were doing enough business to justify gassing up the corporate plane and flying in for a little senior management hobnobbing once or twice a year. At that time there were three or four competitors who were all but tripping over each other trying to get in the door and grab more of their business.

AZ was the best-engineered product line in the business. I don't care what anybody else says. Yes, the others are almost the same, but we're still the gold standard, the Cadillac of the industry. That's what was keeping us on the shelf. Distributors like Southeast almost had to stock AZ. Even so, Gloria was making no secret that she was fed up with us. And it was all operations stuff! That's why I wanted, figuratively speaking, to grab Jake Foster by the scruff of the neck, sit him down, and make sure he listened to the problems that his people were causing.

It was a damn shame what was happening. The relationship between Bud and me, between Southeast and Essential, goes back a long, long way. I've helped him out of jams in the past, and he's helped me. Almost like partners. I'm telling you, our relationship was rock. Yet, given enough pressure, enough abuse, any rock can crack.

Rick Riggins
President

Our paradigm was total customer satisfaction. That was my mandate to the entire Essential Corporation organization. I wanted everyone to put 110 percent into satisfying every customer every day. Furthermore, I know I tried to impress upon people the importance of that goal in many of the meetings with staff, as well as in e-mails and other communications.

So, naturally, it was . . . disappointing to learn from one of our better customers that we apparently had missed the goal by a fairly wide margin. Even more disturbing was the sense I got that nobody on our side seemed to have a good grasp of the issues. I say this with some tongue in cheek, but really, one might have hoped that someone on our side would have made an attempt to smooth things over before the president of the company showed up. How am I supposed to build the relationship if I walk in and find the customer mad as a hornet?

During that dinner with Smoot, I did wonder several times why I was there. Vince Springer had insisted that my presence was absolutely necessary. We had always done these dinners with major customers from time to time, and the company president, even before my tenure, was always present, as were other senior managers on many occasions. That's just the way the Essential Corporation did things. It showed customers like Bud Smoot that he was Number One, our top priority. For me not to attend would send the wrong signal, according to Vince.

Yet, in retrospect, it's worth asking the question: *Was* Southeast Supply really our top priority? Ten years before this the answer would have been an emphatic, "Yes!" Customers like Southeast Supply were Essential's bread and butter. Now, though, the answer was not so simple. In the past few years, we had grown as a company in some exciting new directions. We had picked up BigBox, the fastest growing retailer in North America and a totally new channel for us. Just over the horizon was a tremendous new technology that we were developing, something that I was sure was going to revolutionize the industry. And, to be honest, something I was not sure somebody like Bud Smoot could appreciate.

The truth was, we could lose several Bud Smoots before we would come close to the impact of losing just one region of BigBox. Everything had changed, and was continuing to change. Yet here we were, having dinner at Vince Springer's insistence, as if Bud Smoot was still our king, just like ten years ago. Did we want Bud to be happy? Of course we did. I didn't want to lose Southeast. I didn't want to lose any customer. I really did want them all to be totally satisfied.

So, what am I saying? I'm saying that it was not simple. And I do not think that any of us at the table that night really knew how *un*simple it was beneath the surface.

Jake Foster
Senior Vice President–Operations

By the time I got back to the table, about twenty minutes later, they were having a heated discussion about something completely different. Almost unnoticed, I sat down again. Bud Smoot was talking evenly, yet angrily, rapping the tablecloth with his fingertips to underscore the keywords of his complaint.

"You want a for-instance? I'll give you one. When I got customers calling me to say that they can walk into their local BigBox and buy AZ-

130s at retail for less than I can sell it wholesale . . . well, folks, there is something wrong, and I, as a distributor, tend to get more than just a little bit upset about that."

"Now, now, Bud," Vince said in a soothing tone, "I happen to know exactly what you're talking about, and you know as well as I do that the AZ-130 is not aimed at the professional installer. The 130 is intended for the retail do-it-yourselfer. It's only when you get up to the 150 that you reach the bottom rung of what we consider to be the professional grade."

"That may be what you intended," said Bud, "but there are a great many contractors who do order the 130."

"Well, in any event," Vince continued, "you also have to realize that was a special promotion—"

"Special to whom?" asked Bud. "Special to BigBox, not to us."

"No, of course not! It was available to anyone—"

"Anyone who ordered a hundred thousand units," said Gloria. "Which means BigBox."

I had just picked up my knife and fork (everyone else had about finished the main course) and was about to cut into my cold salmon when Rick, probably desperate to change the subject, asked me, "So what's the status of their 150 order?"

I had been hoping they would just keep on arguing and forget about the lost AZ-150s because what I had found out on the phone was not news they would easily swallow.

"Well, ah . . . there *has* been a problem," I said, quickly adding, "But it's being taken care of, even as we speak."

Attention had shifted to me. Bud had this half-annoyed, half-bemused expression like, *Hey, this oughta be a good one.* And Gloria was glancing from me to Rick and Vince with a look that said, *You see? You see what we have to put up with?*

"It seems that as they were finishing the order, they discovered a defect on a production lot that was part of your shipment. So they've been working to replace the defective part—a wiring harness, I believe—and once they're finished, your shipment will be on its way to you. In fact, the person I talked to at the plant assured me they should have the trucks reloaded by the end of second shift."

"Reloaded?" asked Charlie. "Aw, no! You mean to say, they had everything packaged and ready to go, and then they discovered this?"

"My understanding is that they were just about ready to close the doors on the trucks when one of the hourly people brought it to everyone's attention that the wire connections were coming loose. Of course, that meant they're having to unload the trucks, unpack the cartons, disassemble the unit, replace the part, and then put everything back together again."

"Well, at least they caught the problem before it left the plant," said Charlie. "We would never, *ever* want Southeast or any of its customers to receive anything less than a quality product under *any* circumstances."

If he'd been a slightly better actor, I'd have bought him a dozen roses. As he delivered the line, however, his tone was . . . well, just enough motherhood-and-apple-pie to make you gag. Even so, I appreciated the effort because I certainly wasn't getting much help from anybody else. Rick was just sitting there like a statue, eyes glazed, lips slightly parted. And Vince seemed curiously aloof.

"In any case," I said, "once everything is loaded again, if the truckers can drive straight through, you should still be able to have your order by tomorrow."

"We have your word on that?" asked Bud.

I hesitated.

"Jake will stay on top of it," said Vince. "Won't you, Jake?"

"You bet I will."

"Fine, but I do hope you understand that the problems are not confined to this particular shipment," said Gloria.

"Oh, now please, Gloria," said Bud, "the man hasn't even had his dinner yet!"

To which I said graciously, "No, that's okay. If there are other things we need to talk about, let's discuss them."

Gloria was more than ready to proceed. For the next ten minutes, she chewed my ear about certain modules for our high-end AZ-300 series being perpetually hard to come by, about hassles on some returns, about this, about that. And when she was finally done, Bud jumped in.

"Now," said Bud, "there's something else I want to know . . ."

I was ready to scream.

". . . and it's perhaps more important than anything else. It concerns the future."

"By all means," I said, "let's talk."

"Are you people planning to bring to market any Z3 offerings—and if so, when?"

"Let me field that one," said Rick. "The short answer is . . . maybe."

"Maybe? What do you mean, *maybe*? I asked if you were planning any Z3 offerings. The question would seem to indicate an answer of yes or no."

"Let me give you the long answer," said Rick. "First, we believe that next-generation SOS technology will render all Z-standard products obsolete within the next few years."

"What makes you believe that?"

"Simple logic," said Rick. "Our engineering staff at Essential has concluded that SOS is so clearly superior that there will be no reason for Z products to exist once SOS debuts. SOS does everything better than Z, hands down."

"You think Z is just going to evaporate overnight? Even with those millions of installed units out there still functioning?"

"No, not overnight, but it will happen. Z will go the way of the rotary-dial telephone and the manual transmission. It's just a matter of time. However, having said that, if it appears that the market is slow to accept SOS—and we all know there will likely be some glitches here and there, because no transition of this magnitude is ever smooth—we do have Z3 designs in the planning stages, just in case. And if need be, we can put these on a fast track and launch them in the marketplace sometime . . . well, sometime next year. But as for now, our entire organizational push is behind SOS. Z3 is strictly stop-gap. Two years from now there will be no need for Z3."

Bud nodded slowly and shook the ice in his empty glass and turned to Gloria.

"Reliable is already doing the advance marketing for the first of their Z3 line," she said. "You are aware of that, I assume? My understanding is that Spectrum will introduce their Z3 designs within the next six months, but you're telling me that Essential might have its Z3 out 'sometime next year'?"

"Actually, we're not planning to have any Z3," said Rick.

"*That* addresses my question," said Bud. "Thank you."

"But we will fast-track Z3, if necessary," Rick emphasized.

"Kind of like your AZ-150 shipments," Bud said with a grin.

Rick let it slide past. "I frankly don't understand the interest in Z3. I'll grant you that Z3 is an improvement over Z1, Z2, and Z2-Plus. However, who in their right mind would want Z3 when they can have SOS? It's like choosing radio over television!"

"Oh, yes, I understand that argument," said Bud. "Trust me, we've heard all the praises sung about SOS. I won't argue. There is no doubt that SOS is the future—well, actually there is *some* doubt over whether SOS will be all it's promised to be—and a few doubt whether it will even work in a broadbase setting at all. But here's the thing: Z3 is *today.* Not the future, but *today.* And customers want it *today.* That's not fancy engineering talk, that's not research, that's *reality.*"

At this, Vince and Chuck were looking for a reaction on Rick's face, but Rick's expression gave little away.

"The trouble," said Rick, "is that most customers do not yet comprehend the advantages of SOS, but when we roll out SOS in another few months, they will. We're betting the farm on SOS. It's a strategic decision that we made some time ago."

"Okay," said Bud, "y'all made your bet. Maybe it'll turn out to be the right call. But what I know is that if you had Z3 products available right now, I could promise you as much as twenty to thirty million dollars in orders over the coming year—over and above current levels—because Z3 is what the customers want. Maybe all that will change once SOS rolls out, but I think it's going to take quite a while, to be honest with you. For every customer who might switch to SOS, I see four or five who want Z3."

Rick Riggins sat there trying to be poker-faced, but was succeeding mainly in looking like he'd just been clubbed by a poker. The waiter happened by just then.

"Excuse me," said Bud, "would you please bring me some coffee? And for that gentleman over there"—he meant me—"would you take his plate back to the kitchen and warm it up for him?"

"No, that's not necessary, thanks anyway," I said.

"I am sorry," said Bud. "We should have had them take it back to the kitchen to keep it warm for you while you were gone. Waiter, bring him a menu so he can see if he might like something else."

"No, no, I'm fine!" I said.

"Are you sure? You've hardly eaten a bite," said Bud.

"He's fine," said Rick, answering for me.

"He had a late lunch," added Vince. "Right, Jake?"

"Right," I said. "I'm not that hungry anyway."

Actually, I was starving, but I wanted nothing to interfere with the swiftest possible end to that dinner. In fact, getting the hell out of there seemed to be the only common goal held by the three Essential senior managers who were present.

2

Charlie Packer
Regional Manager–Field Sales

Everybody was honked off after that dinner. Including me. *Especially* me. Because I was the one who was going to suffer the most. It's like, *what are you guys thinking about?* You just took one of my best customers, one of my bread-and-butter accounts, and you made 'em hostile! Why did you even come here? Like, next time, don't do me any favors, okay? Just stay in Grandville, back at headquarters, and do whatever happy stuff you do back there, and leave me alone. But I didn't dare open my mouth. I had to ride with them back to the airport, and I knew better than to vent.

We got into the limousine outside the restaurant. Vince had told me to hire a limo since Mr. Riggins was going to be there. So I did, though I don't think Mr. Riggins would have objected if he'd had to ride in my Lincoln. Anyway, after that dinner, we crawled into the limo like a pack of beaten dogs.

You ride in a limo, it's supposed to feel like, you know, *success*. But that night it just felt like we were cheating somebody. The four of us from Essential got in—Bud and Gloria had arrived in their own cars—and except for instructions to the driver, it was quiet for a minute or so.

Then Mr. Riggins said, "Well, that was embarrassing."

Again, nobody said anything for a few seconds.

Then Jake Foster said, "Yeah, I'd say we were batting a thousand. First we can't service them the way they'd like to be serviced. Next we're undercutting them on price through another customer that, right or wrong, they seem to see as a competitor. And finally we tell them we're not going to have the next big product that they very much want to buy."

Jake said all that calmly, almost like it was kind of funny. Then he looked right at Vince. His finger shot out, pointing at him, and you could tell Jake was mad as hell. He said to Vince, "And *you* were no help whatsoever."

"What's that supposed to mean?" Vince asked.

Jake goes, "The next time you set up one of these let's-meet-the-customer dinners, I would appreciate it if you would brief me on all the issues in advance."

"I told you in advance that they might say something about the late shipments."

"You said it was a concern. You didn't say they were going to be spitting mad. Or was that news to you, too?"

Vince raised his voice and said, "Jake, I have been trying to get the message to you I don't know how many different ways and I don't know how many different times. And if you haven't heard it, then you haven't been listening. I mean, how am I supposed to get my salespeople to go out there and sell more when there are so many problems in operations?"

They were both ready to go at it. I don't mean a fistfight—although anything was possible—but they were furious with each other.

Mr. Riggins broke it up. "All right, all right," he said, "We'll deal with this when we get back to Grandville."

I guess he didn't want them fighting in front of me. So it was like, "Hush up now. You boys go sit in different corners." And it got silent again.

Finally, Mr. Riggins asked us, "Anybody want something to drink?" He was just trying to make peace. He opened the little refrigerator in the limo and inside was beer and soft drinks and ice and a couple bottles of booze and all. "Come on, everybody relax."

Then he poured himself a scotch or something. And Vince had something, and I took a beer just to keep them company. But Jake said he didn't want to drink on an empty stomach. Which actually lightened the mood a little bit. Vince cracked a smile, and Mr. Riggins even laughed.

So we're settled back, drinkin' our drinks. Then all of a sudden Mr. Riggins gets this gleam in his eye. He points out the window and says, "Look! A BigBox!"

And sure enough, we're passing a shopping center—we're getting close to the airport by now—and there's a BigBox store. A new one. Huge.

Mr. Riggins calls up to the driver, "Hey, buddy, turn in here. Take us over to that BigBox."

And I'm thinking, *Aw, come on!* This has got nothing to do with me. I'm in field sales. There's a whole separate part of the organization that services BigBox. I don't *care* about BigBox. I care about Bud and Gloria. Bud and Gloria and those kinds of customers are the ones who pay my mortgage, and when it comes to the company offering BigBox a better price, I'm just as pissed off as Bud because that's business taken out of my pocket. But Mr. Riggins is all excited. He's going, "I want to see if they have the new endcap display."

Endcaps. That's retail. You know, at the end of the aisles, they'll have those promotional displays? Those are endcaps. Apparently it's some kind of big deal for them, but it doesn't concern me. All I want to do is drop them at the airport, turn in the limo, get in my car, and drive eighty miles so I can kiss my wife good night, get a few hours of sleep, and maybe be rested enough to come up with some stroke of genius in the morning that will let me save my Southeast account.

Uh-huh. Right. Mission impossible.

Anyway, the limo pulls up in front of the store. We leave our drinks and get out. Everybody's looking at us like we're movie stars. Like, *hey, we always have a limo to take us to the BigBox!*

Mr. Riggins leads us through the store. Straight to Aisle 7. Every Big-Box in the whole country is laid out pretty much the same way, and Essential's products are always in Aisle 7. Sure enough, between Aisles 7 and 8, there in all its glory is the new Essential endcap.

Mr. Riggins is clearly pleased. He stands there in front of it, hand on his chin, studying it. To his credit, Mr. Riggins has the physique of a statue. Tall. Full head of hair. Kind of a craggy, strong face. He *looks* like a leader. Next to him stood Vince, who is shorter, but also wiry thin. Vince's got salt-and-pepper hair and is somewhat younger looking than Mr. Riggins, but also looks experienced. Anyway, the two of them stood next to each other, like a general and a major. Like they were studying an important battle being fought before them. The Battle of the Endcaps.

Then there's Jake. He's between the two of them, but a step behind both. He's taller than Vince, but shorter than Mr. Riggins. A little pudgier than both. Short brown hair that's gray at the temples. And he's listening. You can tell he's interested, but he's not saying anything. Just standing there, hands in his pockets, observing. You could almost see the wheels turning inside his head.

Well, I'm there—Mr. Beer-and-Pretzels Salesguy—off to one side, trying to appear interested when all I really want is to get on home. Jake glanced in my direction and noticed me, and he took a step over to where I stood.

"I guess we weren't much help to you tonight," Jake said.

"No," I said, "but I'll smooth things out."

"You really think you can?"

"Oh, yeah," I said—confidently, but hoping it was true. "They've been with us a long time. Anyway, as long as there's demand for AZ, they have to stock us to some extent. They may throw their preference to Reliable or one of the others, but they can't dump us entirely."

"Until the switch to Z3," said Jake.

"Well . . . ," I lowered my voice. "Yeah, that could be a bit of a problem, if a year or so from now we don't have some kind of Z3 to sell them."

"But we will have SOS by then."

"Yeah, but Bud says his customers want Z3. Who am I to argue?"

"True."

"Look, no offense, Mr. Foster, but to be honest, I don't give a rat's ass whether it's Z3 or SOS. I just want a product that everybody else in the world wants to buy. That's it. Headquarters has decided it's going to be SOS. Who am I to argue with Grandville? But that is not what I am hearing when I call on customers."

Jake nodded and thought that over a moment; then he changed the subject somewhat. "Is Southeast your biggest account?"

"Definitely one of the bigger ones," I told him. "They're one of the ones I can't afford to lose."

"Are there any you *can* afford to lose?" he asked me.

"Well, let me put it this way," I said. "I'd sure like to have 'em all, but I cover a big area. I have to let some slide. I don't want to, but I have to. By the time I deal with . . . well, you know, the reports, the e-mail, the telephone tag, the problem-solving, the service issues—"

"Service issues?" he asked. "How come you're dealing with that stuff? We've got a whole service and support function."

"Yeah, but you can't tell that to the customer," I explained. "As the salesman, I'm their point of reference, their contact. This is very much a relationship business, in terms of sales. There is a lot of trust built up, and when there's a problem, who's the customer going to trust to get it right? Some service drone they don't know from Adam . . . or me, Charlie Packer, the guy they know, the guy they deal with all the time?"

Jake just looked at me.

"Anyway," I said, "whether they're supposed to or not, that's what happens. By the time I get everything sorted out, relay it and translate it to everybody else, and then do the data changes and the paperwork, and all that, well, it's a lot of time. It can eat up a couple of hours. So I have no choice. To make my quota, I have to focus on the big, solid accounts. There's Southeast, plus a couple of smaller distributors. I've got some OEMs that buy components from us, and I usually write pretty good orders with them every month. And then I've got the larger contractor-installers in my territory. That's the bulk of my business month in, month out. But the second-tier companies, the specialty retailers, the smaller contractors, I just can't get to very many of them. Of course, if Southeast goes away, I'll have more time. But even if I could pick up three or four smaller accounts, together they wouldn't make up for a Southeast-size customer."

Jake just took all this in. He seemed to want me to talk, so I took a chance and said, "You folks back in Grandville, you've *got* to get your act together. All this about the late shipments, the quality issues, the out-of-stocks, and all the rest, you've got to clean that up. It's killing us out here."

I half expected him to get defensive and give me some kind of bull-shit or maybe even take offense. You never know with the big muckety-mucks. In my experience, a lot of them just don't want to hear it.

But Jake put his hand on my arm and said, "I'm with you. I'm a hundred percent in agreement. I'm going to stop at the plant tonight to find out what's going on. I'll get to the bottom of it, believe me. In the morning I'll give you a call, or I'll have someone give you a call with the straight answer. Whatever the issues are, we'll keep after them until they're all resolved. It's going to get better, not worse."

Nice words, but after so many years with Essential, I'd learned not to get too excited about those kinds of promises. But I did appreciate that he was taking the case.

While we were talking, Vince and Mr. Riggins had gone up Aisle 7.

They were examining what was on our competitors' shelf space, then examining what was on ours, whispering to each other. And scaring away customers. The few people in the aisle, as soon as they noticed these two suits approaching, quit their browsing and scattered.

"Let me ask you one more thing," Jake said. "What exactly are your customers saying about SOS? Do you have any sense of what they think about it?"

"Well," I told him, "they're not saying very much. But as for what they *are* saying . . . it depends on the customer. The distributor is waiting to see whether the market adopts it or not. You heard tonight from Southeast; short-term, they're a lot more interested in Z3. The OEMs are mildly positive. But I honestly don't know if they'll rewrite their specs to accommodate SOS or not. As for the contractor-installers . . . well, frankly, most of them seem kind of confused by it all. It's like, hey, the Z products work, we understand them, we know how to install them. Why do you want us to switch to something different?"

Jake was taking this in, but he had this depressed look on his face. Just then I felt a breeze behind me. Mr. Riggins had just passed with Vince striding right behind, trying to keep up. They were done. Mr. Riggins was leading on. He always walks very fast.

We were at the airport a few minutes later, and the company plane was waiting to fly them home. I got out, said good-bye, and watched the three of them walk to the plane. Then I breathed a sigh of relief that the officers were gone and I was back to being a plain old soldier. A one-man army.

With the limo all to myself, I pretended I was some kind of big-deal VIP . . . for about half a mile. The limousine company's office is just down the road from the airport. That's where I'd left my car. I signed the papers, tipped the driver, and took off.

Most of the way home I thought about BigBox. Essential had not had the BigBox business for very long. A few years at the most. I don't mean to make it sound as if everything was paradise before BigBox, but it sure seems to me that something changed after we got our products on the shelf there. It seems like the company became less concerned about customers like Southeast and more concerned about endcaps. Maybe that's incorrect, but that's how it seemed to me. And as the guy who lives or dies over Southeast and other customers like them . . . well, I was worried.

Jake Foster
Senior Vice President–Operations

The company plane was a prop-driven, twin-engine Cheyenne IIIA. Nothing fancy. Seating for six—four seats facing forward, with two seats behind the cockpit facing aft. The seats were the best thing about the plane, as far as I was concerned. They were covered in well-worn, gray leather, and they were very comfortable. I could fall asleep in one of those seats in the blink of an eye. On the way home to Grandville from the Southeast Supply dinner, I slipped into the back row and did just that.

Rick Riggins and Vince Springer sat forward of me, diagonally across from each other with Vince in the aft-facing seat. I was asleep before the plane left the ground, but midway through the flight, we hit turbulence. I was jolted awake, then shut my eyes once more, hoping to drift off again.

Rick and Vince were talking. At first I couldn't hear everything being said, but then Rick raised his voice.

"We have *got* to bring SOS to market," he told Vince. "Do I make myself clear?"

"Rick, there might be a slight delay, but believe me, we're going to be a lot better off in the long run if we take the time to get it right. In the meantime, we've still got the AZ line."

"I don't care about the AZ line!" Rick exploded.

Pause. I couldn't see Vince, but I could imagine his face.

Then Rick resumed, calmer now. "I'm sorry. Let me rephrase that. I *do* care about the AZ line, but with every passing month, it's less important to this company's future than SOS. We have to be out there with SOS. We have to get to market with SOS and establish a front-runner position."

"Yes, but what about Z3?" Vince asked.

Another momentary silence. Then, "I don't know. I don't know if Z3 is even a realistic possibility at this point. But whether we can or cannot do anything with Z3, we have to recognize that AZ is soon going to be history."

"Oh, I don't know about that, Rick. In fact, I respectfully have to disagree with you on that. I really wouldn't rule out AZ just yet. In fact, I'd say that AZ has many years to go before obsolescence. Don't forget, AZ still accounts for a huge portion of total sales revenue, and it's still making money for us."

"But those sales are going to decline, Vince. We know that. AZ is, for all practical purposes, a commodity. It's a *has-been*."

"I wouldn't go that far, Rick. I really wouldn't. We still need AZ."

"Yes, we need it, but we also need to build our position in SOS. Or Z3. One or both. We need new product out there."

"Okay, Rick, but I'm just saying don't rule out AZ."

"I am *not* ruling out AZ."

"Good. Because we could be doing much better if . . .," Vince lowered his voice, and even with my eyes shut, I could sort of feel him lean toward Rick. I knew he was talking about Operations and about me.

"All right, all right," said Rick. "He's doing the best he can. You've made your point. And getting back on the subject, I'd like to know if we can possibly launch SOS in time for Expo."

"In time for *Expo*? Rick, you can't be serious."

"Why shouldn't I be serious? Your marketing people have had more than enough time to get this done. *Why are you not ready?*"

"Because Engineering was late, Rick! We've talked about this before. They kept changing the darn thing—and they're still doing it! I mean, how are we supposed to establish price points, feature-and-option packages, and all the rest when they keep changing the functionality! One week they tell us it'll do this and that, and the next week they tell us it won't! If they would just *freeze* the design!"

In a tone of nearly exhausted patience, Rick said, "From what I am told, Vince, Engineering is making and will continue to make a number of small improvements and fixes as they are deemed necessary. That does not mean we can't launch the product line."

"Rick, we are making progress, but I just don't see how you can expect us to pull everything together in time for Expo."

"I WANT IT FOR EXPO!" Rick exploded. "MAKE IT HAPPEN!"

My eyelids were squeezed tightly shut. I went on pretending to sleep, but there in the darkness inside my own skull, my mind was awake and asking what I had gotten myself into.

Vince Springer
Senior Vice President–Marketing and Sales

When Rick went into one of his rages, you couldn't win. You just had to shut up and stand clear, maybe try to talk to him again in a day or two and hope that he'd be able to see reason by then. Rick had his upside. His energy. His vision. But he also had his downside. He was the kind of leader who made up his mind, and once he did that there was no going back. If he said, "We're going to take that hill," then come hell or high water, you were going to take the hill. Now, when the hill *can* in fact be taken, that's the right attitude. I'll give him that. But what if the hill *can't* be taken? Or what if taking the hill is a really *bad* idea?

I sat there on that plane ride back to Grandville thinking, *How are we ever going to do this? And even if we somehow do, what are the consequences going to be? What will the final cost add up to?*

But Rick had made up his mind, and we were going to have an SOS launch in time for Expo. I would go to my marketing people in the morning and see where things stood, and then I'd pull out my sword and try to get them to charge. What else could I do?

I'll tell you, though, there were times when I just flat-out hated the guy.

Rick Riggins
President

I think I was as frustrated as I'd ever been in my entire life. Nobody knew the pressure I was under.

Essential was a wholly owned subsidiary of Borcon International. It had been an independent company for many, many years, but about eight years or so prior to this point, the board of directors had accepted an offer to be acquired by Borcon. In an operational sense, we still do function independently, as there is very little overlap between us and Borcon's other businesses. Naturally, though, like any other Borcon business unit, we were expected to provide a satisfactory return on the investment Borcon had made in us.

This was, so to speak, my second tour of duty with Essential. I'm an engineer by education, but early in my career I opted for a job in sales.

Later, I also picked up an MBA and moved into management. My first stint with Essential was during the 1980s, when it was still an independent company and experiencing a high rate of growth. I was vice president of marketing during that period.

Just before Borcon completed the acquisition, I left—voluntarily—for a position at a different company, which, by the way, is where I first worked with Jake Foster. I left Essential because . . . well, because frankly I've always had my eye on becoming a company president. I knew that Borcon wasn't going to offer me that position because they intended to bring in their own team. So it seemed like the wisest thing at the time to seek out other opportunities.

Things didn't work out as planned—either for me or for Borcon. The corporation I joined had some fundamental problems, the depths of which were not apparent until I became general manager of a division there. As for the team that Borcon put in to run Essential . . . let's just say their performance did not set the world on fire.

After three or four years had gone by, I heard that Borcon was looking for a new president for Essential. I suppose my early years in sales served me well, because I managed to convince Brandon Claymore that I was the man for the job.

I came back to Essential full of enthusiasm and energy, and I am proud of what I was able to accomplish. Still, if I may be totally candid . . . I cannot say that we met my own expectations. Initially, Essential was more than able to satisfy Borcon's targets for growth. Then, quite honestly, it began to get hard. The economy certainly hadn't helped. Yet neither Borcon nor myself accepted that as an excuse. We were struggling, and clearly, the struggle was only going to get more difficult as the market made its choice between Z-standard products and SOS.

Jake Foster, in my opinion, was a good manager with a first-rate understanding of operations. He'd had some health problems and had been out of the job market for a few years, but I really thought I could count on him. No, I wouldn't say that Jake had been a disappointment, but I'd thought he would hit the ground running—or running faster than what was proving to be the case. Maybe it's unfair, but I thought that by hiring him our operational issues would be taken care of. Obviously, that was proving to be a naive assumption. Was my faith in Jake misplaced? Was the challenge greater than his energy and experience could deal with? I was not sure.

Vince Springer? He had been a terrific sales manager. After I came in, we had also combined marketing under his wing. I grant you that marketing was not Vince's best strength, but he did have some strong people reporting to him. I thought the combination would work. Yet, things weren't coming together.

It was not lost on me that Vince had his doubts about SOS. I had made the decision that SOS was the way we were going to go. Vince, however, had not yet fallen into line. Yes, he was going along, but it was clear he was not behind this in spirit. You have no idea how . . . *aggravating* that can be. Or perhaps you do.

A person like Vince Springer was not easily replaced. He knew all the big customers and had good personal relationships with many, like Bud Smoot. There were only a handful of people in the industry who could match him in that respect, and they were all employed by competitors. Now, let me make myself clear, I did not want to replace Vince, but if it did become necessary, he had the potential to be a two-edged sword.

That said, no company president can abide a senior manager who does not fully support his decisions. Don't you agree? Vince was . . . well, I couldn't say what he was doing. Was he trying to sabotage SOS? That thought actually did cross my mind, though I dismissed it. He just was not moving forward with the entrepreneurial vigor that I thought SOS would inspire. Month after month had gone by, yet his marketing and sales people did not seem to possess the sense of urgency for bringing SOS to market quickly. At the same time, I couldn't rule out that Engineering—which was under Jake Foster's wing—wasn't part of the problem. Frank Harlan, who headed Engineering, was a perfectionist, and he had a tendency to hoard control over development until he was absolutely certain that every little detail was the way Frank thought it should be. Trouble was, we had reached the point at which timing was critical. We had to get SOS out there, I felt, before the market embraced Z3.

To top it off, Borcon Corporate was breathing down my neck. Borcon was not having a good year, and the pressure was on. Nancy Quinn, to whom I reported, was grilling me every time we talked. Why were AZ sales so sluggish? Why wasn't I cutting costs more aggressively? What were we doing to get ourselves back on a growth track? And it was because Brandon Claymore was breathing down her neck.

And then there was BigBox, by far our largest customer—and they acted like it, too. BigBox had turned out to be a whole new set of headaches. Seemed like every week there was some new demand they were insisting upon. Yet, here we were, chasing our own tails trying to find a late order for Bud Smoot.

I mean, can you imagine how I felt? Is it any wonder that I lost my temper once or twice? Everybody always thinks how great it must be to be the company president, to fly around in a company plane, take customers out to fancy dinners, to be in charge, to have all this power. . . .

They have no idea!

Vince Springer
Senior Vice President–Marketing and Sales

When he came in as company president, Rick brought a couple of undeniable qualities to the party. Energy was one of them. It quickly became almost a joke around here that you'd better not get in Rick's way. One morning, Rick was late for a meeting, and he was coming down the hall, talking over his shoulder to Frank Harlan, who was following him to the meeting. Rick was midsentence in what he was saying to Frank, not looking where he was going, and *bam*—he ran into two people and knocked them *both* to the floor. Nobody was hurt; Rick helped them up, apologized, and went on to the meeting, still talking over his shoulder to Frank. But the story got around and the moral was: If you see Rick coming, look out!

That little story actually said a lot about Rick. Either follow him and keep up or get out of the way. Or else he'd knock you down like a bowling ball hitting pins. That sounds great. That sounds *macho*. Kind of like what a lot of people think a leader should be. Trouble was, Rick wasn't always paying attention to where he was headed. Everybody said he was a visionary, but half the time he was looking over his shoulder. And I do think that a lot of people became worried about staying out of his way and not getting knocked to the floor.

On the other hand, nobody can deny that Rick was one of the first to spot the potential of what became the Z-standard, back when he was running Marketing. The Z technology was the basis for our AZ line, which became for many years the company's largest revenue stream and greatest source of profit. You know, there was Z, then Z1, then Z1-Plus, and then a complete second generation called Z2, as well as a whole set of specialized variants, like Z2/H, which was what the retail version was based on. Let me tell you, this company—as well as yours truly, back when I was a salesman on commission—made a lot of money with the Z-series.

You also have to credit Rick for BigBox. That was Rick's baby from the start. Actually, from what I've heard, that was one of the reasons Rick was able to persuade Borcon Corporate to put him in as president. When he interviewed with Corporate, he convinced them that he could deliver BigBox and then proceeded to follow through on that promise.

As a company, we had to make a lot of changes and a lot of sacrifices in order to secure the BigBox account. It would not have happened without Rick's full support and, much of the time, his personal involvement, but when we finally did bring in BigBox as a customer, it was a huge jump in sales. Not just a ramp up; it was a jump. And even better, as BigBox expanded in years to come (which it would, although the days of huge growth were behind it) so, in theory, would our sales. Rick was an instant hero not just internally, here at Essential, but also at Borcon— and specifically in the eyes of Brandon Claymore.

After winning BigBox, Rick was invited down to Claymore's ranch for the weekend, and they even sent the Gulfstream to pick him up. You have probably seen Brandon Claymore's picture. It's been on the cover of any number of magazines, from *Fortune* to *People*. A Texas billionaire who dresses like a cowboy for nearly every occasion. There are all kinds of stories about him and how hard-ass tough he is, like the one about the bull-whip he keeps in his office and how every few months he goes through Borcon headquarters literally cracking the whip. As a joke, you know— though not really. But he can be a real charmer, too. I've met him, and he can win you over real quick.

Anyway, Claymore's got this cattle ranch in the middle of Texas. Don't know how many acres it is, but it's big. Got its own airstrip and a lake where Claymore keeps a fleet of speedboats. If Claymore likes you or wants to get to know you, he'll invite you down to the ranch for the weekend so you can watch him rope a steer. Really, the guy's in his sixties, but he does all that cowboy stuff.

After Rick was invited to the ranch, I am sure he thought the sky was the limit in terms of his career. Then came disappointment. BigBox gave us this enormous jump in sales revenue, but as the quarters went by, we kept wondering, *Where is the corresponding jump in profit?* It just didn't materialize. Yes, we did anticipate some margin erosion. We were giving them special pricing and other terms, and we had to add a considerable amount of staffing to service an account that huge. In fact, we had to add a whole sales and service organization dedicated solely to BigBox. Of course, we expected to make it back on volume. Don't misunderstand, we were making a profit on sales to BigBox. It's just that the gains to the bottom line were much smaller than we expected, and it was the result of all the hidden costs that we didn't factor into the equation—costs that kept rising due to our commitment to customer satisfaction.

The scary part was, now that we had the BigBox account, we couldn't walk away from it. Within a year after securing the BigBox account, Spectrum and Reliable were also in the stores with us. If we ever came to a parting of the ways with BigBox, we would lose market share . . . big time. The vacuum left by our departure wouldn't last a month. We could not allow that to happen. So we were hooked. Even if we weren't making the money we thought we would make, we had to keep going.

Within a few years after bringing in BigBox, the realities had begun to sink in. Rick was no longer smiling. He had based his plan for the company's growth in large part on those phantom profits from BigBox.

I'll never forget the afternoon when I needed to ask Rick a question about something. He was behind closed doors with Jane Grimm, our VP of finance. The question just needed a quick answer and the issue was kind of urgent, so I just rapped lightly on the door and poked my head in—not usually a problem with Rick—and said, "Excuse me, but do you have a second?"

Rick's hands were covering his face. He was sitting there, elbows on the table, rubbing his forehead with the tips of his fingers, and when he dropped his hands to look at me, his face was like a ghost. Completely drained. Jane sat next to him, and her face was the opposite. It was red, like she was embarrassed. Rick had a calculator at his elbow, Jane had her laptop, and there were papers everywhere—printouts of numbers, binders, reports, curled white calculator tape, crumpled yellow sheets from Rick's legal pad. It was the picture of chaos.

"What?" Rick snapped at me. "Make it quick."

I asked him the question. Twice. But he couldn't focus. Finally, I just said I'd catch up with him later, closed the door and tiptoed back to my office.

For a while, Borcon Corporate was patient. As the quarters went by, though, they began to get . . . you know, testy. And finally, Rick got another invitation to the ranch. Only this time, they didn't send the Gulfstream. Rick had to fly down in Essential's company plane, which is perfectly functional, but no treat. So the story goes that Claymore chewed him out for a couple of hours, then he took Rick outside to have him watch as he helped the ranch hands castrate the young bulls. Rick got the point. He had to make something happen.

3

Jake Foster
Senior Vice President–Operations

The plane landed and the three of us walked to our cars. Vince said, "Good night," and drove away. Rick, I could tell, wanted to say something more to me, so I was slow getting into my car. As Vince zoomed off, Rick turned to me and said, "Look, we can't ignore customers like Bud."

"We're not," I said. "And as for the AZ shipment, I'm stopping at Logandale on my way home to see what the hell's going on."

"Good." Then he thought of something and asked, "By the way, you do know what day it is, don't you?"

"Yeah, I know," I told him. It was the 31st, the last day of the month and of our financial quarter.

"You *are* going to make your numbers this month, aren't you?"

"I think so," I said.

But I wasn't sure. What I did know was that enough things had gone wrong during the quarter that it was dicey whether we'd make the projections Rick had given to Corporate. Rough calculations in the back of my mind told me that a few unshipped AZ orders might just be enough to make the difference one way or another.

It had been a bad night. Rick snapped. Slammed his fist down on the roof of his Jaguar. The thump was so loud I wouldn't have been surprised if he dented the steel.

"What do you mean, you THINK so? That isn't good enough! When I ask questions, I want answers—and the answers had better be right!"

I held my own temper and kept quiet.

Rick got behind the wheel of the Jag and peeled out. I followed right after in my Mercedes. A few miles up the highway, I passed him. He had calmed down and was in the right-hand lane doing the speed limit. I, on the other hand, was on a mission and had my foot in it.

• • •

Logandale is the suburb of Grandville that's home to our biggest manufacturing plant, and everyone just refers to the plant as "Logandale." Around 11:30 P.M., I drove down the exit ramp of the interstate and turned at the entrance. The plant was built in the 1970s and looks like two boxes—a glass-walled cube (the plant's offices) dead center in front of a huge, rectangular, windowless steel-sided box (which is the actual factory). The design of the plant was pretty much a straight pass-through. At the narrow ends of the rectangle were loading docks. Materials coming in by truck entered Receiving on the left, went through various manufacturing processes in the middle, and exited as finished products through Shipping on the right. I parked on the right and surveyed the scene.

There were three heavy-duty, overhead doors (like garage doors) set behind a concrete dock with rubber bumpers so that tractor-trailers could back up to the dock and the Shipping Department's forklifts could drive right inside the trailers with pallets of products. Well, that night, there were three, big, forty-foot trailers backed up to the dock, but no tractors—no trucks to pull them. It didn't look good.

I rummaged through my briefcase to find my company ID badge, clipped it to my suit jacket pocket, and got out, ready to do battle. Some steps painted safety-yellow gave access to the loading dock. Climbing these, I went in through the nearest door (all three were raised) and stepped aside just in time to avoid being flattened by a forklift rushing a pallet laden with cardboard boxes marked "AZ-150" into the back of the trailer.

Inside, it was a study in motion—workers grabbing AZ units off a conveyor belt, putting them in boxes, adding the packing peanuts, sealing the boxes, and shoving them down a roller table—where more workers slapped on self-adhesive bar-code stickers for inventory tracking, laser-scanned them into the computer, and sent them on to the teams making up the pallets. As soon as a pallet was banded, the forklift would rush up, lift it, drive into the trailer, drop it, and back out to get another. Two of the three trailers seemed ready to go—their doors were closed—but finishing this last one . . . well, anyone could have seen it was a crash effort.

Everyone was so busy, nobody noticed me at first. Finally I spotted a supervisor. She was at a nearby desk, keying something into a computer terminal.

I went over and asked her, "Are you in charge of Shipping?"

She saw the suit and blinked. Then she saw the company ID badge and read the title, "Vice President–Operations," and she actually flinched.

"Yes, sir!" She stood up straight. "What can I do for you?"

"Is that the Southeast order you're loading now?"

"Yes! Yes, it is! We're just finishing up, Mr. Foster."

"Good. I'm glad to hear that."

"We'll be done soon. Only a few hundred more units to pack."

She went over to where they were packing—I suppose to inspire them. I wandered off a polite distance and watched the forklift zip back and forth. Every so often, the shipping manager would look nervously over her shoulder at me.

At 11:46 P.M., two workers banded the last pallet. The forklift hustled it into the trailer, backed out, and two other workers closed the trailer's doors and locked them down. You could almost hear the sigh of relief pass the lips of the whole department.

I walked back to the shipping manager, who was back at her computer clicking in the final details to officially log the completed shipment.

"See, we made it," she said. "It's on the system. Shipped right on time."

"Well, I wouldn't go that far," I said.

She seemed confused, then sort of got it, and looked a little sheepish. "Yeah, it kind of came down to the wire. But, you know . . ."

"What exactly was the problem? Something about installing the wrong part?"

"Umm, I'm not really sure. I think it was a missing part."

The person I'd talked to on the phone had definitely said they'd installed the wrong part. But wrong part, missing part . . . what's the difference?

"One more thing," I said. "When are those trailers going to be out of here?"

The shipping manager, who a second ago thought she was off the hook, became flustered. "Umm . . . well . . . it shouldn't be too long. Why, is that important?"

I have to admit I kind of snapped at her. *"Yes, it's important!"*

"Oh. Well, let me check."

She picked up her phone and dialed a number, but after a few seconds hung up.

"I'll be right back," she said.

She went off somewhere. It was astoundingly quiet. All the workers had left; the second shift was ending. Finally, when she came back, she told me, "It won't be long. They told me maybe ten or fifteen minutes at the most."

I nodded and said, "Okay, thanks." (I almost added, "Nice job," but under the circumstances, thought that was excessive.) "Have a good night."

"You too," she said cheerily, clearly relieved I was going.

I went out through the cargo bay, same as I'd come in. As soon as my butt was clear, she started hitting red buttons on the wall, and one by one the big steel doors rolled down and slammed the concrete behind me.

Then, as I got into my car again, the thought occurred to me: You know, just to be on the safe side, maybe I should sit here and watch those trailers leave. That way, if it ever comes up, I can tell Gloria I saw it with my own eyes.

As tired and rotten as I felt, it was about the last thing I wanted to do, but I decided to do it anyway. At midnight, second shift came flooding out of the plant, got in their cars, and went home. After they were gone, there were still quite a few cars left in the parking lot; the plant was running a rather sizeable third shift.

Around 12:10 A.M., or thereabouts, a grimy old Freightliner came across the lot. It backed up to the first trailer; the driver got out, hooked up, and in a few minutes away it went.

But it didn't go far. As I was watching it leave, thinking, "one down, two to go," the rig drove slowly past the front of the plant and never made the turn to go to the highway. It just disappeared around the far end of the plant.

Well, that's funny, I thought. But I supposed there was some kind of explanation. Another five minutes or so passed, and back came the same old grimy Freightliner minus the trailer. It then did the same thing—

backed up to the next trailer, hooked up, pulled out, drove past the front of the plant and around the corner. This time, I followed.

When I got to the far end, there was the first trailer, backed up to the dock for Receiving. The second trailer was being backed in, right next to the first.

I whipped the Mercedes around the corner, got out, and caught the truck driver just as he was climbing down from the cab.

"Hey!" I yelled. "May I ask what the hell you're doing?"

He looked at me indignantly and said, "Just what they tell me to!"

"Those trailers are loaded. They're supposed to be on their way to a customer's warehouse."

The driver—a big, barrel-chested black guy in coveralls—shrugged his shoulders. "I don't know nuthin' about that. They told me to bring 'em around here."

It was about then I noticed that he wore an Essential company ID badge. He was no long-haul trucker; he was a plant employee. (As I learned later, the Freightliner was company equipment; they kept it parked in back of the plant, just in case they needed to move a trailer or two.)

"Sorry," I said. "Something's going on, and I'm just trying to get to the bottom of it."

"Good luck," he said in a tone that made me do a double take.

I used the bumper at the back of the trailer as a step and got myself onto the dock, where I was nearly flattened by a forklift, this one backing *out* of the trailer. It was unloading the same pallets that just half an hour before everyone had been rushing to load.

Inside the Receiving Department, it was almost like watching a video of what I'd just witnessed in Shipping play in reverse. The forklift raced back and forth, depositing pallets onto the plant floor, where workers cut the bands, grabbed the boxes, scanned each one's bar code into the computer, then sliced open the seals, removed the AZ units, and then threw the boxes and packing peanuts away. Some of the workers, I noticed, were the same people I'd seen in Shipping. Working overtime apparently, they'd been sent from one end of the plant to the other, to undo what they had just been doing a short time before.

As I walked behind two of them, I was lucky enough to overhear one say to the other, "Man, there must be a full moon out tonight. This is crazy."

"Yep, you can tell it's the end of the month."

"This happens a lot?"

"You can bet it's happened before. Always at the end of the month. You're new, but you just wait a while, you'll see."

They were placing the AZ units they unpacked onto carts, and when a cart was full, someone would push it into the plant. I was about to follow one to see where it ended up when a voice at my shoulder said, "Excuse me. May I help you with something?"

It was another supervisor. I introduced myself, fingering my company ID as I did so. As he read the title, his tone immediately changed from suspicious to nervous.

"Oh! Mr. Foster!" *Yes, what a pleasant surprise.* "Is anyone escorting you?"

"No. No one is escorting me. I'm just trying to find out what the hell is going on here."

"Why, ah, we're just off-loading some AZ units that have been returned."

"Returned?"

"Yes, ah . . . well, let me check the computer, but I believe these were returned because the customer found they were defective."

I said, "Don't give me that. I just watched that trailer being loaded not more than half an hour ago. They never made it to the highway, let alone a customer."

"I believe, sir, these are missing a wiring harness."

"Where are they taking these units? To the Dumpster out back?"

"No, sir, they're going to Section H-4 for refurbishing. Then they'll probably be shipped out again in a day or so."

So it was a numbers game, I concluded. A computer game.

Diane Sullivan
Manufacturing Manager–Logandale Plant

I was considered a rising star at Essential. That may sound like ego talking, but really it's not. I'd had various conversations with Mike, my boss, and with Pamela Cantrell, our human resources VP, and even with Rick Riggins over the years; they had all suggested, hinted, or said in so many words that I might someday be senior management—if I continued to apply myself, achieve objectives, and so on. I think the feedback from just about every one of my performance appraisals was very positive.

I started with the company as a junior engineer, and at one point I worked directly with Frank Harlan. That was when Frank managed Design Services, before he became vice president of engineering, but it was still very, you know, politically correct, even though I didn't see it as such at the time. It was Frank who recommended me for a position in the Hangar.

The Hangar, as you may or may not know, was where the Essential Corporation began years ago. It originally was an airplane hangar, built at an old World War II airfield. The founders of the company bought it and started the company there. I guess it's our version of the legendary garage where so many entrepreneurs start their businesses. My boss, Mike, got his start in the Hangar, and he's one of the few in the company who still remembers those early days.

Anyway, for many years, the Hangar was the whole company. Eventually, though, there was enough business that the company needed more space. So the Hangar became the R&D lab for Essential, and it also served as a production facility for some of Advanced Systems' projects.

My first management position was running the production side at the Hangar. Ultimately, after a stint in production planning that led to Logandale, I eventually became plant manager.

I have to tell you the difference between the Hangar and Logandale is like night and day. It's not just a matter of scale either. The Hangar was pretty much a job shop for building and testing these complex, one-of-a-kind systems created by Advanced Systems. Logandale is repetitive manufacturing, the classic factory, so the adjustment in thinking was kind of a challenge right from the start. When something went wrong at the Hangar, it was only one project and one customer, and you had lots of R&D geniuses close by to help you out. When something goes wrong at Logandale, it often means lots of customers and lots of units of product are affected. Even though the products we produce at Logandale are relatively low-tech, the potential cost of a mistake is much more expensive. You can lose sleep over it—and I often have.

Like the night when Jake Foster showed up unannounced. I was at home in bed. Earlier that evening, I had come home for dinner, then gone back to the plant for a couple of hours, and finally left around nine o'clock, telling everybody to do their best. Now, around twelve thirty in the morning, the phone rang. It was Doug, the production manager on third shift.

"I'm really sorry to call you this late," he said, "but Jake Foster is here and he's asking a lot of questions."

I sat up in bed like someone released a spring. I said, "Okay, I'll be there as soon as I can."

I threw on some clothes and was at the plant in less than twenty minutes. There was no traffic and I was flying. But by then Jake was gone.

I tracked down Doug, and he told me Jake was really pissed off. He said, "I told him you were on your way, but Mr. Foster left anyway. Said something about how he didn't trust himself not to do something he'd regret later. He said he'd talk to you first thing in the morning."

"Did he say why he was here?" I asked.

"I think he was checking on that late order for Southeast Supply. At least that's how it started out."

I had taken a call from Jake earlier in the evening, but he didn't say he was coming to the plant.

"He went everywhere," Doug told me. "He saw what's going on."

"Did he go back to H-4?"

"Yeah. He saw them taking the TD packs off the 130s."

"For crying out loud, Doug! Couldn't you steer him toward the office until I got here?"

"I couldn't stop him! I mean, he's a vice president!"

I took a few seconds to compose myself. Then I asked, "How are they doing?"

"In H-4? As well as can be expected."

"Come on," I said, not trusting anything to chance at this point. "Let's go see."

We went over to H-4, and there they were, every last body we could round up cannibalizing a production lot of nearly assembled AZ-130s, removing the TD packs, so the packs could be installed on the AZ-150s that were going to Southeast Supply.

I went over to Terry, the supervisor. "We going to make it?"

He shrugged. "We should. I called around, and I was able to get four assemblers from day turn to come in early. They'll be here at four A.M., but to get them to do it, I had to tell three of them they could quit early. They don't even care about the overtime anymore; they just want the time off."

"I authorized it," Doug told me. "I know day turn will be mad because it'll probably throw them behind on some other things, but I didn't know what else to do."

"I'll deal with them," I said. Then I asked Terry, "What's your best guess on when you'll be totally finished?"

"On the 150s? If all four assemblers show up, we should be done by six. Then it's however long it takes Shipping to repackage everything and get it out the door."

I turned to Doug. "What about refilling stock on the TD packs? Anyone talk to Kenosha since this afternoon?"

"Their second shift did a special run to get us a hundred or so. They got a guy in a pickup truck driving them here tonight."

I rolled my eyes. "Let's hope he doesn't have a flat tire on the way."

"Diane, you got to talk some sense into those office people," Doug told me. "We've got to have bigger safety stocks on TDs, on the Red-K connectors, and about fifty other things."

"Yeah, like double or maybe triple," Terry added.

"No, come on," I said. "When was the last time we ran out of TD packs?"

"I'm not sure," said Doug. "It's been a while. But that's just it. We never know how we're going to get jerked around by those salespeople when the real orders come in! It's always something!"

"I've tried," I told them. "But whenever we bump the stocks up, the Materials people adjust them back because they're being told to cut inventory."

"Well, I don't know what the answer is," said Doug, "but this makes no sense whatsoever."

"I know! I know!" I yelled. "I hate it too!"

Jake Foster
Senior Vice President–Operations

I was angry at what I'd found at Logandale, especially at the ruse to get an unshipped order onto the books. But these things do happen, even at companies that seem to be well-run. They happen because people are afraid. People are insecure. They don't want to disappoint. They want to look good. The internal culture makes it hard to be honest. It punishes them for bad news. It scares them into hiding problems rather than fixing them. It almost encourages them to fudge. And quite often, the fudging works. Headquarters sees numbers that are acceptable, and nothing happens. Sometimes the perpetrators are even praised for doing such a good job.

I had seen it all before. I had spent most of my career as a manager for DysCo. No, "DysCo" is not really the name. The company doesn't exist anymore, but it was a big, old, well-known corporation with a proud history, the kind of company everyone always thought would be around forever—until it went down the tubes. If I mentioned the name, you'd know it instantly, but let's just call it DysCo.

I came up with that name after reaching the conclusion that DysCo really was dysfunctional. I'm speaking of the management culture, not necessarily the managers themselves, most of whom were (or could have been) at least competent. A few, sadly, were even exceptional managers, though their talents were largely lost at this company. Moreover, the business itself was a good one—had to be in order for the company to survive as long as it did.

On an average day at DysCo, everything seemed just fine. Everybody seemed productive. Everybody was busy. In a typical management meeting, the discussion would sound serious, rational, logical. Managers would give the air of being smart and progressive. Indeed, someone on staff was always introducing some new program to improve something—quality, productivity, customer service, whatever. And in the background, high-priced consultants with platinum credentials would be meeting with senior management, designing the company's incredible future.

It always seemed as if we were pursuing some brilliant strategy, as if we were about to spring some kind of breakthrough that would revolutionize the whole business. As soon as this happened, DysCo would charge to the forefront, "leapfrogging" competitors, as we used to say. As time went on, though, the brilliant strategy (whatever it was—I'm not sure anybody really knew) never seemed to produce any major results. In fact, the ultimate strategy, as defined by the actual decisions being made, seemed to be to keep everything pretty much the same. The programs came and went, and the breakthrough that would revolutionize everything never arrived. Nothing much changed until a competitor did something, and then DysCo would spend billions on a crash effort to catch up.

Most decisions at DysCo were defensive. Managers, senior managers especially, were less concerned with growth and gain than they were with not losing what they already had. Turf wars, as managers fought to keep the status quo, were constant. Tremendous time and energy went into defending one's individual performance rather than figuring out how to improve the overall performance. The cooperation between functions, what there was of it, had a stiff, procedural, legalistic feel about it. We were not one big company; we were a collection of discrete units, each of which did its job tolerably, but independently—fearing the intrusion of outside forces. There were no good incentives, beyond just personal goodwill, for people in different functions to work with each other to achieve the larger goals.

As for those larger goals, they were generally irrelevant and ignored during the course of the daily grind. DysCo spent millions for consultants to create strategic plans for the company, but the plans were never implemented. Copies would be made, the consultants would leave, and these three-inch-thick, spiral-bound copies would sit on office shelves unread and forgotten.

Working as a manager at DysCo felt like being in a labyrinth. Physically, it was your average, bland open-office work environment. In terms of what you could do as a manager, however, in terms of how you could and could not operate, it was anything but open. There were invisible walls between all the functions. As much as possible, people just worked in their cells. Anyone who tried to do more faced any number of puzzles and hazards. Stairways to noplace. Hidden trapdoors. And rumors of secret passages that could allow you past the walls and traps and into the tall towers where the important decisions were made. If you wanted to have any real power at DysCo, you had to find the secret passages.

In my early years there, DysCo seemed like an interesting place to work. I wouldn't say it was fun, but it was intriguing. You know, figuring out where the passages were and who were their gatekeepers. Witnessing the horror of the innocent fools who stepped onto the hidden traps, lost support, and were languishing down in some pit. Memorizing the magic incantations (the "right" things to say to the "right" people) that would get you power and promotions. Yet after so many years had gone by, after I'd learned all the intricacies and was a master of my very own tower, I discovered I was as constrained as ever. It was no longer intriguing; it was stifling.

Why did I stay? I thought about leaving, but where would I go? At the time, I didn't believe it would be a whole lot better at another company. Besides, I was making very good money. My family was happy where we were. I put my résumé out a couple of times, but nothing clicked. So I figured I would retire from DysCo. There were worse fates in this world. Then two things happened.

First, the division I was working for won a contract and became a vendor to General Electric. For a variety of reasons, I became closely involved in this piece of business, and I got to know a number of my counterparts at the GE division we were working for. I spent a lot of time with these people. I toured their plants and facilities. I sat in meetings with them. I worked so closely with them that I virtually became a member of their team. We traveled frequently together and often had long conversations over dinner about business and management. It was through this experience that I finally began to understand what great management really meant.

The contrast between GE and DysCo was day and night. At this GE division, there was an openness, a receptiveness to new ideas and solutions. A week or two into my association with them, I suggested something in a meeting, doing it only to earn points, not even dreaming that my recommendation would be taken seriously. Within a few days, the GE people were asking me to help them implement the idea. Here I was, an outsider, yet my thinking was accepted—even though the change required modification to the way they, GE, did things.

There was none of the screwing around that at DysCo would be compulsory and would delay even minor improvements by months or, often, by years. It was like, *This is the better way. It's going to work. It aligns with our goals and values. Let's make it happen.*

Within a couple of months, we were already starting to see results, which benefited both GE and DysCo. I loved it. What a rush! Yet this was the normal way of doing things for the GE managers. For them, the plan for the business was not some spiral-bound ream of paper on a shelf collecting dust. It was something they had participated in creating and were bringing to life. It was something they could change if some piece of it wasn't working or no longer made sense. They could decide quickly what had merit and what did not, and readily give the green light when a change made sense. The speed was exhilarating.

And I almost lost my job because of it. What a shame I didn't. To keep up with GE, I had to cut a lot of corners in the usual approval process at DysCo, and I hadn't received all the proper sign-offs, as I was supposed to. Using the "secret passages," I got the approvals that mattered, but there was one vice president who was hopping mad that I had not talked to him before taking action. This guy was always a pain in the ass, and he went to my boss and tried to get me fired, claiming that I had exceeded my authority and was making decisions I had no business making. However, GE was such a key piece of business for us that I was merely given a tongue-lashing and told to "cool it."

I do wish they had fired me. This was in the early 1990s, and Jack Welch was bringing to reality his concept of a boundaryless management culture—a culture that gives managers the freedom to run their business the right way, unencumbered by bureaucracy and empowered to pursue excellence. I tasted that boundaryless culture while working with one of their divisions, and I soon developed a craving for it. I kept asking myself, *Why couldn't DysCo be managed the same boundaryless way?*

The average DysCo manager would not have spent even a minute pondering that question, but I became obsessed with it. I began reading everything about GE that I could get my hands on. I read the annual reports and all the books that were available. And I talked with my own staff about GE ideals. About the need for speed in what we did. About the fundamental importance of quality. About integrity, both personally and as an organization. About the passionate elimination of bureaucracy. Clearing away the impediments to success. Self-confidence. Freedom from insecurity. Involvement of everyone. Smashing the "not-invented-here" syndrome. Setting stretch goals that exceeded the expected. Approaching our business with the attitude that nothing is impossible.

I supported the development of these values in every manager who reported to me, and I worked hard to weed out those who clearly did not support those values, who wanted to remain bureaucrats. Together with what I called the "true believers," the people who embraced what I was preaching, we made a sincere effort to create a boundaryless culture inside DysCo. And for our trouble, we ended up with the best darn operations group of any division in DysCo.

Go ahead and laugh. It's almost funny. But that was the limit of what I could accomplish. I was the head of the operations group for one little division, and though I talked to managers throughout DysCo about what I was trying to do, in the end it was only my own group where any real change happened. As for the others? The senior team at DysCo wouldn't even talk to me. Other managers were occasionally intrigued by what I had to say, but they were too afraid to do anything.

That I was even able to accomplish anything within my own group was because of Rick Riggins. That was the second thing that happened. Right after my near termination due to the pain-in-the-ass vice president, Rick came to DysCo and became the head of the division where I was.

In the beginning, we didn't like each other much. To be honest, I was resentful that he had been brought in over me, when I had been expecting to get the top job in the division. And Rick was not a very empowering manager. He was more a command-and-control type, and dubious of what I was trying to do with my group.

Slowly over the months, though, we did develop a mutual respect. What I began to like more and more about Rick was that he wanted change. He was ambitious, and he wanted our division to set the DysCo world on fire. His goal was to become CEO. He came to appreciate me because I was really getting it done, making major improvements in our operations performance, cutting expenses, striving for a first-rate, world-class operations group. He was suspicious of my idealism and my methods, but as time went on, he loved the results.

Rick and I became allies. He let me attempt to create my boundary-less culture within my group, and I gave him lots of positive things that would earn him points with the DysCo senior team.

The problem obviously was that whenever my people or I had any dealings outside our group, even within our own division, we ran smack into the walls and traps established by the rest of the organization. We were forever limited by their stupid rules, their insecurities, their egos.

Rick lasted at DysCo about three and a half years. By then, the senior team had noticed that he was coming on strong, and they screwed him in the reorganization they put together. They stuck him with some losing groups and wouldn't allow him to axe them. It meant Rick couldn't win and almost had to fail.

About then, the grapevine brought word of the president's position opening up at Essential. Rick left. He encouraged me to keep in touch. But the event for which I'd been waiting finally happened. My ship had come in. DysCo awarded me Rick's division. Now, at last, maybe I could mold this division into the winner I thought it could be.

I did try. My staff and I made some progress. We even turned around one of the losers. In the end, though, we never really made the transition. I could not find the method that would take "boundaryless" from buzz-word to everyday reality. I talked and I talked, but that didn't get it done. It required something more, and I just couldn't discover what it was. I knew where I wanted us to go; I just couldn't figure out an efficient way to get there.

In any case, time ran out. I said my ship had come in, but, actually, my ship was the same as that of everyone else at DysCo. And the name on the side of the hull might as well have been the *Titanic*. Within a year of my taking over as the division's general manager, DysCo began to self-destruct. It would take a while before it became obvious that DysCo was not going to survive, that the ship indeed was sinking. The speed and course had been plotted and ordered up on the bridge, and I was just one of the people managing an engine room. It didn't matter that my engine was running better than ever. It wasn't within the scope of my responsibility to suggest the possibility of icebergs.

• • •

My house is outside of Grandville, just off a two-lane blacktop highway. At the end of my driveway, I can turn left and be at my office in fifteen minutes. Or, I can turn right and be at the marina on the shores of Lake Mawgatanapee in ten. The lake is twelve miles long and offers some pretty good fishing. Rick has a big boat out there.

The house was dark when I got home. I was starving and didn't make it past the kitchen on my way to bed. While I was grazing on leftovers, my wife, Sandy, walked in and scrutinized me with a puzzled look.

"How come you're home so late?" she asked.

"Long story," I told her.

"Do you want me to make you something?"

"No," I said, holding up a half-devoured slice of pizza. "This is fine."

"Didn't you have dinner?"

"Not really."

"But I thought that was the point. You know, dinner with that cus-tomer, what's-its-name."

"I never got to eat. They were too busy making my life miserable."

"It was that bad?"

"The good part was they didn't pull out guns and shoot us. Otherwise, it was *that* bad."

"Jake, what on earth is going on?"

I sighed and then sat down at the kitchen table. She sat down as well and put her hand on top of mine.

"Essential is in worse shape than I could have imagined. The politics. The games they're playing. They're so screwed up, it's almost exactly like being back at DysCo."

"Well, you should feel right at home then," Sandy joked.

I shook my head. "I don't know if I can do this. I don't know if I can fight the same battles all over again. Even Rick seems to be against me."

I was hoping for sympathy, but her hand lifted from mine and when I looked at her face, I could tell she was on the verge of being angry.

"What?" I asked her.

"You can quit if you want," said Sandy, "but we are not moving."

"I didn't say anything about quitting—or moving!"

"No, but you're thinking about it."

"Absolutely not!"

"Good. Because I am staying put. The old house is sold. We are finally settled in. I just unpacked the last box yesterday afternoon. I have a part-time job. I've started to make some friends. I'm finally getting to know my way around. And I am not going to go through all that again any time soon. Not until you are officially ready to retire. Besides, I love this house, and you're finally healthy, and I just want to enjoy life for a change. So you can quit Essential if you want, but this," she said, pointing toward the floor, "is *it*."

Then, Cochise having spoken, she got up from the table and put water in the kettle to make tea.

"Well, then," I said, "I guess I'll have to make the best of it."

4

Vince Springer
Senior Vice President–Marketing and Sales

Bright and early the next morning, I had a meeting with my sales managers—the direct reports, that is. There was Felice Torrance, our national accounts manager. Felice handles sales to larger corporations—mostly OEMs—that use centralized buying for all their operations. There was Tom Wright, director of field sales for North America. Xavier Estaban, sales director for international, is also a direct report and would have been there, but, as usual, he was traveling. Finally, Nick Corrigan, sales director for the BigBox account, was at the table. I suppose it speaks volumes (you can take the pun or leave it) that we had a sales director for one account. That's how important BigBox was to us.

Nick was, no doubt about it, out to make a name for himself. He was young—late thirties—and a bit brash. It was one of my challenges to control the rivalry between him and Tom Wright. Well . . . control, but also exploit. I demanded the best from both of them, and sometimes the rivalry helped me get it. Lately, it was Nick who was winning the contest.

In that meeting, I opened by briefly mentioning for Tom's benefit the situation with Smoot and Southeast. I suggested he give Charlie a call to find out more. Then I turned to BigBox. I passed on to Nick some of the complimentary comments Rick Riggins had dropped the night before about the endcaps.

"Well," said Nick, "I've got even better news."

"Yeah, what's that?"

"It is pretty close to certain that BigBox wants to add a Z-based store brand and they want to do it sometime in the next twelve months or thereabouts. Furthermore, I have it on good authority that we, Essential, are currently the preferred choice to manufacture the BigBox store-brand product."

Smiling, beaming with confidence, Nick looked as if he'd just pulled off a major coup. I slumped back in my chair.

"So what's your *good* news?" I asked him.

"Well . . . that's it. That's the good news, the BigBox store brand."

"Do you know what that means? It means, if we win that business, we slit our own throats!"

"How?!" Nick cried. "How can you say that? Okay, okay, I know. Yes, the store brand will compete in a sense with our own AZ products. But don't you see? We'll be supplying that competing brand! We can make money both ways!"

"Yeah, and we can ruin our own brand!" said Tom. "Don't you get it? That's what Vince is saying."

"No, think about it!" said Nick. "We all know current AZ is probably going to decline. This is a way to extend the life of that technology."

"You're sure they want the store brand to be Z-based, not based on SOS?" I asked.

"Yes, I asked them. They told me they would expect an AZ product with slightly different features—we'll have to work with them on that—and they will expect us to upgrade the model to make it Z3 compatible within fairly short order. BigBox said they did not see an SOS-based store brand for three to five years, if then."

I was ready to start pulling my hair out; the more I heard, the worse it became. I said to Nick, "Rick Riggins is just going to love this."

"Hold on!" said Nick. "You folks are missing the point! If we don't supply the BigBox brand, *somebody else will.* They're going to go ahead with this no matter what *we* decide. If we don't jump on it, then the business goes probably either to Reliable or to Spectrum. Why should we *give* that extra revenue and profit to *them*?"

"Because!" I said. "Because I know what Rick Riggins is going to say! I know what Frank Harlan is going to say! Rick is going to see it as a double threat—first against our own AZ products, and second against the adoption of the new SOS products! And Frank . . . ! He's going to sit there on his big, golden Engineering throne and rumble about how he and his engineers will have nothing to do with a cut-rate, low-end version of something that's yesterday's technology! About how we *must* pursue the state of the art or be left behind!"

"That's bullshit!" said Nick. "Ninety percent of the people who walk into BigBox don't care about state of the art, wouldn't even know it if they tripped over it. They want solid, dependable AZ—and they'll certainly buy the store brand if it's a few bucks cheaper!"

"Exactly the problem!" said Tom.

"It's *not* a problem, it's an opportunity. It's an opportunity to make additional sales!"

"As they squeeze our margins on AZ!" said Tom. "And by the way, did you stop to think about the potential fallout that may impact other accounts? Why must everything these days be viewed myopically in terms of BigBox?! It's as if we have no other customers!"

"There shouldn't *be* any fallout. Not with respect to your accounts," said Nick.

"Uh-huh, I've heard that before," said Tom.

"What about the distributors, Nick?" I asked him. "What about the retail outlets those distributors serve? You think *they're* not going to be up in arms if we build a store brand for BigBox to help suck away even *more* of their customers than BigBox does now?"

"Look, I'm not a marketer, I'm a salesman," said Nick. "But I've gotta believe that we're talking about different segments. And if we're not talking about different segments of the market, then shouldn't we be making some choices? I mean, in a worst case scenario, if we lost every distributor we've got, what would that really do to us?"

Tom Wright was about to have a seizure. I put my hand on his arm and said, "Don't worry, we're not going to lose all the distributors. We're not going to lose any of them if we can help it."

"I'm just suggesting a 'what-if'!" said Nick. "Really, if we had to make a choice, who would you rather have, Southeast Supply or Big-Box?"

"*BigBox! BigBox! BigBox!*" shouted Tom. "*You've got BigBox on the brain!*"

"*I eat, sleep, and breathe BigBox!*" Nick shouted back. "*It's my job!*"

"*Why can't you for ten seconds think about the rest of us!*" shouted Felice.

"Okay, okay! Stop! Everybody shut up and count to ten!" I said. After a few seconds of quiet, I continued. "So, Nick, does Marketing know about this yet?"

"I wanted to tell you first," said Nick.

"All right, Nick, I want you to write up a complete backgrounder on this. We're obviously going to have to respond yea or nay, and I'll have to broach the whole thing with Rick."

"Do you want me to work on it with Marketing?"

"No! I'll run it by Rick, and if by *some miracle* he doesn't reject the whole thing immediately, then we'll bring in Marketing. Besides, I need Marketing's full focus on the SOS rollout. Rick laid down the law last night. He wants it to happen in time for Expo."

"Hey, that's great," said Tom. "We're ready for SOS anytime. That's the real growth opportunity, not this. . . ." He cut himself off before it got out of hand again.

I grunted, thinking about the headaches that were coming. After a moment, I said, "Okay, now . . . who's next with some 'good' news?"

Jake Foster
Senior Vice President–Operations

First thing in the morning, I stopped at Logandale to have a talk with Diane Sullivan. I wanted to come on a bit heavy, so I went unannounced straight to her office. Diane was in, sitting at her desk with a tired, stoic expression on her face, but she made an attempt to brighten up and smile when she saw me.

"Well, hello, Jake," she said. "I understand you paid us a visit last night."

"That's right. And I didn't like what I saw."

She bit her lip, then said, "Before you say anything else, please don't judge me or my plant based on the last few days of the month."

"Why not?"

"We're normally much more . . . in control."

"Yes, well, I do want to talk about that, but first of all, what is the current status of the Southeast Supply order?"

"We'll be able to ship the order this morning."

"Really? Gee, that's odd. I thought for sure I'd seen that order ship last night just before midnight. Saw it loaded into a trailer with my own eyes. Now you're telling me it didn't ship? Or could it be that the customer returned it?"

Diane began to turn bright red.

"I can explain, Jake."

"I hope so."

"They were doing everything in their power to finish that order and get it out when someone discovered we didn't have enough of a certain part."

"I see. So tell me, where did you get the parts for the portion of the order you're going to ship this morning?"

She shut her eyes for a moment and sat there silently composing herself. Finally she admitted, "We had to take them from another batch of product that's less urgent than the one for Southeast."

"Perhaps that's one reason why your work-in-process situation is as bad as it is. Look, Diane, what I saw last night—"

"Yes, I know, I know," she said, rubbing her temples with her fingers. "I do accept responsibility for it because . . . well, because I was told to get every possible shipment out the door before the end of the month."

"Before midnight in other words."

"Yes."

"Even if it meant taking it out one door and in the other."

Diane looked at me calmly then and said, "If you want my resignation, I will give it to you."

She surprised me with that. Showed some character, I thought. At least she was willing to be accountable.

"Do you want to resign?" I asked.

"No, of course not."

"The kind of things I saw going on last night absolutely must stop."

I thought that would make her contrite, but it had the opposite effect. Almost defiantly, she said, "Then you're going to have to talk to Mike Zarelli."

Mike was my director of manufacturing, Diane's boss and a direct report to me.

"Why should I talk to Mike?" I asked.

"Because he's the one . . ." she started. Then she caught herself and instead said, "Jake, do you really think I *want* to run my plant this way?"

"How *do* you want to run your plant?"

"I'd run it like a Swiss watch, if I could! But I *can't*! Not with everybody changing their minds about what's important, and who's important, and dumping all these things on us."

"My sense is that you're overwhelmed," I said. "Let's be honest with each other. Maybe running this plant is too much for you."

"No, it's not running this plant that's too much," she insisted. "It's everything else. That's what's too much."

"What do you mean by 'everything else'?"

"I mean dealing with the other parts of the company. Dealing with . . . well, you know, the politics. Trying to please everybody and live up to promises that, a lot of the time, we never made and can't possibly keep." She stopped then. "I'm sorry. I shouldn't be saying all that."

"It's all right," I said. "This is between us. I want to know. I *need* to know."

She started to say something; then, clearly uncomfortable, she fell silent.

"Diane, I don't want your resignation. At least not at present. What I want—what I think we should all want—is a productive, profitable, growing company that is the best in the market for serving its customers. That's no bull. That's really what I'm after."

"Fine. Because that is exactly what I want as well," she said.

"Then why can't you achieve it?"

"You want to know?" she asked. "You really want to know?"

"Yes."

"Well . . . for starters, there's this." She pulled from a drawer a rather thick binder and let it plop onto her desktop. "The forecast from marketing. It's useless. Okay, not completely useless, but mostly useless. They told us we should increase our build of 300s and 450s—and what do we get instead? Tons of orders for 130s and 150s! Don't they understand that if they tell me to build 300s and 450s and then go out and push 150s, we're probably not going to have enough 150s to ship?"

"That's what happened on the Southeast order?"

"And others."

"But that doesn't explain last night's shenanigans—taking work in process, entering it as shipped, and bringing it back in another door."

"That was not my idea."

"Then why did it happen?"

She just stared at me.

"Come on, Diane. Spit it out."

"I don't mean to be impertinent, but I would think that *you* of all people would know why it's happening."

Now I just stared at her.

Finally she sighed and said, "A week before the end of every month, Mike Zarelli calls and grills me about whether we're going to make the numbers. I don't know if you're aware of this, but Mike can be very intimidating. Basically, he tells me he doesn't care how we do it, but the black and white numbers had better show the output that was projected. To quote Mike exactly, 'If it isn't bolted to the floor, it goes on the truck.'"

I nodded slowly, thinking about what she'd said.

"You know, Jake, the first few months I was plant manager here, I did miss on the numbers, and I got screamed at and threatened. So, right or wrong, I turned around and did whatever it took to make the numbers and the metrics work the way people at headquarters expected. Pretty soon, we were always making the numbers. Everybody was happy. I didn't get screamed at, I got praised. I got compliments. I got good performance appraisals. Rick Riggins himself went out of his way to tell me he thought I had a big future ahead with Essential. Seriously, what would you have done?"

"Me? I'd still have kept trying to get it right."

"And I do! I've got all kinds of teams and initiatives and training programs going on, trying to improve productivity, quality, lower costs, reduce inventory and everything else. Every month I keep hoping that we'll get it right for once. That the forecast will be on target. That Purchasing won't keep changing vendors. That Engineering won't keep dumping impossible challenges on us. That Marketing will quit fiddling with the features and options combinations. I mean, good grief, Jake . . . do you realize that the number of SKUs we have to deal with has *doubled* in the past four years? For every basic model number like AZ-130, we may have thirty to fifty different configurations! It's a nightmare trying to keep everything sorted out. And what's going to happen when we add the SOS products on top of the AZ? Nobody's even thought about that. To Marketing and Engineering it's just lists of numbers. To us, all those lists of numbers mean physical objects that have to be made or purchased, quality-checked, stored in parts bins, assembled in the proper sequence, and tested. And when they keep adding parts numbers and SKUs, they're adding orders of magnitude to the complexity—which exponentially increases the odds of something going wrong! Yet nobody will listen.

Everybody just says, 'Deal with it!' Then they wonder why shipments go out late. Anymore, I just keep my head down, and we crank away and do the best we can. Honestly, if Marketing could just get the forecast right, maybe we wouldn't have so many hot jobs screwing us up every month. I really think we could deal with the complexity if the orders were predictable."

I sighed and shook my head. I understood her dilemma because I had been in her place myself years before.

"I'll have a talk with Mike," I told her. "Meanwhile, I want you and your staff to pull up the records on every order that shipped late for the past six months and do a root-cause analysis of what went wrong. Was it an out-of-stock part? Were the same parts consistently out of stock? Was it interference from the hot sheet? What happened? We need to be able to quantify exactly what the problems are. *And* no more shell games at the end of the month. That shit's got to stop. There has to be integrity to the reporting or else we don't know what the hell we're dealing with. Are we clear on that?"

She nodded. Then I checked my watch and stood up. "Look, I have to go. But there's one more thing. Call this guy." I handed her Charlie Packer's business card. "Tell him *exactly* when his customer, Southeast, is going to get the order of AZ-150s. He needs to know the truth."

Charlie Packer
Regional Manager–Field Sales

The second I got off the phone with Diane Sullivan, I said, "Screw it." I'd had enough. She could give me all the assurances in the world, and I'd never believe any of them.

You had to know the computer system to survive at Essential, and I had come to know it very well. I was still in my office at home. So I logged onto the system, entered some codes and my "special" password that I had procured some time ago. Within five minutes, I had the solution.

I got on the phone again and called my ole buddy, Chester. He's in St. Louis, the chief dispatcher for the trucking company we use. I'd made his acquaintance several times in the past, so he took my call right away.

After we'd chitchatted for a minute, I said, "Hey, Chester, you know what? I just heard through the grapevine that our rep in St. Louis happens to have four tickets to a Cardinals game that he can't use—box seats, the best—and I was wondering if you would want to take them off his hands."

"Yeah? Which game is that?"

"Any game you want. You just let me know, and the tickets are on their way."

"Oh. Well, thank you, that's mighty nice of you."

"No problem. Hey, I was also wondering if you could do something for me, help me and my company out of a jam."

"Well . . . is it legal?"

"Legal? Well, it's *pretty* legal. I just need a truck rerouted. See, somebody on our end screwed up, and it's going to the wrong place."

"Uh-huh. You happen to know which truck? 'Cause we got a lot of 'em out there."

"Yeah, I got all the particulars right here in front of me on the computer. The truck I'm interested in left Grandville on Tuesday and is on its way to Orlando."

Chester checked his computer and said, "This the one that's headed for the BigBox Distribution Center?"

"That's the one," I said. "See, somebody messed up, and the shipment on that truck was supposed to go to one of my customers in Atlanta."

"Really? Okay, let me see what I can do."

He put me on hold and came back a few minutes later. "You must be livin' right, Charlie. He got held up on account of fog last night, but he's on I-75 just south of Chattanooga right now. Where you want him in Atlanta?"

"It's the Southeast Supply warehouse. Let me give you the new address. And tell him I'm going to meet him there, smooth out any problems with the paperwork."

See, I figured it was kind of like being in the Army. You could curse the system and be chewed up by it, or you could regard it as a resource and use it to your own advantage. I mean, what was I supposed to do? If we lost the Southeast account, the company would be worse off, I'd be screwed financially, and might even lose my job. On the other hand, if I bent the rules . . .

I made calls from my car while I drove to the warehouse to meet the truck, one to our rep in St. Louis to get the tickets for Chester and then a call to Gloria Kass. I told her that I'd straightened everything out, that her AZ-150s would be arriving within the hour, and she said, "Oh, Charlie, you *are* my hero!"

But not more than a week later, I got a call from Vince Springer. He said, "Charlie, I got some news this morning that . . . well, kind of gave me a shock, and I'm not sure what to do. Anyway, I wanted to talk it over with you."

"What's the problem, Vince?"

"Problem? No problem. Your boss, Bruce Logan, informed me that he's been offered a position in Philadelphia, which he's accepted. So I was wondering how you would feel about moving up to regional sales manager? You see, Charlie, I've always been impressed by your resourcefulness, and I consider it a real asset to the company. The call I got from Gloria Kass just recently is a case in point. If all our field salespeople had the same drive as you . . . well, that's why I'd like to bring you up to management. . . ."

In the end, I said yes, I'd take the job, even though it was actually less money than what I'd made as a salesman. I figured it was more security, and to tell you the truth, I wasn't sure how many more times I'd be able to pull a rabbit out of a hat.

Angeline Ramos
Regional Sales Manager–Retail

One day, Wayne Hill came to me and said, "Hey, we got a problem. Every BigBox in Florida is running low on AZ-150s, and the buyer is mad as hell at us."

I said, "How could that happen?"

"I don't know!" said Wayne. "I just went over our records and the computer says there was a truckload that shipped to Orlando a couple weeks ago, but the buyer says they never got it."

"All right, I'll call Distribution and scream at them. Meanwhile, you put in a new order, and be sure to back-date it far enough that it comes up on their screens in Logandale as being super late. That's the only way it'll ever get priority on the hot sheet."

"I had one other thought," said Wayne. "I've checked around and Southeast Supply has 150s in stock. We could buy some from Southeast and rush them to Orlando, just to tide things over."

"No! That's ridiculous!" I said.

"I just thought . . . you know, as a last resort. Just to cover ourselves. The buyer is *really* mad at us."

I sighed. "Okay, look into it. See how much it would cost. And figure out if there's some way we can do it through a third party. If this ever gets out, we'll be the laughing stock of the whole industry."

5

Mike Zarelli
Director–Manufacturing

I remember simpler times. Used to be that the Hangar was the whole company. There was no Logandale, no Kenosha plant, no field sales, none of that. And for darn sure there was no headquarters. Just a drab old airplane hangar on one side of an abandoned World War II airfield. It was cheap space and lots of it. That was where I started, just about forty years ago, right after I got out of the service.

You might think it would be an awful place to work, this drafty old building, but I liked it there—no nit-picking, not a lot of rules. Just grow the company. Hey, you need help? Go ask the person best qualified to give it. Because we were all there in one big, wide-open space. No place to hide. You were a slacker, everybody knew about it, and you were gone pretty quick.

I got on just fine at the Hangar. Started as an assembler, right out there on the floor. Went to night school, became a supervisor, and then it was right on up the ladder.

Eventually, of course, we outgrew the Hangar. There was just too much business and too many employees to fit them all in one place. So we built Logandale, which I managed for a number of years. But I think that's where a lot of this stuff started—the turf wars, the finger-pointing, the engineers who are holier-than-thou, the salespeople who don't know their butts from a hole in the ground, who make these ridiculous promises and then put the load on us to come through for them. It was a lot easier when we were all together, and you could sit down right then and there, face-to-face with people and straighten things out. Now, if you can do it at all, it takes months. All these policies, all these rules. The Hangar days are gone. We'll never have that again, not in this company.

I survived the Borcon buyout. A number of managers didn't. You know why I survived? Because I'm a "can-do" kind of a guy. Seriously! Whatever is needed, I get it done. With whatever it takes. I don't take "no" or "maybe" for an answer. If it's sittin' still, get it to move. If you gotta kick it, you kick it. Once it's movin', you ship it. You want my so-called management philosophy? That's it. It's that simple. Hey, it's worked for the past forty-odd years, why change it?

Jake Foster
Senior Vice President–Operations

Essential's company headquarters is located in a campuslike office complex in the suburbs of Grandville. It used to be downtown, in a "sky-scraper" that was the tallest office building in a 100-mile radius, but after Borcon bought us, the new management team decided to sell the building and move us out here to the 'burbs. The office campus is very nice. A small group of low-rise buildings sheathed in mirrorlike glass. Lots of lawn and trees. A pond with a footbridge. Ducks. Plenty of parking. My only complaint has been that the campus is, if anything, too tranquil.

My office is on the top floor of our building. Just after I got in, I called Mike Zarelli and said I wanted to have a talk with him. He's two floors below, but said he'd be right up.

Even though business attire in America has relaxed considerably over the past ten or fifteen years, Mike has never taken much notice. That morning as always, he was wearing a bright-white, long-sleeved shirt and a striped, conservative tie.

Mike sat down and I told him what had gone on the night before, both at the customer dinner and at Logandale. As I talked, he jotted notes on a pad of paper, then when it seemed I was finished, he stood and said, "All right, I'll look into it."

I think you could tell Mike that terrorists had hidden a small nuclear device in his office and he would jot a few notes and say, "All right, I'll look into it." That's what he always does. This time, I said, "No, Mike, I want more than that."

He looked up and stared at me.

"I want to know why we're not shipping on time. I want to know why we can't execute."

With a small shrug of his big shoulders, he said, "Who says we can't?"

"I do! When people are playing the kinds of games that I saw going on last night, *they're not executing!*"

Mike turned sideways for a moment, then said, "Jake, I don't mean to argue with you, but we got to keep this in perspective. You know what I mean? Whatever happened at Logandale, those people saved our bacon. You know that? They made their numbers. As far as IT is concerned, as far as Borcon Corporate is concerned, *that* is what matters. Maybe Logandale did it with a wink and a grin that you weren't supposed to see, but the numbers are on the books. And I'll tell you from many years of experience, in this organization, the black and white numbers are what count."

"So you think I should just look the other way? Let it go?"

Another little shrug of the big shoulders. "What would you prefer? That they *didn't* make the numbers?"

"Mike, I want them to make the numbers. Obviously I want them to make the numbers. But I want them to do it the right way—by shipping quality products on time. Not with smoke and mirrors, not with—how'd you put it?—not with a wink and a grin."

Mike just looked at me, not winking or grinning. It's always hard to know what's really going on inside that big, bald head of his.

"Well?" I asked. "Wouldn't you agree? Wouldn't you prefer that they do it honestly?"

"Oh, yeah," he said. "Of course I would. And ninety-nine percent of the time they *do* do it the right way."

It was my turn just to look at him. "I don't think so, Mike. I seriously doubt that percentage."

Mike slapped his palms on his knees and rose to his feet. "Like I said, I'll look into it."

"No! Like *I* said, I want more than that. I want to examine every instance over the past year that an order has shipped late from Logandale and give me a *root-cause* analysis of what happened to make us to miss the promised date. I want that to be a top priority, and I'll expect it from you and your staff within two weeks. Is that understood?"

For a split second, he shot me a surprisingly hostile look, then he calmly asked me a few questions. We talked for another few minutes, he then stood up to leave and said, "Okay. Can do."

Eric Tillwell
Manager–Production Scheduling

I've known Mike for a lot of years. He's a great guy in many ways, but is he a great manager? Well . . . *he* thinks he is.

You know what KISS stands for? "Keep It Simple, Stupid." That's one of Mike's favorite expressions. He loves simple solutions, which is wonderful—if they work. The trouble is that our problems often are not simple. We're dealing with a lot of complexity, and Mike wants simple, yes-or-no, black-or-white kinds of answers. He will not admit that there are situations that require . . . how should I put it? That require a certain level of sophistication and cooperation between a number of diverse interests in order to achieve good results. Broadmindedness, shall we say, is not Mike's forte.

I like Mike on a personal level, but I've also had my differences with him over the years. He can be very stubborn. To people like Jake and Rick, to those to whom he reports, Mike probably seems like a godsend because he rarely argues with people who rank above him. He always conveys this impression that everything is in competent hands and that everything will be taken care of and there are no problems that he can't solve. Now, often the reality is very much at odds with that, but that's the impression Mike tries to put across. On the other hand, if you're under him, it can be hell. I'm glad I'm not one of his direct-reports.

Jake Foster
Senior Vice President–Operations

I had to get ready for a senior management meeting scheduled for later that morning. But after that talk with Mike, I found myself staring out the window, wondering if I was going to have to terminate him—or get him to retire early. I was also wondering who should replace him if that came to pass.

In the midst of that, I heard a soft knock on the door behind me. A woman I didn't recognize was there. She was stylishly dressed, yet she looked terrible, like she was sick.

"Excuse me, Mr. Foster."

"Yes?"

"I'm Vivian Lebeque. I was wondering if I could talk to you in private for a moment."

"Sure. Have a seat."

Before doing so, she closed my office door.

"Mr. Foster, I'm from marketing. I work for Karl Porter."

I knew Porter. He was marketing manager for Advanced Systems, the custom-design, high-end part of the business.

"I'm managing the Firefly Project. You're familiar with it?"

"I've seen the name once or twice in reports, but no, I'm not familiar with it. Maybe you should fill me in."

"Firefly is our internal code name for a proprietary technology we've been developing."

She went on to describe it, but I eventually had to cut her off because of time pressures.

"Okay, but what do you need from me?" I asked.

At this, her head lolled to one side, as if she didn't quite have the strength to hold it up.

"Are you all right?" I asked, worried that she actually might be on the verge of collapse.

She slowly shook her head, waved her hand as if to chase away any concern. "I've hardly had any sleep in three or four days."

"Why? What's going on?"

"Nothing! Which is exactly the problem! We are supposed to take Firefly into field testing, and nothing is coming together!"

She put her face into her hands for a moment, and when she took them down, there was the streak of a tear she had wiped away.

"I'm sorry . . . Engineering promised me that they would have the final configuration ready months ago. I finally found out yesterday that they're not even close. I talked to Sterling Grove"—he manages engineering design services—"and basically he blew me off. Said in as many words that his staff had higher priorities. Said that he doesn't report to

Marketing, that I had no authority over his engineers. Then he even had the nerve to imply that the delays were somehow *my* fault."

"Did you talk to Frank Harlan?" I asked.

"Yes, I talked to Frank. I wouldn't be bothering you with this if I hadn't."

"What did he say?"

"Well, we didn't talk face-to-face, we only exchanged e-mails. But basically, he indicated that he was siding with Sterling."

"I mean, what exactly did he say?"

"I can forward it to you, but mainly he said that SOS was the main focus of their attention right now, and that the final work on Firefly would have to wait until they could get around to it."

I thought about what had been said the night before in the limo. "I'm sorry, Vivian, but that doesn't sound terribly unreasonable to me. We don't have infinite resources—"

"I know! But this is not what I was being told even as recently as six weeks ago!"

"So what's happened since then?"

She waved her hand vaguely again. I could tell she was exhausted.

"I think that they were just stringing me along. Other than that, I don't really know." She pressed her lips together, thinking. Then her head lolled over again, and she pressed the fingers of one hand to her temple to hold it partway up. "Frank and Sterling have always been . . . well, *annoyed* that Karl and I contracted an outside firm to do the feasibility research and some of the basic development. If you want to know the root of it all, that's what started it. A lot of it is political. And to be brutally honest, I just don't have the clout to overcome their resistance."

"Yes, but isn't it also true that the company *does* have other priorities right now?"

"I grant you that SOS is the big deal of the moment. But Firefly could make this company far more money over time than SOS."

"Explain."

"SOS is an important leap over the Z-based standard, no question about it. SOS can do things that Z products never could, and even Z3 isn't as potent. But it is much more complex and error prone than Z and much more expensive. Everyone is gambling that SOS is so technically superior that over time customers will throw away their Z products, so they can take advantage of it. However, that remains to be seen."

"Okay, but what about Firefly?"

"Firefly is almost like a child's set of building blocks. Each module is basic, simple and cheap. Yet if you put them together, you can do some amazing things. While it's true Firefly won't do the ultra-high-end things that SOS will do, it will do a superior job—compared to Z products— of handling the tasks most end-users actually expect our products to perform in real life."

"What are the shortcomings? The liabilities?"

"Well . . . it doesn't work very well with SOS. That's the chief one as far as Engineering is concerned. It does work with all except the earliest Z products, and it will work with Z3."

"Tell me, did our own engineering department develop Firefly?"

"No," she said, "the initial development was done at a little company out in California that we acquired a few years ago. We bought them out mainly to get the Kenosha facility and some OEM contracts. Firefly was just thrown into the bargain, and nobody paid any attention to it until one of Sterling's engineers—who has since left the company—brought it to Karl's and my attention. I immediately could see the potential not just in terms of current customer base, but in all kinds of new applications that would take us into other product lines."

"This does sound very intriguing," I told her.

"Yes, I've always thought so, yet I can hardly get these jerks in Engineering to return my phone calls." She leaned forward to make her point. "Mr. Foster, I have a major potential customer for Firefly ready to work with us on the testing. And I don't mean to brag, but I can tell you it was no easy achievement to set that up."

She told me the name of the company, and yes, it was a big one.

"I even got Bill Albrecht at the Hangar to schedule time to make some prototypes for testing, but Engineering won't fix some critical flaws in the design. They keep saying they will, but then months go by and nothing happens. We've already postponed the production and testing schedule twice. If we have to postpone again, everybody is going to be pissed off, and we may not be able to keep the customer interested. I'm telling you, Mr. Foster, we are blowing it."

With that, the energy that her anger was fueling died, and she slumped back in the chair.

I thought a moment. And my conclusion was, Yes, this was intriguing, but there was no way. There was no way with Rick fixated on SOS and waffling on Z3 that we could muster the will as an organization to pursue this other thing, good as it sounded. But still . . .

"Vivian, I have a meeting today with Frank Harlan and Sterling Grove, and I will bring this up for discussion. But I can't make any promises to you. In all honesty, I'm not sure that this fits with the strategy that's been mandated for the company."

Her eyes instantly welled up with tears, which instantly embarrassed me. I opened a drawer of my desk and got a box of tissues that I pushed toward her. She wiped her eyes and quickly got herself under control again.

"I'm sorry," she said. "I guess I've allowed myself to become personally involved in this . . . which is probably silly."

"No, come on," I said. "It's not such a bad thing to be committed to something you're working on, that you're responsible for."

"Well . . . they can't say I didn't try," she said as she stood up to go. "Thank you for at least listening to me."

And she all but ran from my office.

6

Frank Harlan
Vice President and Director–Engineering

Great engineering is the heart and soul of this company. Always has been, always will be. It is the very essence of the Essential Corporation.

I make a point of telling that to every engineer who joins Essential. They need to understand our value system within the organization. Our so–called culture, as they say. Further, they need to understand what is at stake and what is expected of them. Without the high standards of excellence in engineering that we—and our customers—demand, the Essential Corporation would not long retain its competitive edge in the marketplace.

While it is our duty to service the customer, it must be recognized that customers do not know what is best for them from an engineering standpoint. After all, how many people would be able to design their own automobiles? When the average person buys a car, that person simply wants to be able to get behind the wheel, turn the key and experience a smooth, comfortable ride. Determining how all that occurs is not within that customer's range of competence. It is the very same with Essential's products and services.

We, as engineers, often must make significant choices on the customer's behalf, choices with respect to advancing the core technology of our products. This is why I personally was an early supporter of the SOS standard. SOS offers a wide range of benefits that far exceed the capabilities of all preceding standards. Customers may not recognize this at first, but they will eventually—provided, of course, that marketing does its job and tells them. To ignore SOS is to ignore the state of the art.

Jake Foster
Senior Vice President–Operations

As I said to Vivian, I had a meeting scheduled that morning with Frank Harlan and Sterling Grove on a number of matters. Among them was a custom-design project that had gone significantly over budget—mainly because the project engineers, from what I could tell, kept on fussing with the damn thing to make it ever more perfect rather than finishing it so we could get paid. Then there was Z3, but before getting to that, I brought up Firefly.

"What about it?" Frank asked, as Sterling wiggled in his seat.

"Vivian Lebeque was in my office this morning. She's concerned that she's got a major customer—or potential customer at least—lined up to test this thing and Design Services isn't going to be ready. She's also concerned that, in her view, she's not getting the support she was promised."

"Jake, we're really stretched pretty thin around here because of SOS," said Frank.

"Look, I know how important SOS is. On the other hand, if Design Services made the commitment—"

"The commitment," said Sterling, "was made by Vivian, not by us."

"She claims that you told her you would be ready."

"She totally misinterpreted what I said. She never should have committed to a specific test date until we had signed off on it."

Frank then put a hand on Sterling's arm to quiet him and turned to me. "Jake, why are you taking Marketing's side in this?"

The question floored me. "I'm not, Frank. I'm just trying to find out what the problem is."

"Their priorities are very different from ours."

"Oh, really? Well, that could be the problem right there," I said, and they both looked at me as if I'd come from another planet.

"I personally think," said Sterling, "that the problem is Vivian."

"Why is that?"

"Well . . . if I may speak plainly, she's really become a pain in the ass.

There are procedures that are supposed to keep these kinds of conflicts from occurring, and Vivian keeps approaching us directly!"

"I'm sorry," I said. "I don't follow you."

"She, like all of the marketing product managers, is supposed to go through PDT."

PDT is the acronym for Product Development Team. Feigning innocence, I asked, "Why does she have to go through PDT?"

"Because that is the procedure that is in place," insisted Frank. "PDT is a clearinghouse for all product development activities. She, like everyone else, is supposed to submit her requests to PDT and communicate with other functions through that channel. That's how products are developed around here. We need that kind of open forum and teamwork to be assured that resources are judiciously applied."

Sterling nervously chuckled and said, "Of course, what usually happens is Rick goes to a conference, gets an idea, and sends out an e-mail that says, 'Do it!'"

Frank Harlan shot him a look that froze him in place. Then he looked at me and said, "The point, Jake, is that these procedures are in place for a purpose, and the people in this company are supposed to abide by them. The purpose of it all is to ensure that this company does not waste engineering resources."

I am a believer in choosing one's battles, and I didn't want to fight this one at that particular time. So I just nodded.

"Listen, it's not that I have anything personal against Vivian," added Sterling, "but I'm not sure she should be handling Firefly."

"Why is that?"

"Because for one thing, she's only got an MBA. She's not an engineer. She doesn't have full command of the technical issues involved in Firefly."

I started to object, but Sterling kept on.

"And another thing is that while she is passionate about the projects she takes on, I don't think she's emotionally stable. Last week, she was screaming at me. Yesterday, she broke down in tears. I mean, it's embarrassing."

I again nodded. This time I somewhat agreed with him. Screaming and crying was not exactly the best professional demeanor. On the other hand, I suspect that any human being forced to follow the procedural runaround that Sterling and Frank insisted upon would likely scream and cry by the end of it all.

"All right," I said, "let's for the moment set aside Vivian Lebeque and the procedures and all of that. Right or wrong, a commitment was made to an important potential customer. I still think we need to try to get Firefly into testing by the agreed-upon date."

"I think that's not doable," said Frank, although I was really directing this more to Sterling.

"Why not?"

"I can take bodies off of SOS and put them on Firefly, but what are you going to tell Rick when we miss some critical phase of the SOS rollout?"

"I fail to understand why we cannot accomplish both."

"The way this should be handled, Jake, is we should refer the matter back to PDT and let them sort it out," said Frank.

Now I was starting to feel like screaming and crying, *No! We are the managers in charge. Let's figure out how to get this done.*

I could tell Sterling was about to cave in, but Frank cut him off. "Jake, you are relatively new to the company. I don't think you fully comprehend that there are ways we do things in this organization. These procedures have stood the test of time, and I really think that before we make any decisions, you should talk to Rick about circumventing the procedures in place and advise him of the risks with respect to SOS."

He was trying to push me into a corner, and I was fed up. "I will mention it to Rick, but we don't—*I* don't—need his approval. He's already approved Firefly. Now we should move forward and get Firefly into testing without missing any critical deadlines on SOS."

Frank was shaking his head. But Sterling spoke up then.

"Frank, we can do it. Somehow. There's that technical conference in San Diego next week. We've got a lot of people going to it, and I guess I could tell some of them they have to stay here and work on Firefly. They won't like it, but . . ."

"Hold on," Frank told him, "is that fair to them? What's it going to do to morale? And haven't we already paid their registration fees and airfares?"

"I think there is a lot more at stake here than morale and a few grand in fees and fares," I said. "That's a good call, Sterling. Get them on it."

Sterling nodded. Frank frowned.

"Now, next topic," I said. "Don't freak out on me, but I have been charged with asking you this by none other than Rick Riggins. On a fast-track basis, how much time and how much money would it take to get a Z3 product on the market?"

There was great wailing and gnashing of teeth.

Sterling Grove

Director–Engineering and Design

Later that morning after we'd had the meeting with Jake about Firefly and Z3, Frank Harlan stopped by my office and invited me to lunch. On our way out, we took the stairs. The building has elevators, but they are so slow that a lot of people—Frank being one—always use the stairs instead.

So we were in the stairwell, on our way to the building lobby, and half a flight down, after the fire door had shut, Frank Harlan put his hand on my shoulder—firmly.

I said, "What's the matter?"

"Don't you ever do that again," he said.

"What?!" I asked. "What did I do?"

"Don't *ever* take his side over mine."

"Whose side?"

"You know who I'm talking about."

I listened for footsteps for half a second to be sure the stairwell was empty of everyone else except us. Then I said, "You mean G.W."

G.W. was our code name for Jake Foster. Actually it was a double code. G.W. stood for "Gee-Whiz," which was what Frank called Jake within the handful of engineers and engineering managers like me that Frank deemed his inner circle. Gee-Whiz was some kind of reference to Jake's always spouting off about General Electric and how we should try to be more like GE. Hence, Gee-Whiz.

"Frank, listen," I said. "I just was trying to go the extra mile to keep everybody happy."

"You keep your focus on SOS and the projects that are important. Firefly shouldn't even be on the list. Firefly was forced on us by Marketing, over my objections. Firefly has no place here. And until you shot your mouth off—"

"But, Frank, I think we can do it."

"Rick supports SOS, and that is where we need to focus. If it isn't re-lated to SOS, it doesn't get to the top of the list. Understood?"

"Okay," I said. "But what am I supposed to do after what I told G.W. in the meeting?"

"You can put a couple of people on Firefly, just make sure they're Drones not Talent."

That was more code. "Drones" were engineers who were lower level and did the equivalent of grunt work. "Talent" was the select group made up of the best engineers.

"But," Frank continued, "I do want you to assign someone from Tal-ent—someone like Raj or Howard—to go over what the Drones do and question every potential drawback and document it out the wazoo. My hope is that Firefly dies the quiet death it deserves, but if it ever does go into the field, I want to make sure it's E.B. who gets egg on his face. And it wouldn't bother me if G.W. gets some too since he's taking their side."

E.B. stood for "Easter Bunny," which referred to Vince Springer. I guess the association went something like Springer . . . spring . . . Easter . . . Easter Bunny. There were codes for other people, too. There was P.M. That was Mike Zarelli. P.M. stood for someone late in the day of his ca-reer or, sometimes, in a mild ethnic slur, "Pizza Man." And there was B.G. That was Big Guy, or Rick Riggins. But most of the time, Frank referred to Rick just as Rick. He mostly used the codes for people he didn't trust or didn't like, which was pretty much anyone outside of his Inner Circle. Those were the ones—the people and their functions—who should have egg on their faces. It was imperative to Frank that Engineering never get egg on its face.

"All right," I said, "I'll put some Drones on it, and I'll have Raj pick apart what they do. But what about Z3? Sounds like B.G. really wants to move on it."

"I've got B.G.'s ear," said Frank. "I'll handle it, don't worry."

He finally took his hand off my shoulder—he'd been holding it there the whole time we'd been talking, not hard, but making sure I stayed there with my full attention on him—and instead patted it.

"Just be patient," Frank said to me as we started down the steps again. "In a year or two, if not sooner, G.W. will be history. He doesn't belong here. I can't imagine what Rick was thinking, bringing in an outsider like him who has no background in this industry. He's not even an engineer, and to top it off, he's got health problems."

I understood what he meant. I'd heard about the cancer.

"Meanwhile," Frank said, "B.G. will likely move up to Borcon Corporate when SOS is a success. Or he'll move on because he wants a shot at the big time before he retires. In any case, the odds strongly favor that I'll be running the company."

He smiled at me then. There seemed to be no doubt in his mind that SOS would be a triumph and that he and Rick would get the credit.

We reached the first-floor landing. Frank put his hand on the fire door handle, but didn't pull it open. He just stood there holding it shut. Almost whispering, he said, "You know they won't give it to E.B. because nobody trusts him. And he's the only other contender. Sterling, you just need to remember that every vice president of engineering this company has ever had has come from Design Services."

He winked at me then, opened the door, and we went on to lunch.

Jake Foster
Senior Vice President–Operations

Senior management meetings at Essential usually start at 8:00 A.M.—except when they occur on the first day of a new month or a new quarter. Rick gives our VP of finance, Jane Grimm, a few extra hours to pull together what he terms the "quickie report"—a hastily prepared first pass at the numbers for the latest accounting period, something to let Rick and everybody else know whether or not we were in trouble. Or, more often in those days, how much we were in trouble.

I was a few minutes late getting to the senior management meeting, and they had started without me. Rick is a stickler for starting on time. Senior management meetings were usually held in the small conference room next to Rick's office. They were not particularly formal and we did not have assigned seats per se. Yet everyone tended to sit in the same places at every meeting. Rick always sat at the head of the table nearest the whiteboard, which spanned the wall behind him. Immediately to Rick's right, typically, was Vince Springer, and to the right of Vince was Frank Harlan.

Even though Frank reported to me, he was considered senior management. I suppose it went back to the great-engineering mantra. In other words, since great engineering was one of the core values of Essential and since Frank was the top engineer in the company, and since I was just a manager (as in, *not* an engineer), Frank had to be there. Which actually was fine with me because there often were a number of involved, engineering-related issues to be discussed.

At the far end of the table, directly opposite Rick and as far from him as it was possible to sit while at the same table (a significant fact in the eyes of some) was our vice president of human resources, Pamela Cantrell. Pam was younger than the rest of us, probably early forties. She was black, tall, and elegant. I don't know where Pam bought her clothes, but I doubt it was in Grandville. She dressed exquisitely—always in good taste, but in vivid colors, in yellows, reds, violets. That particular day she wore a suit the shade of tangerines with a white silk blouse and a simple gold necklace.

Jane Grimm typically sat to my left and to Pam's right. Jane was a petite woman in her late fifties who exuded a conservative elegance. She favored dresses with dark colors—navy, black, brown—colors in contrast to her pale white face and hands and her silver hair. Her small stature concealed a strong, clear voice, and when Jane spoke, there was seldom any nonsense in what she said.

When I sat down—muttering apologies for my tardiness—she reached over as she continued speaking, and with her forefinger tapped a row of numbers on the printout at my place on the table, as if to tell me, here's where we are singing in the hymnal.

I quickly glanced at Rick's face to get an impression of the situation, and indeed this told me almost as much as the numbers on the page. He looked relieved.

". . . So," Jane concluded, "as always, I caution you that these are not the *final,* final numbers, as we won't have those until next week at the earliest. However, these are currently the best available, and they should be well within the ballpark, so to speak."

"Which means we made the projections that I gave to Corporate," Rick said. "We're on plan. Of course we did it by the skin of our teeth," and he laughed, "but we did it."

"Hey, if you're over the bar, you're over the bar," said Vince. "That's what matters."

Bear in mind that the plan given to Corporate was pretty pathetic, though they had pressed Rick hard. And here we were just clearing "the bar" by a hair's width.

Rick made a gesture as if to wipe the sweat from his brow, and then cut loose with a grand guffaw that Vince and Frank both mimicked and that the rest of us smiled or chuckled at.

"Okay, moving on," said Rick, "let's talk about what we heard last night over dinner with Southeast. First of all, Jake, what's the status of that order they were all fussed up about?"

I cleared my throat. "I made a personal visit to Logandale after we landed. You're not going to like this, but . . ."

Then I told them. I told them everything. By the end of it, Rick's elbows were on the table, and he was leaning forward, his two hands covering the sides of his face, fingers massaging his forehead.

"I've instructed Mike Zarelli to put together a root-cause analysis of why these orders are not being shipped on time," I concluded. "We have to get to the bottom of this and deal with it."

By now, Frank was giving me an almost pitiful look, and Vince was staring at me in disgust.

"So this order that we swore up and down would reach them by to-day *still* isn't out of the plant!" said Vince. "Man, does that make us look bad! Makes us look like idiots!"

I raised my voice. "I don't like it either! I don't like it one bit, but this is the reality we're facing."

"The reality *you're* facing," Vince said.

"Now, wait a minute," Jane said to me, "what this means, if I understand you, is that an order—a large order—that just sneaked under the wire and is now on the books as a receivable, in accounting terms, is really not. It's still inventory. Work-in-process. Correct?"

"Well . . . I suppose so."

The pen in her hand went into the air, lazily spinning end over end before it plopped onto the center of the table.

"That wouldn't be a part of these numbers," asked Rick, holding up the printout Jane had read from, "would it?"

"We crunched these numbers first thing this morning, based on everything on the system as of midnight last night. So if we back that order out—"

"Oh, now hold on here," said Rick. "Let's not go down that path."

"What choice is there?" asked Jane.

Rick held up his hand for silence around the table. There was a small, pocket tape recorder that Rick used for dictation and to help him keep the minutes of these meetings, which he did with the help of his assistant, Betty Jo. He switched the recorder off now.

"I want everyone to feel they can speak freely," he said. "Now . . . I can't see any merit in juggling numbers that are already in the system, if that's where you were headed, Jane."

"Well, if those numbers do not adequately represent the accounting period—"

"You're opening a big can of worms."

She considered this. "The question that immediately springs to my mind is, what else don't we know about? How many other orders like this are there? Do we have truck trailers sitting in the parking lot filled with work-in-process? Self-storage units around town filled with inventory that's been recorded as shipped sales?"

"No, absolutely not!" I said. "I think we should take this seriously, but at the same time, let's not blow it out of proportion. Look, this was nothing more than the result of pressure—from the top—at the end of an accounting period."

"Jake's right," said Rick. "Let's keep it in perspective. Let's not open a can of worms—"

"Rick, do you realize the trouble this can cause?" asked Jane.

"Okay, okay," said Rick. "If you feel *that* strongly, then take if off the books, or whatever you feel is right. But if it was really only a matter of a few hours, where was the harm? I'm sure that's what the plant was thinking, that it was only a matter of hours, so why not book it? Or, you know, the other possibility is that it was just an honest mistake, some kind of confusion."

"Rick, I saw what I saw," I told him.

Jane turned to me. "Why did you even bring this up?"

"Why? Because I think we, as senior managers, should know what's really going on! Isn't that why we have these meetings? To discuss serious issues? To deal with them? Isn't that why they pay us?"

"Excuse me," said Vince, "but I think what perhaps Jane meant to say is, why did you bring this up *now*?"

"I don't understand," I said. "Why shouldn't I bring it up now? I mean, Rick asked me—"

"Rick asked you the status of an order, which has nothing to do with dredging up all this other stuff. Rick, I hope I'm not overstepping here. . . . Well, in fact, I probably am overstepping, but I just want to say this. Jake, I don't know how they did things at the other companies you worked for, but in this company we're paid to manage our functions. I manage marketing and sales, and if there is a problem in those areas, I solve it. And if some problem about marketing or sales needs to be discussed here in senior management, then I come to the meeting with the answer. I don't lay the problem on everybody else."

"That's not what I was doing."

"Well, it seems to me that you have an operational problem and that you, as head of operations, should solve that problem. Or at the very least, you should evaluate the problem on your own and then come to the table with a complete report and the solution that you intend to implement. If you're a senior manager in this company, you're paid to have the answers."

"All right," said Rick, "let's move on."

"No," I said. "I'd like to respond to that." I turned to Vince. "First of all, I was at Logandale until one o'clock in the morning. Nobody wants a solution more than I do, and I'm not laying off my part of the responsibility for finding one on anyone else. But let me ask you, Vince, what makes you so sure that this is strictly a manufacturing problem?"

Expecting a trap, Vince didn't answer.

"I heard indications this morning that the marketing forecast was way out of line, that they were being asked to do the impossible with respect to fill rates—issues that tie at least part of the problem to marketing and sales."

"Now wait a minute," said Vince, "if you're trying to point the finger at me—"

"I'm not blaming you. Just the opposite, in fact. I'm saying that the number-one issue in this company isn't just late shipments, or poor service, or Z3 versus SOS. The number-one issue is our ability to perform as an organization—as a whole, as a group. And we—all of us— are coasting downhill. We are losing ground relative to the competition. And our performance is going nowhere except off a cliff . . . unless we can work together and support each other."

Well, I thought it had been a terrific speech. I thought I had nailed it perfectly.

But Vince blinked a few times, then said innocently, "I don't think my performance has gone off a cliff."

Arrghh! I turned to Rick, hoping I'd at least made an impression on him—and found he was solemnly scribbling a note on a pad of paper. I don't think he had really heard anything I'd said. When he comprehended silence around the table, he glanced up.

"Are we finished? Can we get off the soapboxes?" he asked. He reached for the recorder and switched it on again. "Jake, I want you to fully—and quickly—investigate the incident at Logandale. Let's try to see if they have some justifiable reason why that order was recorded into the system the way it was. Jane, are you okay with that?"

"Hold on, Rick, what do you mean, 'investigate the incident'? I'm having them look into the total problem."

"Fine, they should do that, too. But I want you to look into this specific incident, since you brought it up. Perhaps you don't know the whole story yet."

"I just talked to Diane Sullivan!"

"Well, maybe she doesn't know the whole story yet. Isn't that possible? There very well could have been an honest misunderstanding between the hourly people over what was what. Okay? Now, Jane, that's all right with you?"

"Well . . . I suppose if Jake, you know, got the wrong impression and Logandale had valid reasons to record that shipment the way they did, then of course the numbers should stay the way they are. But I need to know definitely by first thing next week."

I could hardly believe it. What a brilliant solution! There were no games being played; it was all legitimate!

"Okay, Jake? You'll investigate and, hopefully, find the reason why this shipment was on the books correctly?" asked Rick.

I looked at him. It was very clear what *his* priorities were. His expression said to me, you had damn well better make sure that we have justification for leaving this on the books.

"Okay, Jake?"

"All right," I muttered.

"What's next on the agenda?" Rick quietly asked himself, scanning the list in front of him.

• • •

When I got home that evening, I went fishing. Just went by myself, headed my boat toward the middle of the lake where there was nobody, and when I got there I shut off the motor and drifted with my line in the water. Didn't care if I caught anything. I needed time and space to my-self, so I could think about . . . everything. My life. My work. What I wanted weighed against the dwindling and unknown quantity of time available to achieve it.

I was alone, but it was as if someone else was with me, some other part of me sitting just out of my field of vision, the two of us quietly talk-ing without a word being spoken aloud.

Why are you doing this? asked the voice. *Why are you working for Essential?*

Because. Because I took the job and I have an obligation to see it through. Because Sandy doesn't want to move again. She's happy now. She went through hell with my cancer, and I owe it to her not to mess up her life again.

If you're miserable, Sandy won't be happy for long.

True. But I can't quit. At least not yet.

But you may not have many years left. Not years you can count on. The can-cer comes back, you might not make it to sixty-five. Why do you want to spend the time you do have left working for Rick Riggins?

The answer came with no hesitation: Because I don't want to end my career as a has-been from DysCo. I want to do it right.

There. That was it. The real reason why I'd gone back to work and why I wanted to keep working. All those months, whenever Sandy or the kids or friends or anybody asked me about moving to Grandville and working for Essential, I'd talked about the offer being too good to turn down, about how the cancer had really set us back financially, about how I just wasn't ready to retire. But while mostly true, those reasons were hollow. The solid core of why I was here was that I wanted to go out of the game as a winner, not a loser. More than just "want." I *needed* to win this one.

Okay, said the voice, *but how are you going to win it?*

A chilly breeze came across the water, rippling the calm surface.

I don't know, I thought. It seems almost impossible.

Great. You're as clueless as they are.

Not true. I at least have GE. I have that rock to stand on. I have that experience. I know what it is to be doing it right.

You had that experience at DysCo and it didn't make any difference in the end.

I thought I could do it alone at DysCo. That was my big mistake.

You're alone this time, too.

Yes. And I have to change that. I need allies.

How are you going to get them?

With honesty. With facts. If I keep hitting them with the facts, they have to see the truth. The delusions, the bad ideas, the stupid games have to give way. Rick and the others will have to change, if only for self-preservation. And then there are people like Diane Sullivan who want to change things and have no advocate to help them. If I can just find more like her, I might have a chance. I can be their advocate; they can be my allies.

It's going to take time. And you might not have the kind of time it's going to take. Essential, as a company, might not have the time either.

Yes. I need to figure out a way to make it happen faster. To accelerate the rate of change.

I sat there in the boat, fishing but not fishing, until the sun was below the treeline on the shore. Then I reeled in my line, started the motor and headed in. I knew what I wanted. But I had no idea how I was ever going to make it happen.

DIAGNOSIS

7

George M. Tracy
Consultant

Reed Lawrence is CEO of a company we've worked with. A good client. Anyway, Reed was at an executive conference, and he happened to be seated at the same table as Brandon Claymore of Borcon. I don't know what Reed said about us, but it must have been compelling because a few days later I got a call from one of Mr. Claymore's assistants.

I flew to Dallas and had a brief meeting with Brandon. The meeting did not go well. He sort of "got it" in some ways, but not really, and he soon pawned me off on an executive vice president. That turned out to be a good thing, however. The executive VP—Nancy Quinn—and I had a productive conversation, at the end of which she picked up the phone and called Rick Riggins.

In the established Borcon culture, if you got a call from Corporate, you had to take it seriously—especially if the caller was someone who reported directly to Brandon Claymore, as was the case here. So Rick had to give me the time of day. Now, that's neither my usual nor my preferred way of gaining a new client (mostly that's by referral, the way it started out with Reed—one CEO confiding in another), but out of respect for all, I wanted to follow up. Rick, however, seemed to be genuinely interested the several times we talked by phone, and he asked me to come to Grandville.

Fine. I made the arrangements and flew to Grandville. The minute I walked in, though, it was clear Rick's interest had been superceded by other factors. He seemed distracted and rushed. It was like, "Oh . . . it's you. Yes, I've got to talk to you because I invited you and because Corporate told me I should. Well, let's hurry up and talk because I've got seventeen other things on my mind." I actually wondered if there was some crisis going on in the background, which, as it turned out, there was, but when I gently probed that possibility, Rick assured me that everything was fine. As in, pay no attention to those alarms and sirens going off and the smoke rolling in from under the door; everything is under control.

Particularly aggravating from my perspective was that I had come prepared to make a presentation to the Essential senior management team. But Rick told me flat out that wasn't going to happen, and he was rather vague about the reasons. He thought it would be better, so he said, for the two of us to talk and then for me to meet individually with one or two of the senior team. That was not what we had agreed upon, but I could see that arguing with him was not going to win the day.

After our twenty-minute meeting, Rick shunted me off to talk with Vince Springer. Vince was politely receptive, but after a few minutes I could tell he was just going through the motions to please Rick—much as Rick had been going through the motions to please Corporate. I thought to myself, "Well, it sure looks like a brick wall at the end of this street." When Vince's assistant interrupted to ask him to take a call from BigBox, I immediately searched my briefcase for my OAG and the schedule of flights leaving Grandville, hoping there would be something earlier than the one I was on. You may be the best doctor in the world, but if the patient won't even tell you what hurts, there is not much you can do.

Vince covered the mouthpiece of the phone and apologized to me, saying that the call was important and likely to go on for some time. I nodded an acknowledgment and prepared to leave, thinking this had all been a waste of time, but Vince insisted that his assistant take me down to meet somebody named Jake Foster.

Jake wasn't even expecting me, and at first I didn't think I'd do any better with him than I'd done with Rick or Vince. But then he asked me about my background, and I mentioned that I had worked for General Electric.

"Oh, really? What part of GE?"

"Mostly in Medical Systems," I told him.

"Really?"

"Yes, for twelve years, the last five as general manager."

That caught Jake's interest, and we talked for some time about it. Eventually, though, the conversation came back to consulting, and he told me in so many words that he didn't think very highly of consultants.

To which I said, "That makes two of us."

"Why is that?" he asked.

"Because the way most consulting is practiced, it doesn't work. It's a waste of time and money."

"So, that begs the question: Why are you in the consulting business?"

"Actually," I said, "I'm sort of the *anti*consultant."

Jake was amused by that. "Oh, really? How so?"

"Most consultants approach their work as if they are the experts and their role is to figure out the problems, come up with the answers, and tell management how to run its business. My view is the opposite. It is *management's* job to figure out the problems, find the best answers, and develop a strategy to continuously improve the business—and in fact to implement that strategy and to make adjustments to it as needed. My role, as a consultant, is to enable and accelerate the process through which management makes those things occur. Now, with all due respect, I am no dummy, and I will probably have a good idea of what the answers are before the organization as a whole reaches the same conclusions. I often suggest things that haven't been considered, or that can't be talked about openly. I can point you in the best directions, but the main value my associates and I supply is the medicine for the company to heal itself."

"Heal itself? What are you talking about?"

"I like to use analogies of health and medicine in describing what my associates and I do. Think of the corporate organization as a body, as an organism. When the body is healthy, it nourishes itself, it defends against destructive influences, it grows and gets stronger. When the body is unhealthy—or when it's sick—it doesn't function the way it should, it can't fend off the forces that would harm it, and it doesn't grow stronger, but becomes progressively fat and weak. What we do—my associates and I—is treat the disease that caused the company to become unhealthy in the first place. Most of the time, that means curing the management culture. In fact, we call what we do Enterprise Medicine."

Jake was clearly intrigued by all this. He got up and came around his desk. There was a sitting area to one side of his office with a small sofa and a couple of upholstered chairs. He gestured for me to come with him over there, and we sat together.

"It's interesting, your choice of phrases . . . your analogy of sickness and health," he said. "Do you have a few minutes?"

"Got all day," I said.

Then he told me what he'd been through.

Jake Foster
Senior Vice President—Operations

Sometime after my fiftieth birthday, I noticed I was getting tired a lot. Just didn't have the energy I used to. *Age,* I told myself. *You're not a kid anymore.* Yet, overachiever that I am, I wasn't going to let a few decades slow me down. So I joined a health club. Either in the morning or at lunchtime, depending on my schedule, I would drive to the club and work out. Exercise, the experts say, boosts your daily energy level. Good, I thought, that's just what I need.

My workouts at the club lasted less than a month. It's not like me to give up on something I've started, and I'd already paid the club a year's membership in advance. But those workouts were hell on me. I'd stagger out the door afterwards, then have to sit in my car for a few minutes before I had the energy to drive to the office. And then my energy level did not improve; I was just tired all the time.

Man, are you out of shape, I told myself. *What a wimp.*

Anyway, I quit going. It wasn't accomplishing what I thought it would, and I needed whatever energy I had for my job. The Stairmaster wasn't going to get me to the top.

Almost simultaneous with joining the health club, I had taken on new responsibilities at DysCo, as I was now managing a division. I knew I'd be traveling more than ever, so why try to develop a routine I wouldn't be able to keep up?

One evening, my wife, Sandy, told me, "Honey, you don't seem like yourself anymore." I was slumped in a chair, and she was rubbing my shoulders. "You always seem tired and a little irritable."

"It's just the stress," I told her.

Indeed, I was sure it was stress. And I ignored it. After all, I'd dealt with stress all of my adult life.

One night I was getting ready for bed and Sandy looked at my body and said, "What are those bumps?"

"What?"

"Those bumps." She pointed to one, put her finger on it.

"Oh, I've had those for a while," I said.

"Yes, but what are they?"

"I don't know." I shrugged. "They don't really bother me. I think they're just . . . what do you call them? Cysts. You know the kind. You smack 'em with a heavy dictionary and they go away."

"You want me to get a dictionary?"

"No." I shrugged again. "Honest, they don't bother me. They don't hurt or anything."

Then came the itching. I was in a meeting, and my skin began to itch. So, trying not to draw attention to myself, I scratched a little, here and there, but it didn't help. The itch kept itching. It was a long meeting, and by the end I could hardly contain myself. I hurried to the men's room, took off my shirt, and scratched like mad. Even that didn't help much. It was an itch not on the surface of the skin, but under it.

"Do you have some kind of rash?" Sandy asked.

"No."

"Then it must be the stress you're under," she said.

"You know," I said, "we could use a vacation. At least I could. Get away for a while. Relax. Rest up."

A while later, we packed and flew to Costa Rica. I was itching and scratching the whole way, but I figured once I got away from the stress for a week, I'd be fine.

The first night in the hotel, I had some kind of nightmare about being underwater, and I began to moan or shout or something in my sleep, believing that I was really drowning. Sandy woke me, and I jolted out of bed. She turned on a light. I looked down at myself, and it was as if I'd jumped into a river. I was drenched. My skin had a sheen of sweat. The sheets where I'd been lying were soaked, like someone had dumped a bucket of water on that side of the bed.

"Are you all right?" Sandy asked. "I hope you're not coming down with something."

"It was just a bad dream," I said.

"Are you sure?"

"I feel fine."

A maid came and changed the sheets. I took a shower, got back in bed, and slept until morning. But in the morning I didn't feel fine, and I had a mild fever.

Sandy was clearly disappointed. "Oh, no, not on vacation," she said.

"Must have caught a bug of some kind."

"You know, Jake, you're so stressed out, your immune system is probably low."

"I just hope it's not Montezuma's revenge."

It wasn't. After a day or so, I began feeling a little better. We got out more, saw the rain forest and all, but I could never seem to get the right temperature. I always felt either overheated or chilly, no matter what the ambient air was like.

"You must have caught a cold and your body is fighting it off," Sandy suggested.

We made the best of it, but the night before we flew home, the night sweats came back again and we had to call the maid again to change the sheets.

On our return, I got on the bathroom scale and was shocked. I'd lost fifteen pounds. Sandy and I joked about it, said we'd have to go on vacation more often. I concluded it was probably water loss from all that sweating.

After a few more days, though, I still didn't feel good, and I hadn't started gaining the weight back. Instead, my weight kept gradually dropping.

Finally, Sandy said, "Maybe you should see a doctor."

"No, I'll be all right. Anyway, I have to fly to London the day after tomorrow. There's no time."

"If you're not better by the time you get back, I want you to see a doctor."

"Yeah, yeah."

But I wasn't and I didn't. I just kept going. I was heavily involved in a lot of different things, and even though the load in every way kept on getting heavier, I just kept on going, a tired old locomotive chugging up the mountain—and going slower, and slower . . . and slower.

Others around me began—or I should say, continued—to notice.

My boss: "Jake, you don't seem to be a hundred percent. Maybe you want to think about delegating some of the less important tasks."

"I've just been under the weather lately. But I'll consider that."

My assistant: "Mr. Foster, you've had that cold for a long time."

"Yeah, I just can't seem to shake it. I'm going to get some of those vitamins, the stress-formula kind."

My wife again: "Jake, I really think you should see a doctor."

"Yeah, I probably should."

"Well, why don't you?"

"I'll check my calendar as soon as I get back from the conference. Probably be fine by then."

My assistant again: "Mr. Foster, you're sick."

"No, I'm all right."

"Really, look at you."

I shot a steely look at her. "I don't have time to be sick. I've got too much to do."

Going home from work that evening, I found I was having trouble controlling the car; I was so tired, so feverish, so weak. Somehow I got the car off the highway and parked in the back of a restaurant parking lot. There I just sat for a long time, dozed for a while. It was dark by the time I got going again.

I don't know how I made it home, but somehow I did. I aimed the car into the driveway, coasted to a stop, shut off the engine, and passed out like a drunk. Next thing I remember, I was in the passenger seat. Don't recall moving over there. Sandy was driving the car.

I asked, "Where are we going?"

"I'm taking you to the emergency room."

I didn't have the strength to argue.

They admitted me that night. Did some tests the next day. Before the week was out, they gave me the news. I had lymphoma. Cancer.

I know. You're thinking, *what an idiot. Why didn't he just have the common sense to see a doctor?*

Because I didn't perceive until the very end that anything was seriously wrong. Everything happening seemed to be just a "normal" consequence of my life. It was just stress. Or it was just a cold. Or it was just something that would either go away or I'd learn to live with. The fatigue, the bumps, the itching, the night sweats, the chills, the mild fevers, the unaccountable weight loss—hey, nothing I couldn't handle.

And, yes, I was in denial. Toward the end, as I was approaching the collapse, I knew something was wrong, something really bad. But by then I didn't want to know. It was too scary. I just hoped it would go away.

I missed the final days of DysCo's demise because by then I was going from doctor to doctor, hospital to hospital, trying to save my life and get well again. By the time I was in remission, DysCo was dead. The viable pieces of it had been spun off or bought by other companies. Pieces of my division survived, but it wasn't much consolation to me.

During the long and awful journey toward remission, I spent many hours reflecting upon my life. And since a significant portion of my life had been invested in my job with DysCo, I also did a lot of thinking about what had happened there, what had gone wrong, and why I hadn't been able to make more of an impact.

For years, it had been obvious to me (and a lot of other managers there) that DysCo was screwed up. The management organization had become dysfunctional. And the worst of it was that management—senior management especially—was in denial, just as I had been about my lymphoma.

Friends from work—other managers mostly, some of them fairly high up the ladder—had been coming to see me while I was sick. As I began to get stronger, we even played some golf. My friends could see that things were not as they should be. Not one of them, though, would ever admit that DysCo might not survive. And as individuals, they were powerless against the disease that, in fact, was killing the company. Even at the very top, I later found out, there was for the most part a naive confidence that somehow everything would work out, that nothing was as bad as it really was.

Now, let me make it clear, what happened at DysCo was mainly just bad business—not the outright deception and scandalous accounting that finally came to light and made headlines elsewhere. Mainly what happened at DysCo was a long series of squandered opportunities and strategic blunders that eventually resulted in year after year of earnings erosion—until in the midst of bad economic times, the company hovered on the brink of bankruptcy, and ultimately pieces were shut down, sold off, and DysCo was no more.

Yet the symptoms had been right in front of us, as managers, all the time. We just denied that they were anything to worry about.

George M. Tracy
Consultant

When Jake Foster and I talked in that first meeting, it was as if two strangers in a foreign land had unexpectedly met and discovered that they not only spoke the same language, but they were both doctors and both interested in the same illness. He told me about his battle with lymphoma, about DysCo—and then about Rick and about Essential. He confided in me his doubts that the business could be turned around and made healthy again.

I've had a long career, both as a manager and a consultant. I've worked inside dozens of organizations—and my associates in dozens more—from small companies to large corporations, and over time I began to recognize recurring patterns within them. Didn't matter that these companies were in different industries. There were recognizable patterns—syndromes—that could be observed in all of them, and I saw them over and over again. These were the same dysfunctional patterns that Jack Welch attacked in GE's businesses.

Some of the patterns were what I began to think of as healthy. When management would identify a strategic threat from a competitor and take action quickly and effectively to counter it, that was a healthy pattern. But some were unhealthy. In many organizations, management has great difficulty in dealing with sensitive issues—to the extent that the issues are never resolved. When that happens, for lack of a better expression, the health of the organization goes into decline.

Why the difficulty? Why are some issues so sensitive? For many reasons, but the most important ones come down to human nature. A senior manager pushes for a certain initiative—a new product, a new strategy. Or very often it's the opposite, a continuation of the status quo. That manager's decision isn't yielding the desired results, yet everyone who reports to that manager is reluctant to confront him with the evidence that things aren't going as planned. Why? Because of insecurity. Fear. Ego. People are uncomfortable talking about things they suspect will be uncomfortable for others to talk about. This insecurity has real effects on performance.

The irony, I've found, is that the issues that are the most important to the success of the organization are exactly the ones that managers find the hardest to discuss and deal with. This is especially so in an organization that is underperforming. It's the same as what goes on with dysfunctional families or individuals—the very issues that nobody wants to talk about are precisely the things that they *need* to talk about.

Yet there is often no organizational mechanism to enable honest, ongoing discussion of the really tough issues that affect the enterprise as a whole. There are regular meetings between senior managers. There are meetings between middle managers and first-level managers within functions. On occasion there are meetings between a few functions to deal with specific problems, but the sensitive issues go unresolved.

Even if there are meetings taking place, the easy issues are the ones that will be resolved. The hard issues, the ones that make managers (especially senior managers) uncomfortable, are the ones that will be avoided. They'll be ignored, or put off, or be treated with half measures that are ineffective.

When people are allowed, or when they allow themselves, to avoid unpleasant realities, they usually succeed. Until—surprise!—there is a crisis. And once an issue develops to crisis proportions, they're obviously not going to be able to defuse the danger as quickly or as efficiently as if they'd been dealing with it earlier. Once a cancer spreads, once a cold develops into pneumonia, treatment is far more difficult, sometimes to the extent that radical measures are required to save the patient.

The more Jake Foster opened up to me, the more I could see the same dysfunctional patterns occurring inside Essential as I had seen time and again elsewhere. He could sense that a crisis was coming—indeed, that crisis in many respects was already upon them.

We talked for some time, then had to break off because Jake had a meeting he had to attend. But before leaving for his meeting, he gave me a number of reports and background reading so that I could look over hard data on the things he was talking about. Often it takes quite a while to gain someone's trust, but almost immediately Jake and I both knew that we were allies.

8

Jake Foster
Senior Vice President–Operations

It was the end of the day, past five, by the time I got back to my office. George was still in my office, and I sat down with him, ready to resume our talk. Just as I did that Rick Riggins dropped by.

"I'm on my way out," Rick told me, "but I promised Vince that I'd stop and have a word with you."

"Go ahead," I said.

"It's about BigBox."

Rick seemed unsure whether to say anything in front of George. So I said, "George and I are going to be talking in-depth about the business, so I'm comfortable with him hearing whatever it is."

Rick accepted that and sat down with us.

"BigBox wants to return fifty thousand units of AZ-130," Rick said.

"Hey, that's wonderful," I said.

"And the best part is they don't want to pay the freight charges."

"Of course not. I wouldn't want to pay the freight charges either."

"I'm glad you can joke about it," Rick said, "because Nick Corrigan told Vince that your people in Distribution are having a fit. They want to deny the return."

"Doesn't surprise me," I said. "I just saw a number the other day showing that we've already got thirty thousand units of AZ-130 stacked in a warehouse outside Kansas City. Another fifty probably means we're going to have to rent more space."

"Still, we've got to take them back," said Rick. "We just can't afford to alienate BigBox, especially when we're going to be looking to them in just a few months to take large orders of SOS when it ships."

"Fifty thousand on top of thirty thousand is a lot of units."

"Jake, I don't see what else we can do. We apparently promised Big-Box that if they took the 130s before the end of the quarter, they could return them if necessary. It was part of the deal. We can't go back on it."

"Could that perhaps be the reason why we have those thirty thousand in Kansas City? Might they be returns from the quarter *before* last quarter?" I asked.

"I don't know. I can't even deal with that right now. But I'm telling Vince to stand firm on the freight charges. We can't let that go on."

"You *have* allowed that in the past?" George asked Rick.

"On occasion, we have," said Rick. "Now they're acting as if it's standard policy."

I said, "Rick, it's your decision, but I have to say it sure seems like BigBox is running our business more than *we* are running our business."

Rick looked annoyed. "I am not happy about it, but they are our biggest customer. Biggest by far. They're the eight-hundred pound gorilla, and they can sit on us anytime they want. They expect that if we want the BigBox account, we'll do things *their* way."

"Listen, in many ways I sympathize," said George. "BigBox has a reputation for being hard on its suppliers. Yet you can't say that doing business with BigBox is all bad, can you?"

"Well . . . no," said Rick. "There are a number of pluses in the equation. It's relatively stable demand, especially in a focused group of SKUs. As BigBox grows, so do we. I just wish it could be profitable growth."

"No offense, but that's *your* job, as a company, to service the account at a profit." Then George added, turning to me, "And this puts tremendous pressure on everybody to continuously improve operations."

To which I said, "Not to pass the buck, but it's pretty darn hard for Operations when there is no coordination or, for that matter, forethought given to these special programs and incentives that Marketing and Sales keep passing out just to build revenue."

"Jake," said Rick—tiredly, patiently, yet also in something of a flip tone, "we are trying to induce sales *growth*. Our bosses in Dallas expect to see sales revenue *grow*. So to get sales to grow, our salespeople offer certain customers like BigBox special incentives, special discounts, special product packages, and so on."

"Not to state the obvious," George said quietly, "but if the shipment that results from the special offer just moves back and forth between warehouses, your sales haven't really grown."

"All right then," Rick said, "*you're* the consultant referred to us by Corporate. What would *you* do in this situation?"

"For the moment, probably not much that's different from what you're going to do. I'm not here to find fault, Rick. I'm on your side. For the future, though, there are issues that need to be raised—and raised not only between us, but broadly across the company's management."

"Like what?" asked Rick. "Please continue. I want to hear what impressed Corporate so much."

"All right," said George. "Only let's try to look beyond the current issue. Let's take a step or two back, look at the whole picture, and see if we can create a course of action based simply on logic."

"Fine," said Rick.

"Since you mentioned Borcon, let's start there. After all, Borcon owns Essential, and it acts pretty much like the equivalent of a board of directors and shareholders for an independent company. So let's ask ourselves, what does Borcon expect from Essential?"

"Well, a number of things," said Rick, "ranging from excellent customer service to good corporate citizenship to . . . well, you know, it's all in the mission statement."

"Yeah, but above all, what do they really expect *above all*?"

"Obviously, they expect us to make money. They expect profitable growth."

"Right. Borcon management expects Essential to make money for them. They expect the Corporation's investment in Essential to continue to increase in value, year after year after year. Everything else—customer service, great product design, and arguably to some degree even corporate citizenship—is fundamentally a means toward that end."

"To be even more specific," Rick said, "I have my own expectations and goals for the company. For instance, I expect us to become the dominant player in our industry. I expect Essential to become the standard by which our competitors and peers are judged. And that's not just idle talk. We're making a move right now into SOS, which will be the next big

technological foundation for our products. We have a very good manufacturing capability. We have superb engineering talent—second to none
in our industry—headed by Frank Harlan, who is himself a brilliant engineer. We have, as you know, brought in BigBox to add a major retail
presence to our marketing—and even though they are a pain in the ass
from time to time, BigBox forms an important cornerstone to building
our future. So I think we have the key ingredients for success. Now, if we
can just execute."

George had listened quietly, but now he got up and went to the whiteboard mounted on the wall and picked up a marker. He said, "Well, that's
fine, Rick. The objectives you mentioned sound worthy, and you've
noted a number of resources that are no doubt very important. But let's
take a moment to check all of that against reality . . . against the facts."

He began to jot down a list on the board.

"You say your goal is to become the dominant player in the industry . . . yet I read a report this afternoon indicating that Essential's market
share has actually declined over the past two years."

"Yes, it has, but neither Vince Springer nor myself think that will
continue for very long."

"What makes you think that?"

"For one thing, we're taking a leadership role with respect to SOS."

"Let's come back to that. Do you have other reasons for thinking that
your decline in share will reverse itself?"

"Yes. Over the past few years, we've had to contend with several
low-priced competitors. One of these—Spectrum—has come out with
cheap knockoffs of the lower end of our popular AZ line."

"And what is the plan to counter that threat?"

"There is none because I think that we don't necessarily have to
match them on price," said Rick. "We have superior engineering. We
have a reputation for excellence in the marketplace."

"Which would you rather have, superior engineering or superior
market share and sales? Would you rather have an excellent reputation or
an excellent bottom line?" George asked. "Or, more important, which
do you think Borcon would prefer you have?"

"Oh now, come on, George! Look, share isn't everything. We have
in AZ the Cadillac of our industry. That's why we're in BigBox. Because
they want the best brands in their stores. Yes, we could knock some cost
out of AZ. But that's making it cheaper, not making it better. We could

also manufacture it offshore. But then what do we do with the manufac-turing capacity we already have? We still need our manufacturing plants in order to produce our higher-end products. Without the lower-end AZ volume, what happens to our plant efficiency?"

"Well, what happens if more and more of your customers keep choosing lower price?" asked George. "Is that going to improve your plant efficiency?"

Rick smiled. "No . . . but, as I say, superior engineering will triumph in the long run."

"In a mature product line, Rick, superior engineering means finding ways to boost performance and value while simultaneously reducing the costs of production."

I jumped in here. "You know, you're right, George, and I'm not sure Frank Harlan, brilliant though he is, really gets that."

"Frank and his engineers," George continued, "may be working their hearts out to do things that were appropriate five or ten years ago, but much of that work may be wasted energy in the current market."

"Yeah, maybe . . ." said Rick, "but I believe the point is soon going to be moot. SOS is going to change everything, and the market will pay up to get the added capabilities that SOS offers."

George made another note on the board. "Okay. That's the expecta-tion, that SOS will change everything. If we check the reality, though, SOS is a pretty big question mark."

Rick was offended. "How can you say that?"

"Because it's simply the truth. It's something new that is untested in the marketplace. It's a question mark."

"It's a pretty radical change, even though it is an advance," I added in support.

"All right, but that's to our advantage," Rick argued. "We need that technology change to distance ourselves from Spectrum and the other competitors who can knock off AZ and sell it at a cheaper price point. With SOS, everybody is going to have to upgrade, and that's a huge op-portunity for us."

"*If* the customers do what we expect them to," I said. "If the market adopts it, we win. If they don't . . . well, as George says, it's a question mark."

"Okay, yes, it's something of a gamble," Rick relented. "It's a bet-the-company move. You have to take chances in order to move forward."

"Absolutely," I said. "On the other hand, what I find disturbing is that there are a number of people in this company who are not behind the SOS rollout."

"Well, that's news to me," said Rick.

"I think Vince Springer has been trying to tell you that for some time," I said.

"Yeah, well, he'd better get on board, or I'm going to wring his neck."

"I've heard doubts raised by others," I said.

"Who?"

I shrugged. I certainly didn't want to name names unless I had to. "Various people. Salespeople. Managers."

Rick thought about this. "Do they really think SOS is a mistake?"

"No, from what I've heard everybody say, it's exactly what George described. It's a question mark."

"It's important to take risks," said George, "but if you force a bad risk, then indeed you may end up betting—and possibly losing—the whole company. The important thing, obviously, is to determine the degree of risk and proceed accordingly."

Rick thought about it, then shook his head.

"BigBox wants SOS," he said. "And if BigBox can sell SOS, it'll be a success even if nobody else carries it."

"Perhaps the rest of the management organization doesn't understand that."

"Well, they ought to," said Rick. Then he shrugged. "I don't know if they do or not, but they ought to."

"In any case, that brings us to certain other realities," said George. "For instance, there are the root causes of the issue that brought you here to talk to Jake this afternoon. There seems to be an implied assumption that BigBox is so valuable a customer that just about anything can be justified to keep them happy. But does the reality bear that out? If you have to take back a massive quantity of units and pay for warehousing and possibly also the freight charges, that is certainly going to eat into your margins."

Rick nodded. "No doubt about that."

"I'm curious. Have the involved parties within the company—Marketing, Sales, Distribution, Inventory Control, IT, and so on—ever gotten together to ascertain the true costs of doing business with BigBox?" George asked.

"Well, we have various reports," Rick said vaguely. Then he added, "Okay, okay, you may be right on that one. We *haven't* been as rigorous in that sort of analysis as we could be . . . as we should be. In fact, if that is the kind of project that you as a consultant would be willing to take on—".

"No, no, no," said George. "You miss my point. That's not why I'm here. My concern is whether the managers in those various functions are even thinking about the enterprise-wide costs and opportunities. Are they thinking about what's best for Essential? Or are they mostly worried about the numbers as they reflect upon the performance of their own, individual functions?"

"In other words," I said, "is Distribution up in arms because the added carrying costs are bad for the company? Or are they really mad about the AZ return because of the headaches *to themselves,* and because the higher costs reflect poorly on Distribution?"

"And other questions come to mind as well. How come Vince Springer doesn't approach Jake directly, but instead goes to you, Rick? How come you're the messenger?"

"There's no reason why Vince couldn't approach Jake," Rick said. "It's just that . . . I don't know."

"Maybe it's partly my fault," I said. "Maybe I'm not as approachable as I should be."

Rick waved his hand. "Nah, Vince has always been like that. Since before you got here."

"That's just a little thing," said George. "There are bigger things to see here in the overall patterns across the business. Like that Sales can't work it out with the involved parties as to whether or how the return should occur. Like the distinct possibility that Sales felt compelled to oversell . . . to juice the numbers, so to speak, at the end of the accounting period, as opposed to booking honest numbers. And there was the story Jake was telling me earlier this afternoon about the manufacturing plant that knew it would have to ship late, but took, shall we say, 'special' measures to record a big order as shipped when it really wasn't. You have to wonder, is this car really moving or are people just playing with the speedometer to make it *seem* as if it's going somewhere?"

Rick held up his hands in surrender. "Okay, okay!" Then he slumped back and his head lolled back onto the top of his chair. He stared at the ceiling for a moment, let out a big sigh, and then looked over his shoulder to be sure the door to my office was shut all the way.

"All the things you've brought up are valid concerns," Rick finally admitted. "This company is not as healthy as I'd like it to be."

George and I looked at each other.

"Listen, what I'm about to tell you *has* to be kept confidential. I don't want it to get beyond the three of us. . . ."

Rick Riggins
President

I was extremely frustrated. I had genuinely believed when I took over as president that Essential was capable of dominating the industry. That had been a realistic goal, in my opinion. Even when I explained it to George on that first day, I continued to believe it.

Of course I almost *had* to continue to believe it because I had sold Borcon Corporate on it. Now I was being measured against it. Retreat was no longer an option.

I had not been told this directly by Corporate, but I figured I had one more year left. One more year to demonstrate that I could put Essential on a growth track. After that, if I couldn't get it done . . . well, they'd be looking around to put in someone else. In the meantime, there could be no terrible quarters. No blowups. I could maybe turn in one or two flat quarters and perhaps they would accept that, but nothing that would even hint at a continuing downward spiral.

So that was my predicament. Clearly, even if we were capable of market dominance, my faith was rapidly diminishing that this organization would in fact ever make it a reality. Just *talking* about my goals for the company left a hollow feeling. I do have to confess that in my heart of hearts I was starting to lower my own standards, to hope that we could simply remain profitable, never mind the growth. It was hard at the time even to admit that to myself.

I was not unaware that there were problems. And I was not ignoring them. The whole company felt like . . . like an airplane when it's on the verge of stalling in midair. I felt like the pilot of a plane crossing the ocean, and while climbing to cruising altitude, noticing some of the engines will not go to full power. And then, trying to change course, it becomes clear the rudder controls are malfunctioning. You try to make a small turn to the right, and the plane lurches into a dive. You get it under control and then the radar goes out. One thing after another. At that point, reaching 40,000 feet and flying at maximum speed are the least of your concerns. You're just trying to keep the plane in the air.

I had already tried, as my predecessor had, to get the organization to change, to be more responsive, more progressive . . . to fly! I had put I don't know how much time, money, and effort into teams and research and motivational programs and everything else, yet the ROI on all that had been dismally poor. I was sick of wasting time and money on superficial quick fixes.

I actually wondered if *I* were to blame. I mean, yes, of course I'm the one who's ultimately responsible, as company president, but I also wondered if maybe *I* was the problem. If I had really concluded that was so, I would have stepped aside, but I honestly did not think I was to blame. I could not believe that I was the cause of the problem.

George and I talked for quite some time in Jake's office that afternoon, and at last I got the courage to ask just that. I put it to both Jake Foster and George Tracy, "Do you think it's me? Is the root of the problem something in my personality or something that I am inadvertently doing as president?"

Jake right away said, "No, I do not think it's you." And George agreed.

"What is going on here," George told me, "cannot be ascribed to any single individual. It is far more involved than that."

So I asked him point blank, "What do you think has to be done at this point?"

He said, "There is really only one thing to be done, and that's to treat the disease—the organizational dysfunction—and cure it."

George M. Tracy
Consultant

It was clear to me even after that first day that the company's performance was suffering for a number of reasons. There were problems in the supply chain. Market strategy issues were causing conflicts. The product development process probably was not what it needed to be. I thought it highly likely that, given the loss of market share and the flat sales revenues, the sales organization was less than effective and had to be made more efficient. And undoubtedly there were other issues, conflicts, and problems of varying importance and size as well.

But as I told Rick and Jake, "None of those are what's killing you."

Now, I'm not saying that any of those issues—supply chain, market strategy, and so on—wasn't tough. If they had been easy, they probably would have been resolved a long time ago. Still, even if you totaled the whole list together, those were only the symptoms, not the disease. The disease itself was the inability of the organization as a whole to deal with them speedily and move forward and seize upon new opportunities.

"All right, if that's the disease," Rick asked me, "what then is the cure?"

Well, you have to think about how the disease was able to take hold in the first place. The ability or inability to deal effectively with issues is a function of management, and management is governed by that collection of formal and informal rules, policies, politics, and so on that we call "culture." The disease is rooted in the organizational culture; to cure the disease, you must change the culture.

There is nothing exotic or magical or even mysterious about changing a company culture. But it's not easy. It's not simple. You can't do it with a book. You can't do it with consultants. It's lots of hard work, much of it done under pressure. Mainly, it's a matter of discipline. It's discipline applied on an enterprise-wide scale.

Here's how you do it: In plain language, you first find out what's really going on. You interview management in a confidential manner that allows people to talk honestly. You analyze and quantify what they say. You then bring all the managers above a certain level together in one place. For the next few days, at this "workshop," you oblige them to confront reality. You assign all the managers to teams, each of which focuses upon a specific issue. Every team is cross-functional; it consists of managers from different functions within the organization, according to how relevant those functions are to the assigned issue. To promote free thinking and open discussion, you keep senior managers out of everybody's hair. You encourage cooperation and you discourage intimidation. By the end of the workshop, each team has put together the basis of a plan for positive change relative to the issues it has been assigned to deal with.

From then on, month after month after month, you keep the teams at work. You allow no one to weasel out. You expose intimidation and attempts at sabotage. You hold accountable the teams and individuals on them. If there are managers who don't get the message after a reasonable amount of time, you remove them. You apply continuous pressure to keep the teams focused on their charters. You keep everyone informed. You enable and encourage cooperation and collaboration between the teams and between functions—to the extent that they become "knitted" together in purpose and action on behalf of the whole enterprise. You develop alignments of strategies, functions, processes, and managers so that they become mutually supporting of the same objectives for the entire enterprise. Over the course of about a year, sometimes less and sometimes more, you will have changed how the organization operates. Yes, it's true; you can change a culture in a year. Afterward, for your trouble, you will have alignment between your strategy, your work processes, and your senior team. You will have achieved a number of tangible improvements over the near-term, and you will have a comprehensive plan for long-term success—a plan created not by consultants, but by the people who know the business best, the company's own management.

Another, simpler way of describing the process: You find all the closets in the company. You open every one of those closets. You take everything out, skeletons and all. You put it all in plain sight, in one place. You then deal with the ugly mess. Bury the skeletons. Throw away the junk. And once all that's gone, you organize the valuable stuff that's left, and you use that to forge the future of the company. At the same time, you destroy all the closets, make it impossible for people to hide the truth, so that the mess doesn't get started again.

I explained all of this to Rick Riggins. The last thing I told him was, "Rick, I've done this in all kinds of companies. Some of them had obvious problems, either internally or with respect to the market, that management couldn't come to grips with. Some outwardly seemed fine, but as they went through the process, discovered hidden issues that would have meant big trouble if they hadn't been brought into the open. Many companies were in fact doing quite well, but needed a change in management culture in order to achieve the next level of performance. In all of them, though, there was one constant that made the process successful."

"What's that?" Rick asked.

"The person with your job is the key to it all—the company

president or the CEO. That person has to be a rock. Has to be the book-end that keeps everything in place. If you embark on this process, you must be firm. You cannot waiver. You have to be persistent. If people perceive that you're not a hundred percent committed, their involvement will fade. But if you do remain committed, it *will* work. You—that is to say, you and your managers—*will* turn the company around."

I had to leave. Had to catch a plane home. Rick walked me to my car, and as we shook hands in parting, he said he would think seriously about what I had said. A few days passed. Then one morning my cell phone rang; it was Rick calling.

"We're going to do it," he told me. Then he added, "In fact, we have no other choice. We *have* to do it."

9

Jake Foster
Senior Vice President–Operations

In the middle of George's presentation to senior management, I had the passing thought that maybe I should have distanced myself from the whole thing. With their random glances at me, I got the sense that an "us versus them" situation was developing. Like, *the new guy is putting one down on us.*

Rick had signed on. George was hired, and we were going to go ahead with this. And I was just a vigorous supporter of the process, yet I could tell that they somehow saw me as the instigator, the one they would privately blame when it failed.

At the end of the presentation, George asked for questions and comments. At first, everyone just sat there, like faces on Mt. Rushmore.

"We're about to engage in a process with the intent of transforming the entire company," said Rick. "And *nobody* has any comments?"

Jane Grimm tested the waters. "I think it sounds exciting." You couldn't tell from her face that's how she felt, but that's what she said. "I only have one question for George: You really think you can do this in a year or less?"

"Yes," said George. "I have every confidence that you will accomplish this within that time frame. You and your managers. I'm just guiding the process; you and your managers are the ones who will actually make it happen. And you will get the recognition and all the credit when you succeed."

"Well, I think it's long overdue, if it works," said Jane. Then she added with a grin, "I'm just not sure you know this company well enough to make that prediction."

I couldn't help laughing.

But she looked at me and went on to say, "I think after the bogus numbers we got from Logandale last month, we can use a lot more openness and honesty around here."

Like, *gotcha*. Ouch.

"Anybody else?" Rick asked. "What about you, Vince? What do you think?"

"If you want a reaction, I think it sounds fine in principle, but . . . well, I'm sorry, I just don't see how that's going to help us deal with the day-to-day issues that are important, like, *right now*."

"We are not going to ignore the current day-to-day issues and problems," Rick said. "And obviously they're not going to go away. So we're going to keep dealing with them day after day. But if we don't step back as an organization and look at the whole enterprise and formulate a strategy, that's all we'll ever do—deal with day-to-day problems. We've got to get off the treadmill and figure out where we're going."

Vince nodded. "Okay, Rick. If this is what you want to do, I'll give you all the cooperation I can."

I'll say one thing about Vince. He was a realist. He probably didn't have a lot of faith in George or Enterprise Medicine or any process of change. But he knew it was a done deal, so he wasn't going to fight a losing battle. He would go along. Just like he had with SOS.

"Good," Rick told him. "What about you, Jake?"

"I suspect all of you know where I stand on this; I think it's exactly what the company needs right now. I would just remind Jane and the rest of you that I was the one who brought the Logandale situation to your attention. In any case, I will make sure that every manager in Operations gives priority to the process."

I was looking directly at Frank when I said that.

Rick followed my gaze and asked, "Frank? What are your thoughts?"

"I'm fine with it."

"Is that all?"

"Well, what else do you want me to say? I think it sounds very . . . simple."

"Well, is there something wrong with that?" I countered.

"No. . . ."

"Are you saying, 'This is so simple, it'll never work'? Or maybe, 'This approach makes too much sense! It's too obvious! We can't try this, it might actually work!'"

Now everybody laughed, and even Frank cracked a smile, however briefly.

"If you want me to put my cards on the table," Frank rumbled, "then I will say I think the timing may be inappropriate. Are you going to hold this workshop before the SOS rollout?"

"Yes, it will occur before then," said George.

"Then isn't all this going to be a distraction from the real work of this company? I mean, we have the strategic direction of Essential already set in place. We cannot deviate from that now. To entertain other notions would be a terrible mistake, as well as extremely expensive."

I said, "Frank, you've been here longer than I have. Can you ever recall a time in this company when there hasn't been some kind of strategy in place?"

"That's not the point. I'm just saying this is a critical period right now. Do we really want to create distractions for everybody?"

"This isn't just about strategy," said Rick. "This is about becoming a healthier, more effective organization by aligning the strategy with the work processes that deliver it, and the senior team that leads it."

"Fine," said Frank, washing his hands of it.

Now Pam jumped in. "I have to say I think this includes a great many of the things we in Human Resources have been talking about for years—for instance, the need to listen to our employees. How many times do we really do that? We have tremendous insight and experience within the ranks of our employees, yet we too often fail to give that insight and experience a voice. If we could only achieve real communication and empower all those levels of the organization . . ."

She went on for a while in that vein until her comments began to sound like a lecture. I could see the others around the table mentally turning her off the longer she spoke. Finally, Rick cleared his throat and pointed to his watch.

Pam smiled. She knew her own reputation for being long-winded. "In conclusion, let me just offer my full cooperation. And George, let's get together later today to discuss and coordinate how we are going to conduct the survey and management interviews."

George was taken aback by her use of *we*. "I'm sorry if I didn't make that clear. For reasons of confidentiality and objectivity, the interviews and survey are things that my associates and I will handle."

"Oh . . ." said Pam. "I guess I just assumed that HR would be involved."

"Definitely," said George, "you *will be* involved, just like all the other functions in the company. But with respect to the interviews, it's a simple truth that people will open up much more easily to a third party—to somebody neutral—than they will to someone with authority within the company. We're just trying to get everybody to be candid."

"Oh. Well, okay, I can understand that."

"Let me just make one last comment," said Rick. "Make no mistake that as senior managers we are still in charge. We make the final decisions. We are doing this to bring the company together, not divide us from one another. To borrow some words from Pam, we need involvement from all our managers. We need everybody to be working and thinking about the objectives and initiatives that will make this company dominant in the marketplace."

Great, I thought. *Right on target*. But then I looked around the table and it hit me. They were all jaded. How many other consultants, gurus, gimmicks had been paraded before them over the years? To their eyes and ears, this was yet another management flavor of the month. I thought otherwise. But when would they?

George M. Tracy
Consultant

The opening phase of the process is what we call the "diagnostic." We start by giving a short presentation to the managers, so they know what this is about and what's expected of them. My associates and I then interview all the key managers in the company. Generally, this consists of the company president, plus the direct reports to the president, plus the managers who report to the direct reports. We also include those who might be termed the rising stars of the organization, younger or newer managers who have distinguished themselves in some way.

In addition to the one-on-one interviews, each manager also participates in a web-based survey. The survey has about 100 to 150 questions, typically organized in a general section and then focused on specific issues like customer service or product development and so on. Most of the questions ask the participants to rate their agreement with a value statement on a scale from one to twelve. But there are also some open-ended questions that allow the managers to write in their own comments.

My associates and I then take the input from the interviews and the surveys and organize the information we're getting. Or as we often put it, we "bucketize" the comments by placing similar or related comments together. For example, in the case of Essential, when we got comments about BigBox, we put all those together in a conceptual "bucket" so that we could later go through and sort out the various viewpoints on BigBox and its impact on the company.

It's a bit like a detective—in a nonglamorous, nondramatic way— talking to various witnesses to find the most probable truth. It doesn't take long before a meaningful pattern begins to emerge. In fact, after about twenty interviews, we usually know what's going on, but we keep on interviewing in order to probe different aspects of a problem or to try out potential solutions.

Most managers don't mind talking about the company as an enterprise. In fact, a lot of them love it. A lot of them have never been asked to voice their inner thoughts about the company. Just get them rolling, and they're very pleased to raise their viewpoints above the specific functions they manage and look at the big picture. You can end up with some surprising and valuable observations this way.

• • •

In one of the first interviews, I sat down with the marketing director, a woman by the name of Linda Wong. We chatted for a while about her role in the company. Then I asked her to look at Essential not just from a marketing perspective, but as a total enterprise.

"What's your view of the state of the enterprise as it is right now?" I asked.

She thought for a moment, then said, "Actually, there almost seems to be two companies, not one. There is one company to service BigBox, and the other to service the traditional Essential customer base."

"Are you saying there is a conflict between the two?"

"Well . . . yes, but we haven't recognized that as yet. At present, BigBox seems to have the upper hand and seems to get preferred treatment. That really irks everybody assigned to the traditional commercial-industrial side of the business."

"Do you have a preference?"

"Me? No, I don't. My only question is, where are we going to make the most money? BigBox has not turned out to be the bowl of cherries everybody thought it was going to be. Yet we keep lavishing attention and resources on them."

"And I take it you think this duality . . . this conflict is a problem?"

"Yes, I do. You can see it in the numbers. Ever since BigBox became an account, we've been losing share elsewhere."

"Why is that, do you think?"

"I'm not sure, but I think it's because each side is in conflict with the other."

"If that's true, what do you think should be done about it?" I asked her.

"Well . . . I don't know," she said. "But we at least ought to decide as a company where our best interests will be served. You know, it's like you're on the interstate and you're approaching a Y where the highway splits, with one route going east and the other going west. And it's clearly marked. Miles in advance the signs tell you that you're going to have to make a decision. Do you want to go east, or do you want to go west? But we, as a company, seem to keep pretending that we don't have to make a decision. When the time comes, we'll go east *and* west. We even seem to think that this is more desirable than choosing one or the other. What's more, there is the tacit suggestion that maybe if we try hard enough, we can also go north and south, too. The trouble is that we are only one company with so many resources. If we try to go in all directions, it's not going to work out. So we're zipping along with this nondecision guiding us, and the Y in the highway is getting closer and closer. Meanwhile, because we assume we can go in both directions, we have avoided an assessment of what is the *best* direction for us to take? Where can we do the best job of servicing customers and be the most profitable?"

She lit me up with that. I told her, "That's an excellent analogy. Do you have a sense of which direction should be taken?"

"My understanding is that our goal as a company is to dominate the industry. Fine. Which industry? What segment of the market? The Big-

Box end of the market? The low-end, low-margin, high-volume segment of the market? Okay, great. Then we probably need to shut down Logandale and move manufacturing offshore. Because that's the only way we'll achieve unit costs to make us competitive against Spectrum. But in this company it's total, freakin' heresy to mention that eventuality. It's too emotionally hard to think about that, yet that's exactly what's going to have to happen if we keep messing around with BigBox."

"But in which direction would you steer the company, if you were the company president?"

She shook her head and said, "I'd rather not say."

That surprised me because she'd been so open up to now. So I asked, "Why don't you want to tell me?"

"Because I can't. I mean, I honestly don't know the best strategic direction for the company to take. Rather than just pick a direction, we really need to pull together all the data, analyze the numbers, and then make decisions."

I thought it was a terrific answer.

"There is something else, too," she added. "I think there is some question over whether we should go in *any* of the currently available directions—over whether we should even be traveling on this highway at all. Maybe we should be steering the company toward a completely different highway."

"How come?"

"You look at long-term market trends and clearly there has been a slowing of growth within the industry. I'm sure that's what drove Vince and Rick toward BigBox in the first place. We cannot achieve the growth slope that Borcon wants us to have if we stay strictly within the traditional customer base. No matter how good we are in the commercial-industrial segment, we won't meet Borcon's growth expectations. We have to do something else."

"Are you talking about AZ going away?"

"Partially, yes. AZ is a big part of my marketing responsibility, so I'm well aware that demand for AZ is going to decline over the next three to five years."

"But that's why you—the company—are going to make the move to SOS."

"Right. And yet, even if it's a success, SOS is not likely to make up totally for the decline of AZ. Nobody's allowed to say that, but it's true.

SOS adds some really cool, advanced capabilities, but those capabilities do not lend themselves to high-volume applications. At least not at present. It's estimated that only one out of four end-users is ever going to need the stuff that the engineers here are drooling over."

"Do you think SOS is a mistake for Essential?"

"No, I wouldn't go that far. Clearly, we need to do something. And SOS is that . . . it's *something*. I'm just not sure it's ever going to be worth the money we've put into developing it."

I thought about the way Linda had phrased one of her answers. "You say SOS doesn't lend itself to high-volume apps *at present*. Is there anything that might change that?"

"Possibly. In the tech world, they talk about the killer app—the application that is so compelling everybody's got to buy new hardware to run it. In personal computers, years ago, it originally was the spreadsheet. Later on, it was graphics and then CD-ROM and multimedia and so on. Anyway, if we could come up with a killer app for SOS, then we might really have something. That would change the whole picture."

"Any ideas what that killer app might be?"

"No, haven't the foggiest. But that might be something to sic a couple of engineers on. Have them brainstorm it. See what they come up with. Of course they'd have to keep it practical. They'd have to focus on finding something nobody's thought of yet, but the market won't be able to live without five years from now. It's a tall order. On the other hand, we've got some good minds in this company. They just might be able to pull it off."

"Let's say they don't. Let's say they can't come up with a killer app for SOS. What then?"

She smiled. "Then I suggest we watch the competition to see if they come up with something. If they do, then we quickly do our own knockoff and out-market them."

"All right, but say that the competition can't come up with anything either."

"Well, there is Z3, of course. The engineers don't seem to find Z3 very exciting, but what few numbers I've seen suggest that Z3 is probably what most customers are going to buy in the next few years. And there will be customers and end-users who won't upgrade to either Z3 or SOS, so there will always be a market for AZ, albeit a shrinking one."

"Beyond those . . . ?"

"Services. As a company, it seems to be rooted in our organizational identity that we have to make something. Yet I saw an estimate that Nusult makes more than half its net income from services. Nusult is small compared to us, but if they can do it, why can't we?"

• • •

Linda was a great find. She was honest, open-minded, and highly observant. Good qualities for a potential team leader, and mentally I marked her as a candidate.

Ozzie Brown
Regional Manager–Field Sales

Excerpt from interview comments

If you really want to know the truth, I'm not sure the ops managers comprehend what the salespeople are up against. I mean, we in Sales are out here on the front lines every day, and we salespeople do whatever we have to do in order to survive. Sometimes that means we play it quote-unquote by the book. And sometimes it means we don't because we can't. There are reasons why salespeople don't do what certain senior managers think they ought to.

Very often, we're being asked to take the hill, so to speak, and yet we don't have enough ammunition. Or we have enough, but it's the wrong kind of ammunition. Or there's ammunition on the way, but it never reaches us in time to affect the outcome of the battle. We're on the front line, but we need the rest of the army close behind or we're in trouble. I've got salespeople calling back from the trenches, "Hey, this opposition is tough! We're under attack!" But when I try to relay that back to headquarters, nobody seems to hear us.

If I'm out here in the field, in my foxhole or whatever, I want to be able to look back over my shoulder and see artillery behind me. I want to see air cover over head. I want, you know, a tank that's gassed up and ready to spearhead the assault! Too many times, I instead get some slow, clankety-clank machine with half the guns it should have, and it breaks down or runs out of gas halfway to the objective. Meanwhile, as we're trying to take the hill, we're likely to get a message telling us this hill isn't important, that we ought to be taking this other hill that's way over there. I mean, it gets frustrating.

Our strengths? We still have one of the best names in the industry. We still build a well-engineered, solid product. That should not be ignored. We're still a force to be reckoned with.

I'm not sure we, as a company, really understand what the market has been telling us the past few years.

There is this mantra we get all the time, "We've got to listen to the customer!" Well, first of all, I know from experience that what the customer says and what the customer does are often two different things. They may tell you they want this and that and the other thing, but what they actually buy is just *this*.

Our engineers love complexity. They thrive on it. I'm convinced that even if there is a simple solution, they'll come up with something complicated, something that only they can appreciate and understand.

Sandra Moss
Product Manager

Responding to interview question

If you want to know why there are so many SKUs for AZ, it's because AZ is pretty much all we have had to work with. We've been waiting for SOS for I don't know how long. It was supposed to be out a couple of years ago, but there was one delay after another. Meanwhile, we in Marketing are under all kinds of pressure from the sales force as well as from senior management to try to fill the gap with products that are *new and improved*! So fine, if all we have to work with is AZ, then the best thing we can do is rebundle and unbundle various feature and option packages. It's not *real* innovation, but it might sort of look that way if we're careful about how we word the PR release.

Sterling Grove
Director–Engineering and Design

I was nervous about talking to George. I won't deny it. We were told to block out a couple of hours for the interview, which meant it was going to be detailed, and I wasn't sure what I was supposed to say. Unless you've had someone like Frank Harlan for a boss, you probably wouldn't understand.

Frank's a real command-and-control kind of manager. In fact, he's ex-Navy. He worked in the Pentagon and later in some kind of weapons development program before he came to Essential. He manages with a captain's authority, and he's secretive almost to the point of paranoia. There is one way, which is Frank's way, and if you cross him or contradict him, your career is in trouble. That's the way he is.

Now, you should also know that Frank is a brilliant engineer and his way is usually the right way. Not always, but most of the time. At least from an engineering standpoint.

If you're on good terms with Frank, and you also know your stuff—and the latter has to precede the former—you may be able to persuade him to see your point of view. Occasionally. But there is usually very little leeway with Frank. By the time you've formed your opinion, Frank's already been over the same territory, and he knows the way it ought to be done.

It so happens that my way of approaching a problem was pretty much the same as Frank's way. We had similar technical philosophies and disciplines. Our relationship was harmonious most of the time, and I got along fine with him. I'm a good engineer and, I think, a good manager, but I'm sure that a big reason why I got promoted to head Design Services was because I always supported Frank no matter what. I'm a realist.

When I heard that Jake Foster was bringing in these guys to talk to us and do a survey, the next thing I did was go to Frank and ask him what he thought I should . . . you know, what I should emphasize.

But Frank didn't give me much help at all. He looked at me and said, "Use your best judgment. Say whatever you think is appropriate." Then he kind of smiled and added, "It's Rick's new flavor of the month. It's not going to make any difference in the long run anyway."

Don't think I'm some kind of brownnoser. I'm not by nature a suck-up. It's just that if you're reporting to Frank Harlan, you'd better know what he thinks before you open your mouth in public. It's a matter of survival.

George M. Tracy
Consultant

I interviewed Sterling Grove in his office late in the afternoon. From the start, he seemed uncomfortable, shifting in his seat, sitting with his arms folded, offering only terse replies. After a few minutes of asking him things like how long he'd been with the company and so on, I asked him, "So, what do you think of Essential's future as a company?"

"What do you mean?"

"Well . . . the company *does have* a future, doesn't it?"

"I would hope so."

"Three to five years from now, if nothing major changes internally, what do you think that future will be like?"

"I think we'll be fine."

"Really? Will Essential dominate the market?"

"No, that I can't say."

"If you were to take a guess."

"I wouldn't want to guess. If it's a question about the market, then I think marketing would be better qualified to answer it."

"No, I'm asking you. You're an important manager in this organization, and I'd like to get your sense of the health of the company and its business."

"I think we're fine."

"So there's nothing you would change?"

"I don't have that kind of authority."

"But if you did. Let's say Rick Riggins himself walked in right now and said, 'Sterling, I'm going to Europe for a couple of years, and I'm putting you in charge. But before I go, I want to hear your plans for the company and how you're going to improve it while I'm gone.' What would you tell him?"

He almost allowed himself a chuckle at this, but the crack in the ice immediately froze over. "I . . . I suppose I'd ask him what his priorities are."

"He doesn't have any. He wants to know yours."

"Then . . . I'd have to get together with Frank Harlan."

"Uh-huh. Just with Frank?"

"Right. Oh, well, I mean with Jake and probably Vince, too."

"A team effort then."

"Absolutely."

"Okay, that's reasonable. But, for the sake of argument, guess what: It's not just Rick, but the whole senior team that's going to Europe. Rick's given you the keys. Now, where are *you* going to drive this company?"

Not far, was the general answer he gave. He finally allowed that he'd have to give SOS top priority because that was the next generation, blah, blah, blah. He didn't stray at all from the official company line, and I began to think that this was perhaps what he really thought . . . until I noticed the dark circles on his shirt around his underarms. He was wearing a light blue shirt, and I realized he was sweating buckets. I wasn't. I thought that if anything his office was on the cool side.

I said, "Sterling, you seem *very* uncomfortable. Is something wrong?"

"Oh, no! I'm fine."

"Yes, you're fine, the company's fine, the future is fine. I guess that's why Essential is gobbling up market share and making money hand over fist. Look, we're just talking here. Nobody is going to slam you on anything you say. It's anonymous. I'm the only one who will know who said what. I just want the honest truth."

"What are the others telling you?" he asked.

"The one thing that everyone is *not* telling me is that everything is fine."

"Are you sure this is anonymous?"

"Cross my heart," I said. Then I lifted my tie and showed him the back of it. "Look, no cameras, no hidden microphones. I don't even take very many notes."

"Suppose Frank asks you what I said?"

"I tactfully tell him to take a hike. I tell him that we're not going to get anywhere if people don't feel secure enough to open up and be honest."

"And what if Frank goes to Rick?"

"You mean, what if Frank pressures Rick to pressure me to spill the beans? Then I leave and go home. As I say, there is no point in continuing if people feel threatened. But, Sterling, I've been here over a week and I've not had any pressure in that regard from anybody. Most of the managers I've talked to so far are happy to have the opportunity to say what's on their minds."

"You really want to know?"

"Yes."

He got up, walked around his desk, shut the door, and came back. As he passed me, he muttered something I couldn't make out.

"Sorry? Couldn't hear you."

"I said, you don't know the total Nazi that Frank Harlan can be."

I nodded. Well . . . at least now we were getting somewhere.

"We'll come back to that," I said. "Let's just talk about your perspective on the business."

And we did for the next two hours or so, probably longer. We both lost track of the time.

With the interviews, we're not out to nail anybody. That's not our purpose. Our intent is to improve the performance of the enterprise. Period. On the other hand, there can be personnel issues that cannot be ignored. It was clear in the case of Essential, from talking to Sterling and a number of other people both inside and outside of Engineering, that Frank Harlan was going to be what we call a "project." A project is a specific individual who turns out to be an obstacle to progress. Someone who probably isn't going to get the message very quickly. Someone who may try to sabotage what we're trying to do. Those people are a reality, and those realities have to be taken into consideration.

10

Jake Foster
Senior Vice President–Operations

One morning, George stopped by my office and handed me a document that was a few pages in length, entitled "Overview of Interview Comments." He said, "Here, this is just a heads-up on what we're getting in the interviews. We haven't finished yet, but this will give you an idea of what's coming up as we talk to people."

After he left, I began to read. George and his associates had compiled and sorted the comments by topic. It was quite enlightening.

Overview of Interview Comments

We do have our strengths . . .

"Our engineering is still the best in the industry in terms of technical excellence."

"The move beyond the commercial-industrial and professional markets into retail—BigBox being the prime example—was very momentous for the company. It opened new possibilities."

"We have an excellent reputation in the marketplace. There is a lot of evidence that 'Essential' as a company name is equated with 'industry standard,' and that AZ as a product line is synonymous with quality."

"It's a credit to HR's ability to recruit that this company has some very talented individuals, not just in engineering, but also in sales, marketing, and operations."

But can we achieve market dominance?

"The kind of engineering that was a force in the marketplace five or ten years ago is not necessarily what wins in the market today."

"A decade or two ago, the market wanted more sophistication, more capacity, and more features. Today, the customers still want all that, but they also want easy installation, reliability, and low cost."

"AZ was a major advance in its day, but AZ is the past."

"SOS is the next great leap forward, technically speaking."

"I know SOS is a major advance, I just hope that for Essential it's not an advance over the edge of a cliff."

"BigBox is the biggest customer we have and has a lot of growth potential."

"The cost of doing business with BigBox is so high, I really wonder how much profit we're actually making."

"There is the perception that BigBox is taking business away from our other customers. Whether true or not, the perception is real. We can't dominate the industry with just one channel and one customer."

"Our goal as a company is to dominate the industry. Fine. Which industry? What segment of the market?"

Meanwhile, our competitors are gaining . . .

"Spectrum sells crap. Cheap, low-end crap. Yet that's exactly why they're a force in the marketplace. Because if you can believe the industry numbers, that seems to be what the majority of the customers want. Cheap solutions."

"Engineering seems to view Nusult as our principle competition. Nusult does have the technical edge in some areas, but I'm personally more worried about Reliable. They're kicking our butts right now. Reliable is after our bread and butter, while Nusult just is a high-end niche player."

"All three of our main competitors represent a threat to us. But the one to watch out for is Reliable. If Reliable beats us to market with Z3, which they probably will, we could have a heck of a time countering that in the market."

. . . and we need to move quickly and decisively.

"We need better systems so that we can react faster."

"I'm not sure the strategy, if there is one, is well understood by the majority of managers."

"We need to do more than just play with features and options. We need products that are truly innovative and offer great value."

"Our customers aren't going to wait for us to get our act together. There is no loyalty anymore."

"We have, at best, a two to three year window of opportunity before AZ is totally superceded by Z3 and possibly by SOS. After that, our goose is cooked. This is not the time for confusion and mistakes. We need to move now and do it right."

"We have the resources in this company, we just have to put them to work intelligently."

There are critical issues we must address in supply chain . . .

"At the end of every accounting period, there is this big push to make the numbers. Then once the crisis has passed, everyone covers up the damage resulting from the crash effort and slips back into a business-as-usual mode."

"Everybody in sales plays games with the order tracking system. We all know it goes on, and it goes on because it pays off. I know that there are salespeople who will enter due dates on the system that are impossible for production to meet, but they do it so that their orders get priority. Not everybody uses this trick, but more and more, if you don't, then your own customers suffer."

"Internal systems seem to be set up for the convenience of the IT Department, rather than for communication of useful information to management. Situational awareness and analysis is poor as a result."

"We lack the kind of early warning radar to spot changes in demand. As a result we're always getting caught with either too much of one model or not enough of another. Why can't we fix this?"

"We need to deal with shortages and other problems before they become critical."

"Our production processes are good, but there is room for improvement. We often are more worried about the productivity statistics than with being flexible to meet specific customer needs."

"Our operations are pretty much based on the needs of the moment, not on widely recognized long-term objectives and goals."

. . . in product development

"The development process has become cumbersome and slow. Last year, Reliable beat us to market with the LOX options by a good six months. It's no wonder they're doing so well. They're quicker than we are."

"The problem isn't our process, it's just that we're not using the process we've set up. People aren't following the established procedures."

"SOS is late for one simple reason: Everyone is being cautious. There are more CYA memos and e-mails associated with SOS than any other product introduction I've ever seen."

"Everyone is worried that SOS will live up to its name. But no one will say anything against it because they know it's 'protected' at the top."

"Mistakes are punished in this company, especially in Engineering. What's happened as a result is that fewer and fewer are willing to take chances."

. . . in sales and market strategy

"The plain truth is that sales are not growing, no matter how people try to disguise the numbers on a quarter-to-quarter basis."

"I know for a fact that there are some salespeople who will juice the numbers at the end of the month, getting some customers to take product, knowing that they can return what doesn't sell at the beginning of the next month."

"The return policies are absurd. Yet we let it go on."

"We bend over backward for BigBox. That account gets anything the retail people want, and there is a lot of resentment over that."

"A lot of the messages from headquarters are like so much noise. Some are even contradictory. I got two e-mails the same day, the first telling me to curb customer entertainment expenses, the other telling me that we need to build better relationships with our key accounts. So what am I supposed to tell my salespeople to do? Treat their customers to McDonald's?"

Need for cross-functional cooperation

"The organizational structure of Essential is very traditional—vertical, by function—and I question how effective that is in this day and age."

"I sometimes think that in this company a higher percentage of important decisions are made in the hallways, the restrooms, and the stairwells than in the conference rooms."

"There is poor communication and cooperation between the various functions of the company. This hurts all of us."

"Hidden agendas rule."

"There is almost a tribal mentality between the different groups and departments, though no one would ever admit that publicly."

"People who try to cut through the bureaucracy and work across the boundaries between the functions are entering a no-man's-land—with all the incumbent perils."

"Because of the turf wars, we've set up this defensive maze of procedures that are supposed to preserve order. Mostly these just serve to slow things down and prevent the root causes of problems from being dealt with."

"Work is expedited based upon the political leverage of the people involved."

"Each function tries to do what's best for its own situation, to optimize for its own performance, not for the performance of the company as a whole."

George M. Tracy
Consultant

Yes, of course, the names of other managers come up during the interviews. That's healthy and good. It enables people to express legitimate thoughts and concerns in a confidential manner, without worries about stepping on the other managers' feelings . . . and without fear of reprisal. Comments about specific managers, for obvious reasons, are not made public, but they are shared privately with the managers in a summarized form.

Now, the task of revealing to senior managers the regard in which others hold them is best handled tactfully. With empathy . . . yet with honesty. Remember, nobody is out to nail anybody. It's to be expected that you will have some who will mouth off, but we don't consider that in itself to be meaningful. What *is* meaningful is if you hear the same things over and over from a variety of people throughout the organization. When that happens, there is most likely something behind it. It's part of the process of healing and getting stronger and moving forward that the organization has to deal with certain individuals.

I stopped by to see Frank Harlan one morning, and I had with me a summary of comments that had been made in reference to him.

I said, "Do you have some time for us to talk?"

"By all means!" he said graciously. "Have a seat."

Frank had been one of the early interviewees, and he had filled my ear with all manner of opinions. His dislike of Jake Foster and how Jake was out of his element at Essential. His firm support of Rick Riggins. The vital importance of SOS to Essential's future, the vital importance of the Engineering Department to Essential's future, etc.

"As you know, Frank, we've been talking to all the key managers in the company, and we've been encouraging them to speak their minds about Essential, both as it is now and its future direction. In those talks, your name has come up a number of times—which is not surprising because all the senior managers and many others come up in the discussions. In your case, however, there were quite a number of comments regarding your management style that . . . well, were of concern, and I thought should be brought privately to your attention."

Frank nodded slowly as he gave me the evil eye. "And what were those comments?"

"Well . . . here." I slid the single sheet of paper across the desktop toward him. "This isn't word for word, but it's the gist of what my associates and I have been hearing about you from the other managers."

Comments on Frank Harlan

Frank Harlan has his engineers totally intimidated. Nobody will offer a view that does not have his stamp of approval.

He's a brilliant engineer without question, but I think Frank learned management from a third-world dictator.

It's well understood that if you challenge him or even just speak your mind publicly, your career is as good as over.

If you don't agree with him, Frank will move you off the good projects and onto the dogs. You might as well put out your résumé and move on at that point.

We've lost a number of exceptionally talented engineers mainly because of Frank. Many of those who remain are just sticking it out until retirement.

Unless you're one of Frank's chosen few, working in Engineering can be very unpleasant.

I could tell he was becoming agitated as he read to the bottom of the list. Finally, he looked up at me and said, "People in Engineering actually said these things?"

"Not just Engineering, but managers in other parts of Operations, as well as in Sales and Marketing and other areas of the company as well."

Frank casually flicked the paper back across the desk at me.

"I'm not terribly surprised," he said. "Engineering is a profession that requires logic, discipline, and precision. I run a tight ship, and I'm not surprised that there are some who resent and resist my high expectations. If you will give me their names, I will have a talk with them one on one."

"Well, Frank, that's not the purpose here. What's come out of the interviews is that the perception of your management style precludes open and straightforward discussion and that this is having a detrimental effect upon the performance of the company as a whole."

"Hogwash. If the intent is open and honest discussion, then give me the names and I will engage in such with those individuals."

"I'm sorry, but the comments were made in confidence—just as you made comments in confidence about Jake and Rick and other individuals. It would undermine the whole process to break that confidence."

"Don't I have the right to confront my accusers?"

"Frank, please!" I laughed. "Nobody is accusing you. Now, it's true there are some significant issues here that have to be dealt with. One of them is the perception—"

"The perception that I'm some kind of Hitler or something! All right, if you won't give me the names, let's go through the list and I'll refute these one by one."

"Frank, it's not going to accomplish anything for you to argue with me. It is the rest of the organization that is the important thing."

"Yes, well, let me tell you that I am personally quite satisfied with the way Engineering is managed. If others are not, they can at least have the guts to come and talk to me about it in person. Furthermore, as to my performance as a manager, the only person I have to satisfy is Rick Riggins."

I found that last statement puzzling. "Don't you mean Jake Foster?"

"Jake Foster is not an engineer, and he lacks the technical basis to evaluate this department's performance. Though I may report to him on an organization chart, I consider my real boss to be Rick Riggins."

"Uh-huh. I think that would come as a shock to Jake . . . and also to Rick."

"Then you miss my point. I'm just saying that formalities aside, it is the president of the company who has indicated he has confidence in my abilities."

"I'm sure that's the case, Frank. Nevertheless, Engineering doesn't just deal with the company president. Engineering has to accommodate and work with and satisfy many different constituencies throughout the company as well as in the marketplace."

"And we do."

"There seems to be some disagreement there."

"Not so far as I'm aware."

"Okay, but you see, that is why I'm bringing it to your attention."

Frank folded his arms across his chest.

"You see," I said, "I think there may well be some genuine misunderstanding about the role of Engineering as a part of the total scope of Essential's strategy."

Something seemed to click inside Frank at that moment. It was a small click, but it was noticeable. He unfolded the arms crossing his chest.

"So you're saying that the real point of all of this is . . . communication?" he asked.

"Well, yes. But more than that. Communication for the purpose of bringing about meaningful change and improvement."

"There are a number of things that I would like to have communicated to others within the company. I do agree that the needs of Engineering are frequently misunderstood, and our contribution is under-appreciated."

"That's not really it, Frank. We're concerned with the health of the enterprise as whole. Let me explain it once more. . . ."

In the end, he did seem to acquiesce to the larger goal. He even confided that perhaps he was a bit heavy-handed at times as a manager. It was a small mea culpa, but it was there. He gave me his pledge, grudgingly, that he would give "this whole thing" a chance. I didn't take it at face value, but it was a start I felt.

Jake Foster
Senior Vice President–Operations

There was another part to the diagnostic, the survey. It was conducted via the Internet and, like the interviews, the survey was also confidential. George and his people gave a control number to each manager so that he could tally the numbers by function and management level (and so that no one could skew the results). But beyond the control number, which was kept under wraps, it was anonymous.

The survey had more than 100 questions. For most of them, the respondent answered by marking a scale of numbers ranging from 1 to 12, according to agreement or disagreement with a statement or to state the degree of some condition. Here are some examples:

Survey Questions

To what degree does "turf protection" interfere with effective performance in this company?

How effective are the handoffs between functions in the development of new products?

What is the nature of upward communications from personnel to higher levels of management with respect to controversial issues affecting Essential?

How good is the cooperation between functions within Essential?

How would you describe the effectiveness of the Company's response to emerging markets and opportunities?

Does management communicate a clear and consistent message regarding strategic direction to all Essential personnel?

What proportion of your daily time is spent on productive tasks versus "firefighting" to deal with mistakes and unanticipated problems?

To what degree does Essential effectively allocate resources to deal with shortcomings and capitalize on opportunities?

What is the level of morale within Essential?

Do personnel receive proper training and development to give us a competitive performance advantage?

Once all the managers had responded, it was fairly easy then to convert the data into bar charts for each question. By sorting the charts, patterns began to emerge. You could see where there was a predominance of agreement among managers, and even more important, you could identify areas and issues in which opinions diverged. The latter was vital because then we could identify where the illusions lay—or, more to the point, where we needed to sweep away the false impressions and illusions in order to deal with the underlying realities.

So George had the broad yet subjective information gathered via the interviews and also the quantified measure of the management issues within the company. Combining the two, we had a comprehensive assessment of the state of management, if you will, inside Essential.

Vince Springer
Senior Vice President–Marketing and Sales

The diagnostic—both the interview comments and the survey—was a real eye-opener. And an ear-opener. I resolved from that to do more listening. Clearly, there were things that I was missing as a manager, things that I needed to do a better job of responding to.

Pam Cantrell
Vice President–Human Resources

The diagnostic process disturbed me. I'm not a control freak, but I do feel that HR should have had more involvement. On the other hand . . . well, it did serve to help bring issues out into the open.

Jane Grimm
Vice President–Finance

At one point while reading through the comments, I jumped to my feet, put my fist into the air, and shouted, "Yes!" Fortunately, I was at home in my living room when I did that. But I felt that finally—*finally!*—we might just have the wherewithal to slay this invisible dragon that was slowly killing us.

Frank Harlan
Vice President and Director–Engineering

I had no idea we were an organization of whiners and malcontents. I actually questioned the validity of many of those comments. Someone— and I think we all know who that someone was—had an agenda and was putting words in people's mouths. Because if so many managers were so dissatisfied with the company, then why didn't they quit? Okay, I grant you that there have been some who did quit, but those were not the people we wanted to keep. We never lost any manager or professional we really wanted to keep, not in Engineering at any rate. Furthermore, it is commonly suspected that certain of our competitors were engaged in raiding practices. . . .

Mike Zarelli
Director–Manufacturing

You want the honest truth? I was embarrassed by the whole thing. I sat there trying to figure out who said what, thinking, "Now, who would say something like that?" And if I could ever know for sure who said some of that stuff, they'd be on my shit list forever.

Rick Riggins
President

The interview comments really brought it home for me. I read all of them. At first, I was a little angry about some. But the more I read, the more I began to recognize how much I'd lost touch. How much was beneath the surface. And that galvanized me. We would come to grips with this.

11

Diane Sullivan
Manufacturing Manager–Logandale Plant

I got a call from George asking that I come over early the next morning for a meeting in the executive conference room at the top of the building. When I got there, I found not only George but also Jake Foster and Rick Riggins. I thought, *Oh great. Are they going to promote me or fire me?*

It turned out to be neither. Rick said, "As you and the other managers know, we're going to hold a three-day workshop off-site at the Dellwood Lodge on the north end of the lake."

I said, "Well, there's a joke going around that it should be one heck of a party."

"A three-day party is not quite what we had in mind," Jake said, "which isn't to say that we won't have some fun moments."

Fun. Right. Well, I thought, anything is possible. "So," I said, "I'm sure you didn't have me come over here just to remind me of that."

Rick Riggins looked at me dead seriously and said, "Diane, this three-day workshop at the Lodge is going to be the pivot point for how we manage this company in the future. This is it. We, all of us, are going to change the nature of 'business as usual' inside Essential."

"And after careful consideration, we would like you to play a prominent role in that process," said George.

"How do you mean?" I asked.

"At the workshop, we are going to set up a number of different management groups that we call Advocate Teams. They will be cross-functional; each team will include managers from all functions relevant to the task it is to address. The role of every team will be to advocate—and indeed to actually bring about—changes within the company that will ultimately secure our future and make Essential preeminent in the marketplace."

"Okay, so I'll be on one of these teams?"

"Diane, we want you to be coleader of the Supply Chain Advocate Team."

"And who would be the other coleader?" I asked.

"Adam Bernstein. You know him?"

"Yes, I know Adam. He's a marketing manager. Well, that sounds fine. Um, are you going to supply the boxing gloves, or should we bring our own?"

"You're saying you don't think you can work with him?" asked Jake.

"No, not at all. *I* can work with anybody. It's just that . . . may I speak plainly?"

"Please do."

"I've long felt Marketing is often as much of a thorn in the side of Manufacturing as an ally. And that also goes for Sales to a large degree."

"Diane, why do you think we're doing this?" asked Jake.

"Oh, don't take that the wrong way," I said. "I think it'll be great—as long as they don't strangle me before the end of the workshop."

I was joking of course.

"No rough stuff," said George. "Especially because, as you and everyone else will discover, this isn't simply a three-day workshop. The process we initiate will go on, month after month—and even year after year."

"In all seriousness," Jake said to me, "this is your chance to show me and the rest of the company what you're made of. In our discussions, you showed real concern and you convinced me that you really want to run an honest, first-rate plant. Well, this is the best opportunity you could have to work through the problems and get Logandale turned around."

"I'm ready," I said. "I'll get it done."

George M. Tracy
Consultant

Everyone has a role to play in the process. The role of the company president is to set the goals and then to be the firm hand pushing everyone else in the desired direction and keeping everyone honest. We often call him "the bookend," meaning he is the one who keeps all the others upright and in-line.

Most of the managers who participate are members of Advocate Teams. These teams are made up of managers from different functions and are organized around a single topic. Examples might be sales effectiveness, market strategy, or supply chain. The topics are selected based on the interview comments and the survey, and then are approved by senior management as being key to accomplishing the company's strategic goals.

As a first order of business, each Advocate Team writes a charter describing how the team will approach the assigned topic, and then develops a set of objectives in support of what needs to be accomplished. From then on, each team works to advocate change—hence the name—that will bring about significant improvement and enable the enterprise to achieve the president's stated goals.

Linking all the Advocate Teams together is the Core Team, which is made up of all of the Advocate Team leaders. It is, in effect, a team of team leaders. The role of the Core Team is to join the separate efforts of the Advocate Teams into a united effort. We call this the "cross-team knitting." That is, the efforts of the different teams become joined together, interlaced into a seamless whole. The knitting begins with the interactions of the people on the Core Team.

The Senior Team is made up of the company's senior managers. They are the "yea or nay" decision makers. They grant the approvals when these are warranted. Many or sometimes all are also what we call "sponsors" who sit with the team members. They may offer insight when asked to do so and advise when the team is obviously wandering off course. Otherwise, they are supposed to stay back, especially in the early going, refrain from meddling, and let the Advocate Team leaders guide the discussion. Of course, the Senior Team, which includes the president, makes the final decisions on what actions are carried out. But that happens later, in the months following the initial three-day workshop.

The main purpose of the workshop is to bring everyone together and establish clear communication around common objectives, which of course need to align and balance with the larger goals as defined by the president. We want this process to permeate the management organization. So, during the workshop, we often have the Senior Team meet separately from the Advocate Teams, both to keep them out of the hair of the other managers and to get them to focus on the larger strategic picture. In my experience, one of the common problems is that the senior people won't let go of control over the day-to-day stuff—which preoccupies them and prevents them from thinking about the enterprise itself, what's best for the business as a whole. In any case, we often try to get them off to themselves for a while, but not always.

At Essential, one or two members of the Senior Team had such paranoia about what might be going on at the Advocate Team meetings (as if terrible things might be said, revolutions plotted, etc.) that, after talking with Rick, we felt it would be better to include them in the Advocate meetings as sponsors, so long as they didn't obstruct what was going on. There is frequently tremendous fear about dealing openly with the problems and past mistakes of the business, and often the fear is greatest among certain individuals of the Senior Team. We figured that if we could just get the senior managers to allow the opening of the closet doors, whatever was inside probably wouldn't be as scary as they thought.

Position	Name First	Name Last	Market Strategy	Sales Effectiveness	Supply Chain	Product Development	Vendor Management
PRESIDENT	Rick	Riggins	CS				
VP FINANCE	Jane	Grimm					S
Controller	Leo	Jacobs				X	
IT Manager	Gordon	Villers			X		
Systems Analyst	Mandy	Koslowski		X			
VP HUMAN RESOURCES	Pamela	Cantrell		S			
HR Manager	Kevin	Lee		X			
SR. VP MARKETING & SALES	Vince	Springer				S	
Director–National Accounts	Felice	Torrance				X	
Director–Field Sales Force	Tom	Wright	X				
Regional Sales Manager	Charlie	Packer			X		
Regional Sales Manager	Kathy	Ambrose		X			
Regional Sales Manager	Ozzie	Brown		L			
Director–Retail Sales	Nick	Corrigan	X				
Regional Sales Manager	Don	DiPrenza		X			
Regional Sales Manager	Angeline	Ramos			X		
Director–International Sales	Xavier	Estaban	X				
Director–Marketing	Linda	Wong	L				
Marketing Manager	Adam	Bernstein			CL		
Product Manager	Sandra	Moss				X	
Product Manager	Patrick	Tyler		X			
Marketing Manager	Karl	Porter	X				
Product Manager	Vivian	Lebeque				CL	
Product Manager	Andy	Innis					X
SENIOR VP OPERATIONS	Jake	Foster			S		
Director–Manufacturing	Mike	Zarelli	X				
Manufacturing Manager–Logandale	Diane	Sullivan			CL		
Manufacturing Manager–Kenosha	Bill	Albrecht					X
QC Manager	Heidi	Jordan					X
Director–Materials	Larry	Oletta			X		
Manager–Production Scheduling	Eric	Tillwell			X		
Manager–Distribution	Chris	Finnegan		X			
Manager–Purchasing	Wendy	Orman					L
VP & DIR–ENGINEERING	Frank	Harlan	CS				
Dir–Engineering & Design	Sterling	Grove				CL	
Engineering Mgr–Product Design	Tony	Natuzzi				X	
Engineering Mgr–Process Design	Hank	Urban			X		
Engineering Mgr–Est. & Pricing	Brenda	Pearl	X				
Dir–Adv. Systems Engineer	Will	Younger					X
Dir–Research & Development	Rahzi	Kotsami				X	
TOTALS*			7	7	8	7	5

Note: X = member; S = sponsor; CS = cosponsor; L = team leader; CL = coleader.
* Not including sponsors.

Rick Riggins
President

George Tracy and I spent a lot of time together during the diagnostic phase, much of it spent talking about the business, about management, and about my role in what was to come. We talked about all kinds of things, but one key point that he impressed upon me was the periodic need for the senior executive to cause creative disruption.

You have to disturb the status quo at appropriate times so that the rest of the organization can awaken from its complacency, and you have to do it in a way that creates positive change. You must even be willing to dismantle policies and strategies and so on that you, the executive, may have put in place. The art of leadership involves a constant quest for the better way. You must never allow your own ideas to become justified and perpetuated just because they came from you.

The so-called caretaker managers don't allow for creative disruption. Caretakers do not want to disrupt the status quo. For one thing, they often want their own accomplishments to remain in place. They encourage the complacency, yet improvement, almost by definition, is disruptive.

George M. Tracy
Consultant

In a healthy management, it's not a question of who is right. It's a question of what is right. Enterprise Medicine is about making that change in thinking throughout the organization, from decisions based on *who's right* to decisions based on *what's right*.

Having said that, though, it's absolutely critical that the company president determine in his or her own mind the destination toward which the company has to head, the financial goals to be set as targets, and so on. The role of the company president in the process is not only to instigate the creative disruption but, above all, to provide the stabilizing sense of direction for everybody as this process of change progresses.

12

Adam Bernstein
Marketing Manager

The Dellwood Lodge is an old-fashioned resort that sits above the lake. It's rustic, but nice. Behind the lodge, a broad lawn sweeps down to the water's edge, where there is a marina with boats for fishing and excursions. The main building is made of rough-hewn logs and inside is a stone fireplace that's big enough you could cook an elk on a spit. There are a lot of meeting rooms for businesses like ours, and all the recreational amenities as well—an eighteen-hole golf course, tennis courts, and a stable with riding horses—not that we would be using any of those.

We arrived and checked in the afternoon before the workshop, and at 5:30 P.M., we were to meet at the marina. Tied up at the dock were a number of excursion boats, the kind with two pontoons supporting a flat deck, covered by an awning and all that. There was one of these boats for each team—Supply Chain, Sales Effectiveness, and so on.

After we'd boarded the boats, we put out into the lake with one of George's associates at the wheel of each boat, the person who would be with each team during the workshop. Anyway, the boats cruised out across the water toward the middle of the lake, and it was like we had our own little navy. Jokes and wisecracks flew back and forth across the water from boat to boat. Everybody was smiling, chatting away, enjoying the late afternoon sunshine.

All of a sudden, all of the boats cut their motors and the whole flotilla slowed nearly to a stop. Rick Riggins, with a megaphone, gave instructions to throw ropes from one boat to another and tie them together so as not to drift apart. Once we had done that, all the boats were close enough that we could hear Rick without his having to use the megaphone, and he talked to us.

"I suppose you wonder what we're doing out here," he said. "Well, in part, it was to make a simple point, but I'll get to that in a few minutes. First, I want to talk about the purpose of what we're going to be doing over the next three days.

"Tomorrow morning, we're going to begin charting the future course of our company. Collectively and individually, you will be involved. And you will be responsible for creating and executing a strategic plan for the business that will evolve from our discussions and discoveries.

"Our purpose is threefold. First, we need to articulate common objectives. Not marketing objectives or engineering objectives or what have you, but common objectives for Essential as a business. I will be giving you the numbers and the strategic targets that I think we need to hit. But you, as a group, need to set forth the objectives that will get us where we need to be in five years. These need to be balanced. They need to take into account our competition, our core competencies as an organization, our markets, the financial requirements of Borcon—all relevant factors.

"Second, we're going to talk about all the stuff nobody wants to talk about. We need to do that. We need to get into the open all the issues that are holding us back. We're going to talk about the future of AZ versus the future of SOS. We're going to talk about why Manufacturing is having trouble with the Marketing Forecast. There are no taboos. If it concerns the business, it's open for discussion. George Tracy tells me that as we do this, it'll quickly become a lot less scary than it seems.

"Third, once we have the objectives written down and all the issues on the table, we need to define the problems and obstacles standing in our way. We need to get down to the root-cause level of what these problems are about. For instance, though I don't want to pick on anybody, why can't Operations deliver to the customer on time? I believe what you're going to find out is that these problems are not one-dimensional. The problems Operations gets blamed for have ties to issues throughout the company. If you don't believe that, I think you're going to get a quick education.

"This isn't a training exercise we're engaged in. This isn't hypothetical. This is the real thing. What evolves over the next few days will be the beginning of the future of the Essential Corporation. We are going to figure out where we need to be in terms of customers, markets, sales force, products, logistics, and everything else. This is more than a workshop. This is setting the foundation of what Essential will be in years to come.

"You were invited to participate because you—each of you—occupy a key management position within this company, and the rest of us need your experience, knowledge, and commitment in order to be successful. And you will be putting into action the plans and decisions that come from this process. So for everybody's sake, including yours, please give us a hundred percent and do a great job.

"One last thing. Why the boats? Just to make a simple point. I believe, based on the evidence collected in the interviews and surveys over recent weeks, that as a management organization we've been adrift for some time. And I further believe we've been drifting in separate directions without the benefit of ropes to keep us together. What's more, I don't like the direction we've been drifting. I think the ultimate consequence is as certain as that spillway about half a mile ahead. The current of the lake has been taking us inevitably but imperceptibly toward it as I've been talking the past few minutes. If we don't take action, sooner or later, we're going over.

"Now, I don't know about the rest of you, but I'm ready for hot hors d'oeuvres and a cold drink. Let's power up the boats and navigate to where we want to go."

Christopher Finnegan
Manager–Distribution

Make no mistake, I saw myself as one of the warriors in this process, not as one of the chiefs. I wouldn't even go so far as to say I was a warrior in the front ranks . . . or even wanted to be. Hey, *they* were doing this, so I was there.

My sentiment was like, *Okay, great, let's chart our friggin' destiny and get back to work.* All through breakfast that morning, I kept getting paged. I had three different problem situations that were going on simultaneously in different parts of the continent. None of them were life-or-death, but all of them required some input from me. I mean, that's a manager's life these days.

At the same time, I can't deny being influenced by this coming together of all the significant managers in the whole company. On a normal basis, I see Rick Riggins maybe once or twice a month—not to speak with him, but I see him in the building. If I wasn't wearing an ID badge, I think he might know my name, though I wouldn't bet my life on it. Anyway, here we all were, in one place at one time, all talking about the company . . . and perhaps doing something about it. I'm not against any of that.

The morning of the first day of the workshop, everybody—all of the teams—met in the main banquet hall of the lodge. There were some introductory comments, then George Tracy took the microphone and began by talking about the survey.

Well, right off the bat, *that* was something. Borcon Corporate as well as our own HR people, among others, are always doing some kind of survey. I don't mean every day, but it's not unusual. What *is* unusual is to hear back how the survey turned out and what the results mean. You put an hour or even longer into filling out this silly thing, and then it flies off to Surveyland where somebody goes, "Hmmm . . . oh, my . . . yes, very interesting," and then files it away in a drawer with all the other surveys nobody talks about. Well, if it was so important to get our thoughts and opinions about this subject, why didn't you then tell us what the outcome was?

This time, hey, what do you know! They took a survey, and they're actually talking about it! And it's only been a few weeks since we took it, not months and months later when you can barely remember the thing.

So George was up there describing what he termed the "Worst Nows." These were a group of charts showing, in effect, where we have the most agreement on what the biggest problems are.

For instance, turf wars. The survey had a number of questions asking about turf protection and about the cooperation (or lack thereof) between functions. Large percentages of the managers who took the survey indicated that they thought there was a lot of "us versus them" in the company. As I recall, something like 70 percent of the managers thought that cooperation between functions in the company ranged from "poor" to "somewhat acceptable." The rest thought it was "acceptable," and there was nobody in the whole company who thought internal cooperation was "excellent." Think about it! There was not a single soul who would rate cooperation as excellent. Doesn't that speak volumes?

Another for instance: There was a question in the survey asking, "What percentage of your time is spent 'firefighting' to deal with mistakes and other unanticipated problems?" Something like 50 percent of the managers said they spent either a high percentage or a significant percentage of their time fighting fires. I'll tell you, I was in that 50 percent. Again, think about it. What are the costs of all those fires that everybody's fighting? What if you could prevent at least some of them? I mean, among other benefits, some of us might start to grow hair again. And in all seriousness, think about the drag this was having on us—the costs, the way it slowed down responsiveness, the friction with customers, the inability to think beyond today or this week or this month.

One more thing. George made a comment that echoed something I was already thinking. Even though the survey didn't directly bring it out, you had to wonder to what degree the turf wars were causing the fires.

George had another set of charts from the survey, too. These were the "Least Consensus About Now," Basically, these showed where we have the least agreement.

Take, for instance, the question, "How effective is Essential's senior management team at making key decisions and communicating them throughout the company?" When you looked at this by management rank, you could see that the executives tended to rate themselves "very effective," whereas when you got down to managers like me the typical rating became "somewhat effective" or "poor."

Similarly, there was the question, "How well do you understand the company's overall strategy?" The higher-up the management ranks, the more the manager claimed to understand the strategy "very well," but as you came down to the levels of people who were supposed to implement the strategy, the answers were more like "somewhat understand" or "don't understand."

The survey numbers were sliced and diced by function as well. One of the questions was, "How good is upward communication on controversial issues within your function?" For most functions, like Production and Sales, the responses showed communication from lower ranks to higher was mediocre at best. But in Engineering, the bar on the chart was a fraction of the others, as there was barely any upward communication.

For me, it all rang true. Of course, you could say, "Anybody could have told you these things without a survey." To which I would say, "Yeah, but this puts it in some kind of totality. It's quantified. You can't dismiss it as hearsay. It's out there in front of everybody's noses." That last was, I think, the most important. It was no longer buried away. It was in the open now.

At the end of his talk, George projected some graphics that kind of served to reemphasize Rick Riggins' theme from out on the lake. Did we want to drift, or did we want to power up and steer our best possible course? George depicted this in a most romantic and poetic motif—the X/Y axis graph with scatter plot, always a sure bet to enrapture management audiences everywhere. But the message was clear.

What we wanted was not to be down there in the lower-left corner. We, as a company, wanted to be in the upper-right corner. We wanted 70 percent of the managers—or more—to be able to say honestly that cooperation between functions was excellent. We wanted a consensus to reveal that turf wars were nonexistent. We wanted the vast majority of managers to report that the percentage of time spent firefighting was small to minimal.

So the choice was this, according to George—and according to logic. On the one hand, we could drift along the bottom of the chart, over time, waging our turf wars and fighting our fires. *Or* we could work hard to eliminate those kinds of things and move to the upper right of the chart . . . to become the kind of company where everybody understood what was going on, what was supposed to happen, and committed themselves to making the right things happen. To become a great company, if I can say that without blushing. And that's what we were here to do . . . in a practical, measurable way.

What really got me was the way people's body language changed. At first, a lot of people were sitting back, kind of skeptical (not unlike me), anxious to get on with this, to get it over with so that they could get back to the "real" business of managing their everyday problems. But as the session went on, you could see this change, with people leaning forward, obviously listening with interest. By the time Rick Riggins took the mike to deliver his talk on the goals for the company, we were into it.

Rick Riggins

President

Excerpt from presentation remarks

Let me give you a situation analysis of how this company is positioned at present . . . and our overall strategy and goals for the future.

For the past few weeks, George Tracy and his people have been talking to all of us, and from those discussions, a clear picture has emerged showing what you think the major issues are and, to some extent, how we need to deal with them. At the same time as George and company were gathering the subjective data in the form of your thoughts and comments, many of us were also pulling together hard data and taking a tough, objective look at our sales, operations, and financial performance.

When we combine these, we don't see a pretty picture. In the past, not all of us have been able to see the picture, for whatever reason. Many have perhaps not wanted to for fear of what might be staring back at them. My conviction though is that we as an organization need to see the truth and we need to see it together. So let's do that. Here are the realities facing us.

Over the past five years, Essential has invested over $50 million in SOS, by far our largest research and development expenditure ever. Yet, now, as we approach the market launch for SOS, a number of us are wondering whether SOS is going to be the magic bullet we've counted on. Is SOS a sure thing? Many have their doubts. We need to resolve those doubts one way or another.

Meanwhile, within the past several years, our competitors have achieved parity with our principal moneymaker, the AZ line. We still like to think of AZ as the Cadillac of the industry, but the market is telling us more and more that customers see it as a Chevy that's competing against Toyotas and Fords. That may be hard for some of us to take, but it's the truth.

In an attempt to differentiate AZ from the competing offerings, we have tremendously expanded the array of models and features and options combinations to the extent that even I have trouble keeping them straight. Some of you have suggested that customers are also finding all this variety to be confusing and not the competitive edge we had thought. Moreover, Operations is caught in the middle of all this and is having one heck of a time managing the supply chain. At least some of the difficulty is due to the complexities imposed on them. Do we really need so many SKUs? How can we—not just Operations, but *we* as management—achieve greater efficiency and lower costs in the supply chain?

Then there is BigBox. All of you know that I championed the effort to win the BigBox account. Well, I'm here to tell you that it's been a disappointment. We have a real challenge on our hands. How can we manage this piece of business so that it delivers the net income that we've long sought from it?

For lo these many years, Operations has been the scapegoat. Whenever there have been problems, Operations has tended to get most of the blame. Yet none of the issues I've just described falls discreetly within the domain of Operations. The issues and dilemmas we face are company-wide in scope. The solutions—and I do believe that there are good solutions, based in part on the comments of many of you—are also company-wide. We need to end the blame games and the finger-pointing and move forward. That process is what we're starting today.

But forward to where? In what directions do our greatest opportunities lie?

In decades past, we put our trust primarily in technology. We assumed that great products would make us successful, yet as time has elapsed, our technological edge has faded. I won't argue whether our technology is superior or whether our engineering capabilities are better than theirs. Perhaps they are. Even so, I ask you, is technology *alone* going to guarantee our success? Our competitors have been gaining on us not because they have better technology but because they are market driven and they've been able to move faster than we have. We cannot ignore that reality.

What must we become? Let me give you the strategic view. Our long-term strategy for success will be based on three principles—or what I call the Three Bests.

The first of these is being the Best in Product Innovation, which comes from a genuine understanding of the end-users' needs and values.

The second is having the Best Relationships with Customers—and through those relationships, an intimate knowledge of customers' needs in various channels now and in the future.

The third is delivering the Best Fundamental Values to the customer. By fundamental values, I mean quality, costs and pricing, and any other values that are a high priority with customers in targeted segments and, therefore, key to winning those markets.

Now, "best" is a relative term. I chose it for that reason. We want to be the best not in some idealistic, abstract sense. We want to be the best in those three standards in measurable terms—using empirical data from customers, market sources, and world-class benchmarks.

Where are we today? In your binders, you'll find some scorecards we've put together. You'll go over them in more detail later, but let's take a quick look now. Take customer service . . . are we easy to do business with? We may think so, but relative to Reliable and others, we are a long way from being the best.

How about sales effectiveness? Check where we stand with respect to sales force time spent in front of customers—way at the low end of the range. Now, to fix that, do we just go yell at the sales force: *"Get more face time with customers!"* That's kind of what, with the best of intentions, we've done in the past. Hasn't worked, has it?

Perhaps the reason the sales force can't get more face time in front of customers is because Manufacturing can't get the orders straight. And perhaps the reason Manufacturing can't get the orders straight is because Marketing keeps fiddling with the SKUs. And perhaps the reason Marketing keeps fiddling with the SKUs is because Engineering can't quickly deliver new designs that are genuinely innovative. And round and round we go. Does any of this sound familiar? It should; you told us.

Well, today we get off the merry-go-round. We look at the scorecards, figure out why we're stuck in the lower-left corner of the graph, and how we're going to move to the upper-right corner of the grid, where we want and need to be.

Those Three Bests are an unbeatable combination. If we can indeed become the best in all three of these in markets where we compete—best innovation, best relationships, best fundamental values—it adds up to the grand prize . . .

Market dominance. That's what we're after. And if we grow our performance continuously by all three of those standards, that's what we will achieve over the next five years.

Our specific goals as a company include the following:

With respect to growing the business . . . *to become dominant in the most desirable market segments.* Notice I said, "most desirable," not "all segments."

In financial performance . . . first, our goal is to be either number one or two among Borcon International business units in terms of return on invested capital. And, second, to deliver the highest return on invested capital of any company within our industry segment.

In specific numbers . . .

The goal is to grow total sales from $1.1 billion to $2.3 billion—roughly double the current total—in five years.

We need to triple our operating income.

And we need to double our return on invested capital.

Yes, the bar is being raised. I know that many of you are asking yourselves right now, "Is Riggins *crazy*? Given where we are now, given the issues and problems that he just outlined, aren't these goals a disconnect from reality?"

The answer is, no. Not at all. I've done the math, and these goals *are* attainable. Take a look at this spreadsheet. If we assume a two-percent growth in traditional markets for Z products, over five years we see these markets grow from their current $2.75 billion to a little over $3 billion. If we can just hold our own, we gain $114 million in sales simply from market growth. *But* if Essential can take share away from others, notably Spectrum and Reliable, we gain a lot more.

For decades, Essential's total share hovered around fifty percent. Spectrum and Reliable have chipped away at that over the past few years and pushed us down to about forty percent. If we can simply regain that ten percent we lost—actually a twenty-five percent improvement over five years—we gain $304 million. So we get $418 million from market growth and taking share from competitors on top of the current $1.1 billion. I'm not saying it will be easy. And it's true we don't yet know how our AZ base will fare with Z3 and SOS on the horizon. But we *will* find ways to make it happen.

Now, that is only in *traditional* markets. Look at the untapped *global* markets, which are growing at a five percent rate. If we can achieve a ten percent global share—just ten percent (and by the way I think a twenty to thirty percent share is not unreasonable)—we gain from that ten percent about $351 million. Add in new application segments and new related business, which will be created in the months and years ahead, for another $432 million . . . and there you have the $2.3 billion in sales.

Later we'll go through the same process for operating income and ROIC, but the point is the same. Even with a fairly modest set of assumptions—a return to our traditional share domestically, a ten percent share internationally, innovative new products to bring in additional streams of revenue—we can achieve dramatic results.

And we can do it. I will even tell you that we *must* do it, if Essential is to have a future—and it is our job as professionals to ensure that future through the growth of the business. That's what we're paid to do.

You want to know the only thing that can stop us from reaching those goals? It's us. You, me . . . everyone in this room. *We* are the biggest obstacle to our own success. The competition hasn't been beating us; we have been beating ourselves.

That's the truth. None of the problems identified in the interviews or in the data is insurmountable . . . *if* we change the way we interact and work together. Most of the complaints you voiced would not exist . . . *if* we had had the kind of management organization in the past that we are going to have in the future.

Your job—our job collectively—is to create a common set of objectives and establish the foundations for initiatives that will enable us to achieve the goals we need to reach. We have a long way to go. No question about that. We're not going to get there tomorrow. Or next month. Or maybe not even next year—but we'll be heading in the right direction. A three-day meeting like this, in itself, is not going to get us there. This workshop is the bon voyage. It's the beginning of the journey. My advice? Come along or get left behind. Today, we depart from the past.

Tom Wright
Director–Field Sales Force

My reaction, sitting out there in the seats, listening to Riggins talk was, *You've got to be kidding!* He wanted to *double* sales in five years? And *triple* operating income? You want *this* outfit to do these things? Come on!

I heard some of the others talking as we went to lunch. They were being guarded about what they said—and not very loud—but they clearly regarded this as just too big of a stretch. For *us* anyway. Then I got to thinking about it. What if we *could* do it? I didn't see how it was possible, but suppose there really was a way? That would be . . . *something*. That would be . . . *cool*.

13

Ozzie Brown
Regional Manager–Field Sales

To me it wasn't all that complicated. Rick Riggins had said, "We're going to double annual sales in five years." Okay, sounds good! Now, what do we have to do to make it happen?

You know, it was like, "Folks, we're going to climb Mount Everest!" Hey, that's great! Now, first of all, how do we get to Tibet? How much money do we need to get there? What kind of equipment do we need to buy? What kinds of skills do we need to learn? What's the best way for all of us climbers to get into shape?

Same thing with doubling sales. No need for a panic attack. Let's take it back a few steps and figure out rationally what we have to do.

Well, if we were going to double our sales and still meet the other performance targets, we would obviously need a much more efficient sales organization—working in concert with a much-improved company feeding us the right things to sell, executing well on quality and delivery and so on. But as far as the sales effectiveness, which was my charge, what had to happen?

Basically, my own thinking was simple. Effectiveness came down to two things: sales people and the systems that support those people. That's why the team included Human Resources and also one of the IT managers.

As with any sales force, Essential's sales organization had some strong performers and some weak performers. We also had some people who looked like strong or average performers but who were in fact average to weak. They looked better than what they were because they knew how to manipulate the systems to their own advantage. Obviously, if we were really going to double sales, we needed people who could really get it done, not people who played a good game of appearing to get it done.

The political part of it was that the strong performers were understandably coveted and highly prized by the local sales managers. Everybody wanted to hang onto their stars, yet there were star salespeople who, many of us suspected, were being under utilized. They were stuck in nongrowth areas of the country, handling accounts that really only needed a good order taker—while we, as a company, were missing opportunities in high-growth areas that were underdeveloped. Reliable, in particular, was picking up the gems while we were continuing to allocate our best talent where they couldn't do us the most good.

In a business like ours, in which relationships were important, you didn't want to move people around without taking a great deal of care in how you did it. It was expensive, the person you were moving might not want to be moved, and even once you got the right person in the right place, it would take time for the move to pay off. Even a star needs time to develop a new account.

So there were lots of issues big and small that had to be identified. The workshop was a time to come together to deal with all that—and I've just mentioned the personnel part of it. There was a whole technical side as well. Like, once we get the right people into the right places, what kinds of tools should they have in order to make the most of the situation?

As I say, the goal was fairly straightforward: "Climb Everest!" The complicated part, which would require months of work, was figuring out, where was Tibet? Or for that matter was Everest even *in* Tibet? Maybe it was in Nepal! Or India! Or wherever! And how do we get there? How do we set up the base camp? And who should buy the oxygen tanks and the pitons? And what skills do we need to do this? How much training? All of that. That's what we were figuring out.

Linda Wong
Marketing Director

George had coached me prior to the workshop. He and I were of like mind on the most important aspects of what we were out to do. Highest on the list was that whatever future market strategy resulted from the process, it had to be based on facts. It had to be driven by hard data. Furthermore, it had to allow for all of the available facts to be given consideration, and we should always be careful that extra weight not be given to some so-called facts over others just because they happened to suit a particular agenda. This was very refreshing to me. In the past, so many decisions at Essential were based not on the real facts, but on who carried the most weight in a particular meeting.

Each Advocate Team had its own space, a room where the members could go to work. I don't know if it was planned or whether it was just the luck of the draw, but the Market Strategy Team got what the lodge called the Terrace Room, which was on the upper floor of the main lodge. It had big plate-glass windows affording a grand view of the lake and the hills rolling off into the distance—suitable background I suppose for those trying to gain a sense of the big picture.

I have to say I was tense going into this, not so much because of what we were dealing with, but because both Rick Riggins and Frank Harlan would be at the table with us. They were cosponsors of my team. Actually, I almost welcomed Rick being there, but Frank Harlan gave me the jitters.

I hadn't worked very often with Frank, not directly, but I knew his MO. I knew that if you crossed him, then Engineering would never support anything that was linked to your name—or if Engineering did support it, then Frank would find a way to have you removed or distanced from it. Anyone who didn't believe this had only to witness Vivian Lebeque; she had discovered it the hard way. And if you wanted to work your way out of this purgatory, the way to do it quickly was to not support someone Frank didn't support (and then, of course, not repeat the prior mistake). What made Frank especially tricky to deal with was that he always had solid technical reasons—or at least they sounded solid—behind his approvals or disapprovals. I wasn't terrified of him (though some people were), but as I say, he made me nervous because you could never discount what he might do to you. In theory, all of that kind of stuff was supposed to be on the way out. But would the power plays and ego games really stop? There was no way to be sure. I assumed that Frank would be on good behavior during the workshop. It would be later on that we—I—would have to worry about.

Frank had successfully built Engineering into an ivory tower, isolated from reality. Yet maybe if he could be brought down from that tower and made to look at all the facts—not just the technical ones—and put them into context, then he might see the light. I mean, it was possible. He was a bright guy. He might change his tune.

After we'd broken into separate teams for the afternoon session, I found myself looking down the table at Frank Harlan. For the briefest of moments there was eye contact between us. We were just settling in and not everyone was seated yet. The others at the table were talking, joking with each other. Somehow for that second it was if it was just Frank and I in the room. And it was weird. I sort of smiled at him, but he stared right at me with this deadly serious scowl, so cold it sent a chill through me. Nobody else saw it, just me. And then Rick Riggins came in and sat down next to him, and Frank was amiable and chatty, almost a different person.

Well, there was no backing out at that point, and I launched right in.

Nick Corrigan
Director—Retail Sales

If Linda was nervous, she didn't show it. I was quite impressed by her. She came well prepared, and in that initial breakout session, we got right down to it.

The first order of business was the team charter, which is a statement of the team's mission, key objectives, scope of operation, and a listing of major issues to be addressed.

Linda walked in with a draft of the main points for the charter, which she had worked on with George. She went over these and asked for reactions, and within a relatively short time, we were agreed upon what we were doing and were ready to get into it.

I mean, it was terrifically straightforward: To develop fact-based strategies to guide the business! Hey, let's get it on! After all, how many battles had I had to fight that had nothing to do with the facts? It always came down to what Rick thought, or what Scott thought, or what Frank thought. If we could make decisions based on the facts, I knew I could win.

Market Strategy Team Charter

General Charter and Mission

To develop market strategies that enable the company to achieve and maintain a leadership position within the market, to identify opportunities for innovation, to ensure a desirable price-to-value relationship for our customers with respect to existing and new products and services, and to maximize our financial and operational performance.

Key Objectives and Scope

Develop a fact-based market strategy that is well understood and broadly accepted by the organization.

Develop a deep, comprehensive understanding of the market. Aspects of this understanding must include competitors, customers (as well as end-users and the market channels that serve them), our core competencies, and all important details related to products and services (such as market size, market share, growth rates, profitability, and product life cycle).

Enable our market strategies to evolve dynamically in response to change within the marketplace and actions by our competitors.

Our emphasis will be to understand the needs and preferences of end-users, innovate new offerings to suit those needs and preferences, deliver these offerings with values that customers and end-users hold highest, and to do this better than our competitors.

Create strategies that leverage our best strengths and support corporate objectives for growth and performance.

Our scope is worldwide, although our primary geographic focus will be the North American market, as it presently is the largest. Our responsibility covers all products and services marketed by Essential.

Jake Foster
Senior Vice President–Operations

As a senior-management sponsor of a team—the Supply Chain Team, in my case—a big part of the role was to keep quiet and stay out of their way. But there were some side benefits to being there. For my part, I got to learn what these managers really thought. And how they thought. And how they interacted with each other. It was quite valuable to witness that firsthand.

One of the better exchanges came early on in the workshop. Even though they were supposed to be coleaders, Adam Bernstein and Diane Sullivan were sitting at opposite ends of the table. Charlie Packer, the sales manager who had been at the Smoot dinner some weeks before, was between those two poles, and everybody else was spread out according to alignment with one of those "extremes."

They were talking about various issues, and Diane said, "Well, here's something at the top of my agenda, something we in Production have been struggling with month in and month out, year after year." She held up a hard copy. "The marketing forecast."

"A struggle?" asked Adam, smiling as he said it. "How could our rigorously prepared, always-on-the-money forecasts ever present a struggle for you?"

"Well," said Diane, "if you want a 'for instance,' let's look at last month. The forecast predicted that sales for AZ–150s would be flat with the previous month, and that, on the other hand, sales for AZ–300s and 450s would be twelve and fifteen percent higher, respectively. So what happened? We got these huge orders for 150s, while orders for the 300s and 450s tanked. My question is, how come the sales force is out there pushing the 150s when you're telling us to ramp up production of 300s and 450s?"

"Look, first of all, we in marketing don't work with a crystal ball," said Adam. "We take all kinds of information—from the sales force, from industry reports, and lots of other sources—and we analyze it. Then we make our best guess as to what's going to happen. Last quarter, we were not pushing 150s. On the contrary, we were putting marketing dollars into 300s and 450s, where the margins are better, so naturally we assumed that there would be a payoff in terms of higher sales for those lines."

"Then what went wrong?"

"It's not that anything went wrong exactly, it's just that things didn't turn out exactly as planned," said Adam.

Charlie Packer jumped in here. "Diane, if you look at the end of the quarter results, you'll see that the final sales revenue numbers were actually pretty close to what was forecast."

"Yeah, but I go back to inaccuracies in the mix. I mean, when we ramp up and build the 300s and the 450s and they don't sell, you're tying up a lot of working capital. And you're taking production time that could have been used to build other kinds of product, like the out-of-stocks and the 150s—the stuff we keep getting yelled at to rush out the door. Don't you realize that we, as a company, keep getting nailed on these customer service issues when, despite our best efforts, we have these out-of-stocks and poor fill rates?"

"Yes, absolutely! I very much do understand that," said Angeline Ramos, one of the regional sales managers for retail (which mostly was BigBox). "But is it really the fault of the forecast? Why can't operations respond according to actual demand?"

"Yeah, really," said Charlie, "what do you want us to do? I suppose you want us to say to customers, 'Gee, we're sorry. Our factory is only building 300s this month, so I can't take your order for 150s right now. I'll stop back in a month or two when the factory is ready to build 150s, is that okay?'"

"For crying out loud, Diane, these days we should be happy for every order we can book!" said Angeline.

"But I still don't understand why you salespeople can't do a better job of selling what's called for in the forecast. Isn't that the playbook we're all supposed to abide by?"

"Well, try telling that to the customer, Diane!" said Charlie. "To be perfectly blunt about it, we in Sales can't understand why your factory can't build what the customer wants when the customer wants it. For instance, why are you building so many 300s and 450s when we haven't made the actual sales?"

"Because we can't just push a button and have the finished order instantly appear. It takes planning. Parts and materials have to be ordered. Machine time has to be scheduled. We've got workers coming to the plant every day to run those machines, and we like to keep them busy. We prefer to have them actually *do* something for the money we pay them. It's called *productivity*."

"All right, all right. But, seriously, what do you expect us to do about it?"

"Well, you don't seem to understand. When one of your salespeople books an order, we're expected to ship it in seventy-two hours," said Diane. "Seventy-two hours is not enough time to produce it from scratch. If we don't have enough of an item already produced when the order comes in, chances are good it's going to ship late. That's why we *have* inventory. And we base that inventory level on Marketing's forecast. Even if your sales-dollar forecast averages out over time, we still have to deal with these endless imbalances in physical inventory. We're always getting whipsawed—too high on some models, too low in others. And when your people try to intervene and expedite individual orders, it just kills my productivity metrics—and makes it all the harder."

"Actually, if you want to know the truth," said Charlie. "I do sympathize with what you in Production have to deal with. But you *do* have to deal with it. I'm not going to have my salespeople turn down firm orders because they're not in the forecast. A sale is a sale, and when we can book it, then you have to produce it. It's as simple as that."

"Really, Diane," said Adam, "what's more important to this company, actual sales dollars or a productivity number?"

"Those productivity numbers may not seem important to you," said Diane, "but ultimately they do have an influence on costs, and on whether you can offer a cost advantage over competitors."

"No disagreement there," said Adam. "I know productivity is important. But can't you see our side of it? This company could have great productivity numbers, but if they don't translate into higher sales, higher customer satisfaction numbers, and higher profitability, then what's the point?"

I decided to add some perspective here. I said, "Diane, I do think that Adam and Charlie have a point. The productivity and efficiency numbers are important, but they're not an end in themselves."

"Of course not," she said. "But, for one thing, I am judged by them. Just like *they* are judged by sales booked for the month and so on."

"I understand, and eventually we can deal with that on a senior level. However, let's set aside for a moment what I'll call the tyranny of the metrics. Diane, I do think there are things you could be doing to better cope with the whipsaws in demand for specific SKUs."

"Such as?"

"Flexibility. As in more of it. Quicker changeovers. Shorter setups. Smaller lot sizes. Whatever will give manufacturing more flexibility to respond to fluctuations and surprises that are deviations from the forecast."

"That's not going to be a quick fix," Diane said.

"No, not at all. We're not here to come up with quick fixes."

"Well . . . good," she said. "My point is just that we're talking about . . . you know, a really substantial change from the way we've done things in the past."

With a big grin on my face, I said, "Hey, Diane, I think you've got it!"

14

Tom Wright
Director–Field Sales Force

The format for the workshop was basically presentations in the mornings and team meetings in the afternoons. The afternoon of that first day, after we had broken out into our respective teams, everything—to me at least—seemed almost cut-and-dried. Thanks mostly to Linda Wong's advance preparation, we fairly quickly nailed down the team charter and all the preliminary groundwork stuff. My understanding is that some of the teams weren't as efficient as we were, and even by the afternoon of the second day at least one of them was still trying to figure out what they were supposed to be doing. I think that was the Vendor Management Team, but don't quote me.

Anyhow, the first day was almost a piece of cake, and the next morning, we were the first to present, which was a compliment to all of us as a team. The order in which the teams made presentations to everybody else depended upon how well prepared the team was—with best-prepared going first. That was us.

The afternoon of the second day didn't go as well. We were pulling together all the sales data and attempting to organize a big spreadsheet, a comprehensive matrix with product models and SKUs matched up with market channels and end-users. We were doing that so we could see our entire business, and we were eventually going to map out a total strategy. I think George called it, the Market Chessboard.

By midafternoon we were starting to get a general idea of what this chessboard would ultimately look like. There were four major product groups as they currently existed: the AZ-130 line, the AZ-150 line, the AZ-300 line, and the AZ-400 line. And there were the many variations of each of those, which worked out to be hundreds of SKUs. There were replacement parts because those were a significant source of revenue, particularly on the more expensive models. There were system design services. And so on.

But there were also the new lines and technologies that did not yet exist. Like SOS. And there were the Z3 questions. And then there were mystery products, like something called Firefly that, frankly, I'm not sure I'd ever heard of before. Didn't even know it was potentially a product, that's how low a profile it had.

Across the top of the matrix were the categories of buyers of those offerings, the market channels. The major ones included retail outlets (mostly BigBox, but some smaller chains as well), original equipment manufacturers (OEMs), and distributors. In addition to those—and surprisingly large in volume, as a group, once we started looking at actual figures—were what Linda called the "professional resellers."

The professional resellers tended to be little companies that took various AZ components we made and combined them with other manufacturers' components to design, install, and maintain various systems. Often these were highly specialized—for police and fire departments, for commercial buildings, and so on. In fact, some of them were actually in competition with us, with respect to the high-end stuff that our Advanced Systems unit produced.

Now, in addition to the professional resellers, there was a related group called the "contractor/installers." These were the people who physically installed the product. Sometimes these installers bought from distributors. Sometimes they were engaged by the resellers who did the custom design work (and they would buy from the reseller and mark up the unit when they in turn sold it to the end user—the building manager, the local fire department, or what have you). And sometimes, in the case of the larger contractors who were regional or nationwide, they would buy direct from us in order to get a price break.

As we went along, I found it to be increasingly interesting. Most of it was quite familiar, stuff we've been dealing with every day for years. Yet . . . different, too, because we'd never seen it all laid out this way, and it was almost mind-boggling in scope. The total market ranged from the local contractor and do-it-yourselfer who ran into the nearest BigBox to pick up an AZ–130 or 150, all the way to multimillion-dollar systems that linked AZ–400s along with some rather exotic equipment to do all kinds of far-out things.

My overall impression, formed as the afternoon wore on (and later confirmed in weeks and months ahead), was that as a company we had kind of wandered here and there in the marketplace. We had lavished attention and resources on some channels while ignoring others—but without regard for the relative payoffs. I was personally gratified that our blind allegiance to BigBox was finally coming under scrutiny. On the other hand, I have to admit there were channels and specific accounts that were far less important in the grand scheme of things than I thought they were prior to building the chessboard. I know I had personally pounded the table to get support for some of them—promotions, special privileges, whatever—simply because . . . well, just *because.*

We would be building and working with the chessboard for months, but even that first afternoon at Dellwood it soon became obvious that we had unintentionally created something unnecessarily complex and strategically ill-conceived. All of a sudden I heard Mike Zarelli, the manufacturing guy, blurt out, "Holy schmoley! This is one big fouled-up mess!"

Except he didn't say "fouled" up. All I could say, which I did privately to some people, was that I was sure glad we were finally tackling this stuff after years of meandering around without really understanding the consequences of the actions we'd been taking.

Bill Albrecht
Manufacturing Manager–Kenosha Plant

The moment I heard that Wendy Orman would be leading the Vendor Management Team, I knew it was going to be a waste of time. Sure enough, we didn't get a damn thing done that first afternoon at the lodge. Wendy did ninety percent of the talking, and the rest of us tried to get a word in. Maybe not quite that extreme, but it felt like it.

I guess they put me on the Vendor Management Team because the Kenosha Plant is almost like a vendor. We're mainly a feeder plant to Logandale, although we do make some finished products. Because we supply Logandale, we get jerked around a lot. See, I wanted to be on

Supply Chain, to get those problems worked out, but in their wisdom they put me with the VM Team.

Technically, vendor management is a part of the supply chain because the total chain extends from suppliers through customers. For the sake of practicality, the Supply Chain Team was organized to deal with the flow of orders from Logandale to customers, and Vendor Management was set up to deal with the upstream issues, of which we had a few.

Mike Zarelli had authorized a root-cause analysis of why Logandale was shipping late, and the analysis showed that about thirty percent of the time it was because of something to do with a vendor—a part being out of stock or in low supply, a part or a subassembly arriving later than expected, or a nonconformance issue, those being among the major ones.

In my opinion, less-than-optimum performance on the part of vendors (and Kenosha for that matter) was more of a symptom than the problem itself. That is, I felt it was wrong to blame the suppliers—many of which frankly were better than us when it came to supply chain management—for problems that, I believed, originated with our own policies. And many of those policies were the result of our own manager of purchasing, Wendy Orman.

Let me give you an example. Wendy's number one priority is low price. Notice I said it was Wendy's priority, not necessarily mine, and not Diane Sullivan's or Heidi Jordan's in QC. Wendy is always putting work out for bids, and she will switch suppliers in the bat of an eye if it means even a few dollars of savings. There are times when we'll be running low on a part at Kenosha, and somebody will call the vendor to ask, "Where is it?" And the vendor will say, "We don't have the contract anymore."

So we call Purchasing to find out who does have the contract—this week—only to find that it's some little outfit in Wherever that's just getting up to speed on who we are and what we need. Or it's a big outfit that doesn't really care about us because we're just a little plant in Wisconsin, and if it comes to pleasing one of their Fortune 500 customers or the folks in Kenosha, guess who gets the short end of the stick? Besides which they only got the business because they were cheaper than the other vendor; how much extra effort and overtime do you think they will put into pleasing us? Yet when something isn't right, we blame the vendor and maybe switch the contract again rather than try to communicate and improve relations.

Wendy Orman has managed Purchasing a long time, and she has

trained all her people to be like her. Every year Wendy gets a bonus based on how much money her department saved the company. Wendy then turns around and throws a party for her department honoring the people who have been the most aggressive about cutting costs. Everybody has a great time. The people in her department love her. Some of the rest of us, however. . . .

Many of us have complained about Wendy in particular and Purchasing in general. The complaints never get anywhere. Wendy is a great talker. She will talk your ear off. She will talk until you've forgotten why you were talking to her in the first place. She is always negotiating everything. She doesn't leave McDonald's without negotiating the price of a hamburger. And she is the Queen of Vagueness. You think she's agreed to something, and it turns out what she's promised is a lot of nothing.

So here she is at Dellwood! The leader of the Vendor Management Team! I briefly suggested that we work on ways to take advantage of value-added supplier relationships that would help us with inventory management, just-in-time capabilities, that kind of thing. Heidi Jordan talked for thirty seconds about ways to qualify vendors in terms of quality and performance standards, rather than just price. Will Younger thought we might tackle a better make-versus-buy strategy for the company. Andy Innis just sat there and doodled. And Wendy Orman talked for hours on end about everything else.

Well, our team was last to present the next morning. That meant we were the least well prepared. The second afternoon, with a lot of coaching by the guy from George Tracy's group, we finally hammered out a team charter, the core of which was aimed at better ways to qualify suppliers. We all had a feeling where that would end up: better ways for Purchasing to find the lowest bid.

Mike Zarelli
Director–Manufacturing

At first, I didn't know why they put an old-time manufacturing guy like me on the Market Strategy Team. I half suspected maybe it was to keep me out of the way of one of the other teams, like Supply Chain. But I went along.

Anyway, I was looking at this map of the market, this chessboard thing they were creating, with everything identified. I suppose I shouldn't have said what I did. It just came out. That we were, you know, "fouled" up.

I was a little embarrassed—everybody looked at me. And then they all laughed—and they agreed!

Then somebody, I think it was Tom Wright, said, "It's no wonder with all this complexity that Logandale has its troubles." I think he said that in sympathy, like he was trying to make me feel better, but I didn't take it that way.

"There's nothing wrong with Logandale," I said.

The mood around the room just switched instantly.

"What do you mean, there's nothing wrong with Logandale?" Nick Corrigan asked me.

"Well, there isn't. Not fundamentally. It's a good plant."

Everybody kind of looked at each other, not sure whether they wanted to take me on or not. Then Tom said, "All I can say is I'm glad we're starting to take a look at all this before we launch SOS."

"Why? You think Logandale can't handle SOS? Let me tell you, we've got some of the best CNC equipment in the country at Logandale. And skilled operators, too. You'd be very hard-pressed to duplicate what we've got at Logandale; I can assure you."

"Have you looked?" asked Linda.

"What do you mean by that?"

"Have you considered other manufacturing options in addition to Logandale?" she asked.

"No . . . not really," I said. "Why should I?"

"Suppose there's not enough capacity at Logandale? Even if there is, what are the production costs going to be compared with other sources? And to take Tom's point, if you've already got snafus and production bottlenecks at Logandale, how smart is it to add new demands on top of what's there?"

"Listen," I said, "we're making plans now to produce SOS at Logandale."

"And I'm saying perhaps you—perhaps *we*—should consider all alternatives."

"What, you think we should build SOS in *China*?"

Linda Wong stared back at me.

"I'm sorry, I'm sorry. I didn't mean that the way it sounded," I said.

"It's just that . . . we've invested in Logandale for decades. Why don't we want to get the most from that investment?"

"Could it be that we've continued to invest in Logandale because we've never allowed other options to be considered?"

"Hey, wait a minute," said Karl Porter. "Isn't this the Market Strategy Team? Aren't we getting pretty far off base, talking about operating strategy?"

Rick Riggins had been silent this whole time. Now he shook his head and said, "Our cost position directly affects how aggressively we can price, and pricing is certainly a central element of our market strategy. It all connects, Karl." Then he went on.

"I don't see any reason to automatically presume that Logandale will always make what we sell. I think we have a responsibility to consider all options, including cost advantages of offshore production. At least for some products."

Right away, that took some wind out of me. I sat there for a moment seeing every face of everyone I knew at Logandale.

Meanwhile, Linda was saying, ". . . Because you know that Spectrum is thinking globally and always has since it entered the market. We also know that Reliable has outsourced much of its manufacturing to Asia."

"Those are facts, Mike," Nick told me.

"No, come on!" I said. "I can't believe I'm hearing this. Are you seriously suggesting we shut down Logandale and buy from *foreigners*? What's going to happen to Grandville? This is our home! I mean, we *live* here. We're Americans! The people at Logandale are our *neighbors*. Every box coming out of that plant is labeled 'Proudly Made in the USA!' In all its history, this company has *never* allowed final assembly of the product to be done anywhere but Logandale."

"Mike, do you even *know* what the difference in costs would be?" Linda asked.

I shrugged my shoulders. "No, I don't."

"You need to look into it, Mike. We need to know that kind of thing."

"Mike, I'm not saying we're going to shut down Logandale. Not at all," said Rick. "But you've got to be aware that if we can't match costs with Reliable and Spectrum, both of which are sourcing from overseas, Logandale won't survive anyway. And we, as a company, won't be around either. We need to compare the costs of making versus the costs of buying. We have to face reality."

I finally nodded and said, "Okay." But it was very difficult for me. Yeah, yeah, I know as a manager I'm supposed to be objective. I know this trend to manufacturing in Mexico and Asia and everywhere else had been going on for a very long time. I just never thought it would ever get to Grandville. Hell, I was there when Logandale was built! It was *my* plant! I felt embarrassed to be so "soft" about this, and I kept quiet. I hated it, though. I truly hated it.

Nick Corrigan
Director–Retail Sales

At the mention of the possibility of offshore manufacturing, I knew my opportunity was at hand. If they could consider that heresy, then it was time for me to push for another. So I did a quick gut check and leaped.

"There's something we need to add to the list of considerations for the future product mix. About six weeks ago, BigBox came to me and suggested that we be the producer for a BigBox store brand of AZ. Now, I happen to think this is an incredibly important opportunity—"

"Wait a minute," said Rick. "Didn't we nix that? I thought I told Vince Springer we weren't interested."

"Well . . . I didn't exactly hear that from Vince," I said. Which was the truth. One of the peculiarities of working with Vince Springer is that unless he specifically comes to you and says "yes," you are to assume the answer is "no." I had never actually heard "no" from Vince on the Big-Box store brand. In fact, I had not heard anything from him since raising the issue in that staff meeting. You have to understand the "Springer style" to know that this in itself was an emphatic reply that the default answer of "no" was loudly in effect.

However, as I said to Rick and the others, "I've been stalling BigBox because I feel strongly this is something we should consider thoroughly."

"I have to tell you," said Rick, "that I fail to see how in the world we can possibly benefit from building a BigBox store brand. More to the point, I fail to see how we can't avoid being screwed by it in the long run."

At this, I could see out of the corner of my eye Frank Harlan building up, ready to pile on.

But George cleared his throat and said, "Rick, we've agreed in many discussions that you and the Senior Team may consider *many* ideas, but that doesn't mean you have to follow through on any particular one and make it happen. All we're talking about is putting some numbers to the concept, laying out the pros and cons, and evaluating the possibilities."

"Exactly," I said, "and I think it makes sense for us to do that—before Spectrum or Reliable jump in and take this for themselves."

Rick was straining to hold himself back. Finally, he said, "Okay, we agreed my role and Frank's would be to advise but to otherwise stand clear and let you people do your work, so . . ."

Meanwhile, even as we were talking, Linda Wong had quietly, nonchalantly added BigBox AZ Brand to the list, along with SOS, Firefly, and everything else. When we looked at the board, there it was.

That was the first moment when I really knew we were changing as a company, when a controversial idea could be added to the agenda and allowed the chance to survive an open discussion based on the facts—and not be dismissed on reflex because it conflicted with some belief held by Rick or another senior manager. We were on our way.

15

Sterling Grove
Director—Engineering and Design

On the afternoon of the second day, in trying to create a better product development process, we were trying to put some scale on what we had to deal with. We had made a list of all current product development projects, both those that were active and those that were stalled or on hold for some reason. It added up to a couple dozen projects of various sizes. Which was a lot, given that Essential is not a gigantic company. In a separate list, we included projects that were contemplated or definitely would be needed at some point in the future. We had also categorized all these projects by the major technology they involved—AZ, SOS, Firefly, and Z3. Finally, we were trying to estimate time requirements and completion dates and so on.

We were using a flip chart on an easel to do this cataloging, and each time we filled up a sheet, we tore it off and tacked it to the wall using masking tape. The walls were covered with these sheets, and all of us were scanning these, trying to keep everything straight, as we analyzed the merits of this one or the value of that one—pondering how we were going to organize a system to deal with all of them.

I was thinking about all this, and only half listening, when I heard Vivian Lebeque say, "You know something? If you look at our history, we've tended to have two kinds of development."

"Successful and unsuccessful?" someone asked.

"I was thinking more like 'major' and 'insignificant.' We've typically had the push for the next big revolutionary breakthrough—like SOS. That's the major development that gets most of the attention and resources, and along with it is some kind of emotional mandate that it has to be great.

"In the background, though, is the second type of development, which is a hodgepodge of various projects, most of which are based on one wish list or another. That's most of what's posted on the walls right now. These generally have to do with minor improvements or adding features to existing products, and we nudge these projects along quarter by quarter until one of them is finished, at which point it dribbles out into the marketplace to meet its fate. Usually the impact is nothing significant, but we've spent years making it happen."

I thought about it. "She's basically right. That's been our pattern."

Tony Natuzzi, who works for me (he's the engineering manager in charge of product design) seemed annoyed. "Well, are you suggesting that we *not* pursue the next big advance? Should we *not* add new features to products?"

"I'm suggesting a more focused outlook," she said. "What if we simply said to ourselves, 'Look, twenty to thirty months from now, we're going to have a major new offering on the market. It doesn't have to be revolutionary. It doesn't necessarily have to be great. It just has to meet specific criteria—business criteria.'"

"Like?"

"Like it has to have realistic potential to add at least ten million dollars to total sales within two years after introduction. Like it has to be a product or service in a growth segment of the market. And so on. But the main thing is we set up a continuous cycle so that we always have a major new offering every twenty-four months."

"Every twenty-four months? You mean like clockwork?"

"Well . . . Yes, like clockwork," she said.

Everybody in the room looked at each other.

"Excuse me, but I think you're out of your mind," Tony Natuzzi told her. "You can't put development on a rigid timetable!"

"Right, so maybe it's a time frame rather than a fixed deadline," said Vivian. "We launch a major new product every eighteen to thirty months. And we come out with a major product upgrade with new features and so on every twelve to twenty-four months. Something like that."

"Why does it have to be a product?" asked Sandra Moss, another marketing manager. "Why do we have to be locked into this mind-set about products? Why can't we think about services?"

"Because that's not primarily who we are," argued Tony. "We're a company that makes things."

"No, I don't agree with that. The only thing this company has to make is money," said Vivian. "A service, a product—whatever. The idea is that every two years, more or less, we come out with something new that has significant growth potential and that we can do it well and profitably."

Rahzi Kotsami, our research and development manager, got into it now, asking, "How do you know, Vivian, that there is going to be a new technology available every two years? We can't predict or schedule those kinds of things."

"I didn't say it had to be based on a new technology. Maybe it's based on old technology," she answered. "The goal is simply a major new offering on some kind of disciplined, regular basis."

Felice Torrance, our national accounts manager, weighed in. "I think Vivian's idea has a lot of merit. It would put everything we do into framework. Once we got into the cycle, it's conceivable we could become very good at executing that way."

"Think of what it would do for the growth of the company," said Vivian.

"I also think it has merit," I said. "My question is, what do we do with all these things we've already got going. We've got to deal with everything we've got listed up there on those sheets on the wall before we can even think about some kind of major new product."

"But look at what's up there," Vivian said. "There are four projects dealing with AZ. Why are we still working on anything that has to do with AZ?"

"Basically because those projects were started a long time ago and nobody has told us to stop," I said.

"Or," said Tony, "every time we did try to stop them, somebody would complain and say, 'You can't let these die on the vine.'"

"Let's not forget," Vince Springer chimed in, "that AZ is still going to be around for a long time to come."

"Does that mean we have to keep dumping development resources into AZ?" I asked.

"Well, you talk about nixing AZ development, but at least AZ still makes money. As long as we're putting everything on the table here, what about Firefly?" asked Tony. Of course, he said that knowing it was in Vivian's camp.

"You want to know something?" asked Vivian. "I don't know why we're developing Firefly. If SOS has been determined to be the next big thing, then why are we fiddling around with Firefly? Personally, I don't enjoy having my time and energy wasted on something nobody supports."

There was a moment then. Everyone considered the impact of what she'd just said, that she was in effect offering to throw away something in which she had put a lot of her own time and energy. I felt a little embarrassed.

"If you want to know the truth," I said, "I've always thought that the technology underlying Firefly had a lot of promise."

Vivian closed her eyes just for a second and mumbled something that sounded like, "I never thought I'd hear that from you."

"The problem," I said, "is that . . . well, the powers that be have chosen SOS, and if you look at these lists we've made, SOS is associated with probably half of what's up there."

"Fine," said Vivian. "All I've ever wanted were straight answers. Professionally, I don't think that SOS is going to be the salvation of the world, but if SOS was the decision—"

"Let me say one more thing," I interrupted. "I never liked the way that SOS became the development priority. And even now, I wouldn't automatically say it's the right way to go."

Vince Springer sat up straight when I said that. "Hey, Sterling," he said, "I know I'm supposed to keep a low profile in all this, but I've got to ask you one thing. What do you really think of SOS?"

"As an engineer, I think it's a technical masterpiece," I told him. "Most of the company will never have a true appreciation for the hoops that Engineering had to jump through in order to make SOS work. Purely from a technical standpoint, it's far and away better than anything that's out there—or will be out there for a long time to come. I'm very proud of my role in developing SOS, and I know Tony is, too. Yet, from a business standpoint . . ."

I looked around. Everybody was facing me. Might as well get it off my chest, I thought.

"From a business standpoint, I doubt that the majority of our customers will be able to make full use of the potential that SOS has to offer. And there are going to be some major teething problems and support issues, especially in the early going."

"Funny thing!" said Vince in a loud, almost too loud, voice. "That's exactly what I've been hearing from most of the customers I've talked to!"

"Yes, but Vince," said Sandra, "in all fairness to Engineering, we in Marketing did a research study that indicated there was a very strong interest in the kinds of capabilities that SOS now offers."

"Yes, I remember that study," said Vince, "and first of all, it was four or five years ago, before anyone had thought of Z3. And it was a study of high-end users, the minority who will be able to use what SOS offers—"

"They were considered the gateswingers, the ones first through the gate, who forge the trail that others will later follow," said Sandra.

"Yeah, let me tell you one other thing, and then I'll shut up," said Vince. "From bitter experience, I've learned that customers will tend to tell you, 'Oh, yeah, I want this and that, and this and that, and this and that' . . . And then when you actually make it all and try to sell it to them, they only buy this thing that costs a buck-thirty. There's more than one company that's gone broke giving customers what they've asked for, but won't pay for."

After that, I think we were all a little depressed. Vince indeed did shut up. The rest of us were left looking at each other, as if to ask, where does that leave us?

"Um, excuse me," said Tony. "May I remind everybody that we are not here to pick and choose or otherwise make decisions about SOS or Firefly or AZ or services or anything else. That's not in our charter. We're here to create the organizational process that will promote efficient development of products that will support the goals of the business."

"You're right," I said, "and we have strayed a bit. But, don't you see? It's all related. It's all connected."

"Exactly," said Vivian. "It's all connected. That's why we're here. That's why at some point we need to do more than sit in a room by ourselves dreaming up our little process. We really need to talk to Market Strategy."

Vivian Lebeque
Product Manager

The opportunity came sooner than I thought it would. We were finished for the night. It was fairly late in the evening. Sterling Grove and I were walking up the hall together, congratulating ourselves on how much we'd got done. The doors to the Terrace Room, where the Market Strategy Team was meeting, were open, and as we passed, a fresh breeze was coming through. Both Sterling and I stopped and looked in.

Most of the Market Strategy people were still in the room. Rick Riggins had his chair tipped back and his feet on the table, his hands clasped behind his head. Linda Wong had taken her shoes off and was walking around in her bare feet. Nick Corrigan had turned a chair around to the table and was sitting with his elbows atop the back of the chair. Bottles of beer and cans of soda delivered by room service were scattered about the table and the room. And they had opened the doors to the terrace, hence the nice breeze drifting in from the lake outside.

The lights were slightly dimmed, so everyone could read the two spreadsheets that were projected side by side on the wall. George Tracy was off to one side, quietly typing numbers on one of the laptops. Reading the numbers to him from a printed report was Xavier Estaban, the head of international sales.

Sterling and I stood in the doorway a moment and were ready to turn away when Rick noticed us and waved.

"Come on in," he invited.

So we did.

"We're just kicking around some what-if possibilities," Rick said. "Grab something to drink and have a seat if you'd like."

"Where's Frank?" asked Sterling.

Rick and everybody else looked around. No Frank.

"I think he went to bed," said Nick.

"How did everything go today?" George asked us.

"We made a lot of progress," Sterling told him.

"You want to give us the highlights now or wait until tomorrow morning?" Rick asked.

"We can tell you now," I said.

So Sterling and I gave them the rundown, explaining how we would structure the development process so that it produced a major new offering on a regular cycle.

When we were all done, Rick Riggins, who had been nodding thoughtfully throughout, said, "Maybe we can refine that a bit. Suppose you applied that to SOS. I mean, collect all the potential features, options, upgrades, and so on that are possible for SOS and then prioritize and process them the way you've described."

"Well, we were thinking on much broader terms than just SOS," I said.

And Sterling added, "Yeah, forget about SOS."

Then he caught himself.

"Oops. Did that come out of my mouth?" he asked, trying to turn it into a joke. "Where's the bar of soap?"

Rick didn't laugh. "We put fifty million into SOS. We're not going to forget about SOS."

"No, of course not!" I said, trying to come to the rescue. "Nobody's forgetting about SOS. It's just that we felt the better way would be to look at the business in a more open-ended way. The market doesn't care that we spent fifty million on SOS."

"But I care," Rick said. "And I care because Borcon cares."

"Excuse me," said George, "but you know, Rick, that fifty million is spent. It's gone. It went to money heaven. The question before everybody now is whether SOS, regardless of what's been invested in it so far, is going to make money for Essential."

"Yes," I said, "and if it isn't, let's find the opportunities that will deliver the performance to meet the goals you've set."

I thought that was as diplomatic a way as I could put it. Rick, however, frowned. We talked another five minutes or so, but Rick became increasingly sullen.

The spell was broken. When we'd come, Sterling and I, they'd been playing with their what-ifs and having about as good a time as you can have in business, yet the doubts over SOS still put a damper on everything. Frank Harlan wasn't even in the room . . . yet he was in the room.

Rick Riggins
President

I'll tell you, I was doing my best to let this be an open forum—to set the parameters, to guide, and also to stay out of the way. But I knew what I'd promised Borcon about SOS. In increments, they'd signed off on the fifty million, but each time I went back to ask for more, they made their point all the more strongly that the return had better be worth it.

When I got to my room at the Dellwood, I sat on the bed wondering about all this. On the one hand, I was never more convinced that George Tracy was right. Good things were starting to happen. On the other . . . if those good things didn't bring about a successful launch of SOS, it was going to be ugly.

Finally, I silently said to myself, *Rick, you've decided to ride this horse. You at least have got to stay on and ride it a little farther to see where it takes you.* And then I turned out the light and went to sleep.

On the morning of the third day, each advocate team gave its next presentation. Each team described what it was attempting to do, what its goals would do for the business; a range of high, medium, and low expectations of what might be gained as a result; and how its gains supported the overall goals I had set at the beginning of the workshop. Not bad.

Now, in the background, George Tracy and his people had worked with the teams in creating their presentations. Nevertheless, if you considered the magnitude of the issues the teams were dealing with, the scope of the changes being contemplated, the acceptance of the responsibility for making the change happen, it was nothing short of impressive what our people were coming up with. This was no house of cards we were building.

As had been the case the day before, the best-prepared team went first, and first to present on the third day was the Sales Effectiveness Team. What Ozzie Brown and his managers presented was a very compelling case for how they could double the selling ability of the field sales force in a matter of a few years *and* actually lower our SG&A expense. I sat back and listened—and was just blown away.

Ozzie Brown
Regional Manager–Field Sales

Excerpt from presentation remarks

How can I stand here with a straight face and tell you we can do these things? Well, if you want to increase sales without adding expense and your sales force is your primary instrument for gaining sales, then, quite logically, you have to make the sales force more productive. But you only have a finite number of hours for the sales force to work. Therefore, you have to make the salesperson's hours more productive.

Before the workshop, Kevin Lee in HR reminded all of us that a couple of years back we had done a time analysis of our sales force—that is, how they really spent their time during typical days. Well, we went to Vince Springer and dug that out of the files and gave it a close look.

Turns out that most of our salespeople spend only twenty percent of their time actually selling, and we're talking about good salespeople here, not the goof-offs who wash out after a few months or a few years. Twenty percent—which actually wasn't the shocker to me that it might be to others. I'd read some things over the years indicating that twenty percent of a typical salesperson's day actually selling to a customer was a fairly normal expectation for our industry and the type of sales force we had.

What is the rest of their time—the other eighty percent—spent doing? A lot of it is spent helping customers. But rather than selling, the salespeople are problem solving. They are handling logistic issues; they are listening to customer complaints and dealing with others inside the company to resolve logistical issues; they are following up and calling here and there for answers and so on—all legitimate stuff, in one sense. But by spending all this time solving problems, they are not out there making new contacts, building new relationships, bringing in new orders. They aren't actually selling.

There are other disturbing things as well. For instance, the normal salesperson in our company spends an inordinate amount of time reading and dealing with e-mail. And then, of course, there is travel time. And there are reports and paperwork—administrative matters that go far beyond what is required to close a sale. And so on.

It's not like they are out playing golf every afternoon. Most of the unproductive work is either stuff that they inflict on themselves or administrative burdens that management dumps on them, but it is not work that results in increased sales.

So if the Sales Effectiveness Team could reduce or eliminate tasks from the non-sales-increasing category, this logically would enable more time for new contracts, new customers, and new sales. That's assuming, of course, that we also install the proper incentives and system to enforce the raised expectations. But we honestly believe—and we have set this up as a major goal—that we can double the typical Essential salesperson's selling time in front of customers within twelve to eighteen months. We can do this mainly by improvements in four significant areas: productivity tools to help salespeople save time, better training to make them more effective in the field, reducing the number of fires they have to fight by better customer service performance, and giving Sales reasons to trust that the rest of the organization will really respond when there are customer problems.

Rick Riggins
President

I looked around the room as Ozzie presented, and I swear even the engineers were intrigued. All of a sudden, a small, delicate hand shot into the air, and Linda Wong began making some comments, talking about how the sales-effectiveness move was going to fit perfectly with some of the things we'd been talking about in the Market Strategy meetings. The reason was that with our chessboard of the market, we were going to be identifying the hot, higher-growth segments. Now, if we could just make sure the salespeople didn't spend their time chasing old customers or the low-growth segments, but instead focused on the best targets. Well, wouldn't that be something?

More and more people started chiming in, and pretty soon, totally unexpected, it was like a group discussion crossing back and forth across the whole room, across the whole company. In fact, though I hated to, we had to cut it off so that we could get the other presentations going.

Right in the middle of that, as one manager was reacting to another, the ideas were feeding on ideas. It was like we'd reached some critical mass and gone beyond. I forgot my doubts and became very enthusiastic. I thought, "This is without a doubt the best thing we could have started in this company. We are definitely on our way."

TREATMENT

16

George M. Tracy
Consultant

If all we did was conduct a three-day workshop, our "medicine" would be worse than useless. Every workshop or seminar that's any good leaves you with a high at the end. But the high wears off.

If my associates and I said good-bye to Essential after that third day's presentations and we just assumed that all of those great initiatives would continue and everything would be just fine in the future, what are the odds that the workshop would have any long-term impact on the company? Probably close to zero. Within a short time, all of the old habits would return, the familiar powers would regain control, and nothing would have been accomplished. In fact, the company would be worse off because any manager who had believed even just a little that this process of change was for real would become disillusioned. It would be very difficult to get anyone to believe in anything more than the status quo.

There has to be continuing follow-through. So at the end of the workshop, we schedule the first of a series of monthly meetings. These monthly meetings are like a smaller scale version of the workshop. Each of the advocate teams makes a presentation to report progress and discuss issues with each other and the Senior Team. These meetings continue month after month after month. They become a normal part of the business.

The monthly meetings are what we call "pressure points." You need pressure to make real change happen, and the meetings function to impose a discipline. You have to be ready to present, to report progress. There is a great deal of peer pressure coming to bear. Now, attendance is not mandatory for every manager in the company; that would be impractical. But the company president is always there. Senior managers are there, as well as the leaders or coleaders of the core teams, and anybody else who needs to report something of relevance. It's a big deal. And we do everything we can to make sure it's perceived that way.

From the time the managers leave the workshop through the weeks that follow, everyone is—or should be—preparing for the next meeting. Yes, it's real work. It is, however, work that many managers very much want to do because it brings about real improvement and it directly relates to their real jobs. And, over time, the total workload on the manager tends to get easier because the nonsense rituals, the daily b.s., get discarded. You're doing far more of the work that really matters to the business and far less of the stuff that mainly was a waste of your time.

That's not to say everything starts getting better instantly. On the contrary, there is usually a struggle that goes on for some time.

Diane Sullivan
Manufacturing Manager–Logandale Plant

I left the workshop as energized, if not more so, as I'd ever felt while working for Essential. I believe it was a feeling shared by just about everyone who attended. We had a real chance to make this company the best in the industry, maybe one of the best companies ever. And as part of the bargain, I felt, Essential was going to become an interesting, dynamic, terrific place to work.

Bright and early Monday morning, when I got to the plant, I found out both of the EP presses had gone down. One had broken on Friday afternoon, the other on Sunday. So they hadn't been able to finish the AZ-300s they were running. Doug came to my office and explained the situation.

I asked him, "How long before we can get them up and running again?"

"Well, the one that broke Sunday has a cracked bed. It was the backup unit. We might as well replace it. In fact, should have replaced it years ago."

"And the other?"

"That's the 'good' one. John says he can have it back in operation in six to eight hours—after he receives the master cylinder he needs."

"How long 'til we get the part?"

"That's the bad news. The cylinder may have to come from Sweden, and because of the weekend, we haven't been able to place the order yet. Even if we airfreight it, we're probably looking at Wednesday at the earliest before we can get the EP running again. That's assuming the manufacturer in Sweden has one sitting on a shelf somewhere."

"Isn't there somebody in North America who has one in stock?"

"We called around late Friday but couldn't locate one. We should know more later today. But those presses are very specialized and very old. You know, the hell of it is, we only use the EPs to make the 300 series. That's why it's never been economical to replace them."

"Yeah . . . well, that doesn't help us now. What about subbing it out?"

"There's a job shop in Cleveland we've used before. I've got a call in to them now. There's also a machine shop across town that might be able to repair one of the cylinders we already have, at least as a temporary fix."

I considered all this.

"Say, how was that workshop you went to?" Doug asked me.

It took me a second to understand what he was referring to. You know, job shop . . . machine shop . . . workshop. I said, "Oh, the workshop. Yeah, it was good."

"By the way, I hate to tell you this, but there's a rumor going around that Borcon is going to force the company to close the plant."

"What?"

"The word on the floor is that's the reason management was holed up at Dellwood for three days, to make plans to shut down Logandale."

"How could they possibly come to *that* conclusion?" I threw my hands in the air, then said, "Spread the word that there are no plans to shut down the plant."

"I'll try. But you know how they are."

Then the phone rang. I said to Doug, "Let's touch bases later," and picked up.

It was Mike Zarelli.

"If you take a look at the calendar," he said, "it's almost the end of the month, and as usual, I just wanted to check with you to see what our order fill rate was going to look like on the report and, you know, pick a time for us to get together to go over the numbers."

Almost automatically, by reflex, I started to tell him that everything was peachy and we'd make the numbers and all . . . and then I stopped myself and thought about how for three days last week we had talked about change, and honesty, and not covering up problems. So I told him about the EP presses being down.

"Diane, that's not going to reflect very well upon either of us," he said.

"Mike, I'm just telling you the situation."

"How come you didn't have a spare master cylinder on hand?"

"I don't know! In any case, we don't. We're doing our best to get one."

"What's this going to do to our productivity numbers? You know, don't you, that Corporate reads those reports—"

I shut my eyes. He always said that. Every month. Corporate reads those reports. Like Corporate has nothing better to do.

Well, Diane, I told myself, *welcome back to the rat race.*

Jake Foster
Senior Vice President–Operations

I knew very well Mike Zarelli was an old dog and what we were attempting amounted to a new trick. I thought it entirely possible that as we neared the end of the accounting period, he might resort to his old pressure tactics. So I talked to George about him, and we agreed he merited watching. One afternoon I went to his office for a little heart-to-heart.

"How's everything at Logandale?"

The first thing out of Mike's mouth was that Diane had assured him she would make the promised numbers.

"Oh, really? Well, that's nice, but it's not what I meant," I told him. "I want to know what kind of progress is being made on fixing the supply chain issues. How's the supply chain advocate team coming along?"

That he didn't know.

I said, "Look, we're serious about this. If Logandale reports bad numbers this month, I actually don't care. I want *honest* numbers to be reported. No fudge factors, no midnight magic tricks."

Mike tried to be poker-faced, but I knew he was unconvinced. He said, "Well, that's what *you* say. But what about the guy in the corner office upstairs? What is Rick going to tell Dallas?"

"You let me worry about Rick—and let Rick worry about Corporate. Rick has told me he will take the heat from Dallas. The important thing is that we make progress on the real issues. I want you to give all the support you can to the Supply Chain Team—and all the others, wherever their needs overlap your authority."

Mike stayed poker-faced. "Well . . . okay, if that's the way we're really going to do it. I'm all for it."

Just to be sure, I talked directly with Diane a number of times—not just about Mike, but about the team and the issues and a lot of things. At the end of the month, it did seem that Mike lightened up from his usual tactics.

Only a week and a half past the Dellwood workshop came the evening of the thirty-first of the month. I made a point of stopping by Logandale. It was a quiet night. Second shift was working without frenzy. I even overheard one guy grousing to another about how they'd been working less overtime the past few weeks. *Good,* I thought. Even that was progress.

But the gain would not be painless. In the coming days, the Logandale plant would report the worst numbers of any month in the past ten years. And it would get worse before it got better.

Nick Corrigan
Director–Retail Sales

I had wanted to believe that Vince Springer was truly on board, truly committed to making this new culture a reality. He was clearly pleased by what the Sales Effectiveness Team was doing, and he said so on several occasions. It was a mixed bag, though. He gave hints that he was less than happy with what he was hearing on the market strategy side of things. Judging from his past, it was hard to tell if he was really on board or whether he'd stonewall as time went on. You know, he'd seemed to be on board with SOS and he wasn't.

My sense was that he was waiting. Actually, most of us were—myself included. I wanted this to be permanent, but who could tell? Maybe this would just be another of Rick's kicks. Maybe it just wasn't practical for us. Maybe a company as screwed-up as ours demanded a screaming autocrat. I didn't believe that—no way did I believe it—but it was a possibility. They were all possibilities.

One day I met with Vince privately to talk about BigBox. I brought up the BigBox store brand of AZ, and Vince made a face.

"What's wrong?" I asked him.

"If honesty is the management style *du jour* around here, then in all honesty I don't know that you should keep that a priority," Vince said.

"But what we talked about at Dellwood—"

"If I were you, I would refocus on the established AZ models. Isn't there some way you can get BigBox to take more of those?"

What a crock, I thought after the meeting. *Back to the same-old, same-old.*

17

George M. Tracy
Consultant

Senior managers are always either the solution or the problem. They're physicians or unwilling patients. They are either helping to cure the disease, or they are doing things that prolong the infection.

What is difficult for some to figure out is that it is impossible to win as an individual. You can't just build a great sales force, for example, and expect to be successful. Your personal success cannot be fully realized unless the organization as a whole is successful. The senior manager's job isn't to manage a single function; every senior manager's job is teamwork—working with other managers on the senior team and other functions to ensure the success of all.

To more than a few, that realization doesn't come easily or quickly. Occasionally, it doesn't come at all.

Sterling Grove
Director–Engineering and Design

Frank Harlan seemed to go into hibernation after the workshop. He was there, but he wasn't there. Which was unusual for him. He's a very controlling kind of person. Some might say he was a control freak. Because of that, everybody had for years gauged and planned according to what they thought Frank would approve. Now Frank was mysteriously quiet.

You couldn't tell what he wanted. And he seemed to hide in his office a lot, clicking and fiddling at his workstation with his back to the door or with the door shut. He was absent at meetings he would normally attend. It was odd.

Still, everybody knew the priority was SOS. We still had a lot of detail work to do prior to the SOS launch, and we had already assigned some of our more talented people to dreaming up new features and laying the preliminary groundwork for SOS-2. Even without Frank wandering around telling people what to do, we were busy.

In the midst of this, I began working with Nick Corrigan and Patrick Tyler on the BigBox brand of AZ. I mentioned it to Frank, and he kind of rolled his eyes and muttered something like, "Fine, but you know what the real priorities are." For Frank, even that was a generous allowance of discretion. So I decided to run with it.

So as not to take any resources away from Frank's priorities (SOS), I personally got involved. To my surprise, the experience turned out to be exhilarating. Even more so than the workshop.

The project was code-named Grasshopper. High on the priority list was taking out component and material costs without significantly reducing functionality. To make it cheaper without necessarily making it crappier. I knew from the start this was not going to be easy. I mean, yes, we could certainly get the costs down, but to do so without turning the product into a piece of junk was going to be difficult. Besides, through the years we had already gone over the design, which was fairly bulletproof at this point, and taken out as much of the cost as we sensibly could.

However, we in Engineering had never gone through the process while working in any kind of close association with Marketing. In the past, Marketing had come to Engineering and said, "We need to hit a certain price point, see what you can do." So we would take it, and some months later we would hand it all back to Marketing and say, "Okay, there you go. It's now a buck cheaper."

This time, with Grasshopper, we began working with Marketing—and with Manufacturing—on a much closer basis. This was partly as a result of the workshop and an outgrowth of what George was encouraging, but it was also for expediency. Nick had been saying that BigBox was getting impatient and we had to get something to them quick if we wanted to capitalize on the opportunity.

Well, in one of the first meetings about Grasshopper, Patrick Tyler from Marketing produced a study that had been done a few years before by an industry association. I had never seen it before—and I'm not sure anyone else at the table had either—but it was based on surveys that rated the usefulness and value of different features of Z-standard products from various end-users' points of view.

"Huh," I said, looking over my copy, "where'd this come from?"

"Oh, it's been in our files in Marketing for a long time," said Pat. "George Tracy noticed it and thought it might be useful. But I don't know. It's kind of old."

The study was over fifty pages long and densely written, probably one reason why it got stuffed into a file drawer. At first glance, it didn't seem all that significant, but later, as I read through it (which took a while), I discovered that it showed exactly how different groups of users valued specific features of Z. This kind of thing was tremendously valuable because features and options add cost, and if you want to take cost out, one way to do it is to home in on the features that users really want and scale down or eliminate those they don't care about.

There were only two problems with it. One was that, as I said, a number of years had passed since it was published. That didn't invalidate the study. Most of its findings were probably still accurate. On the other hand, I wasn't sure whether we should base a new product—even a low-end one—for a major customer on data that wasn't current.

The other problem, which went hand-in-hand with the first, was that the study did not specifically address the retail segment. That's because when the data were collected, retail was much smaller—this was before BigBox and the other big chains came in—and was not seen as being as significant as it is now. The lack of a retail segment breakout was a serious fault.

I talked to Pat Tyler the next day after I'd gone over the study and told him what my concerns were.

"Well," he said, "this association has come out with other studies since then, but nothing quite like the one I gave you. Still, I guess I could give them a call."

"Yes, by all means," I said. "Call them!"

George M. Tracy
Consultant

We do something we call "sweep the floor." We encourage people to open up all the file drawers and computer directories and so on and take an inventory of everything that could be a useful resource. You'd be amazed at the gems that are often hiding here and there at various places in the managerial organization—not so much because anyone deliberately hid them, but because functions are not in the habit of sharing resources or even of talking to one another.

That's what happened with the end-user study Pat Tyler produced. Someone joked that because it was so valuable, it had been locked up for safekeeping. Only one or two people knew of its existence . . . until we swept the floor.

As soon as I saw it, I knew it might be one of those gems we often find. One of the reasons I thought so was because of the end-user perspective. In the past, you might say that Essential's products had been "designed by engineers for engineers." Nothing against engineers, but they're not the ones who actually use Essential's products. And not to rant against Frank Harlan, but clearly the end-user was not at the top of his professional agenda.

Sterling Grove
Director–Engineering and Design

Pat Tyler had an assistant track down the author of the end-user study, and by the end of the day, Pat was on the phone with a woman in Virginia, just inside the DC Beltway, who was the association's head of research. But apparently, they sort of got off to a bad start with each other. No, for various reasons, there had not been a follow-up study to the one we had. Yes, there were other reports and surveys that were more recent and lots of them. Which ones did he want? No, they didn't have anything specific to the retail segment, but they did have data on retail that they had been tracking. No, they couldn't break it out. No, heaven forbid, we could not access their database. We would have to pick and choose from the available reports and then perhaps we could piece things together to draw our own conclusions. Finally she agreed to fax to us the latest list of abstracts showing what was available.

But the list was as disappointing as the conversation had been. There were some freebie reports, most of which we already had, and everything else on the list was pricey and even downright expensive, never mind that none of the reports (which ranged from a few hundred to a few thousand dollars) squarely addressed what we needed, based on the short paragraph that accompanied each title on the list. It was frustrating because I had a sense that the information we needed was probably somewhere in their database, but not in the form we needed it.

"Let's call her again," I said to Patrick, "and this time I'll get on the phone with you."

I don't know why I thought I could do any better than he had done alone, but I wasn't going to give up without another try. We called and got through to the research head—Mary-Ruth was her name—but her attitude had not improved. For some reason, she was acting as if we were trying to find fault with her research. She actually got a bit short with us, as if to say, "I faxed you the list of what's available. If you want to pay for any of the studies, fine. If not, I've got other things to do."

So I got kind of cranky in return. In so many words, I told her, "Look, our company pays your association huge dues every year, and if we don't get some cooperation here, I'm going to talk to our company president about whether we should renew our membership." It was a bluff, but it somewhat got her attention. Finally, Mary-Ruth allowed that while she could not permit us to access their database by Internet, if we came to the association's headquarters, she would set us up at a data terminal and we could explore it to our hearts' content.

"Fine," I said. "We'll be there."

Yes, *we*. And yes, I know, it was probably overkill for both Pat and I to go. But we didn't have an excess of time to get this right, and to be honest I didn't totally trust Pat to bring back exactly what was needed. At the same time, he knew the marketing lingo far better than I did, so it was important for him to be there.

We cleared our schedules, flew into Dulles a day or two later, rented a car, and drove to the association headquarters. Mary-Ruth was not quite the pill she had seemed to be over the phone, but I was just as happy we didn't spend a lot of time with her. She took us down to the basement of the building and introduced us to Melwin, who was in charge of the database from a technical standpoint.

Melwin at first wasn't sure what to make of us. I don't think he got very many visitors down there in the basement, especially from outside the association. He was polite and helpful, though reserved. But once Melwin determined that I knew something about databases, that was it. We were in. Then, to seal our relationship, I at one point complimented Melwin on a couple of things—all right, it was shameless buttering up— and after that the guy couldn't do enough for us. What a find he turned out to be. He knew that database forwards, backwards, and sideways— which data were dependable, which were suspect, how to combine different sets. And I had guessed right. There was far more in there than Mary-Ruth had let on.

We didn't see Mary-Ruth again. By two in the afternoon or there-abouts, we had what we needed. Melwin put it all on a disc and handed it to us. Then I asked him about the billing because I assumed there would be a charge for this.

"Don't worry about it," he said. "Your company is a member of the association, right?"

"Sure."

He shrugged his shoulders and smiled. "Then you're covered."

We had taken him to lunch, so for the price of a grilled-chicken salad and an iced tea, plus our own travel expense and time, we got exactly the data that could allow us to design a hit product. It was a day well spent.

Pat and I worked with the disk a little on the plane ride back to Grandville using my laptop, and I took the disk home with me and worked with it after dinner. At the office the next day, Pat and I met first thing, and within an hour or so, we had the product specs for Grasshop-per pretty well nailed down. I mean, it was really coming together quickly, now that we had good information. A lot of times, this sort of thing would have taken weeks or months or even longer, but here we were, zeroed in and just about ready to show this to everybody else. And we knew we were on solid footing with the direction we had taken. Pro-vided that people read the research, there was little room for argument with the decisions we'd made. I still wanted to put some cost engineers on it to see how far we could get the unit costs down, but there was no doubt in either my mind or Pat's that Grasshopper was going to be highly competitive once it reached the marketplace.

As we were winding down, Pat even suggested, "You know, we might just be able to have actual product on the shelves at BigBox by middle to end of next quarter."

"That would be great," I told him. "Of course, I want to hear that from the production people before we get carried away. But I really think we have a winner here."

"I was thinking," he said, "what if we gave our own AZ offerings the same treatment? We've been assuming for years that there's nothing more we can do with AZ, but that may not be the case. What if we came out with a kind of Super AZ that's low cost but focused on the core functionality that the biggest groups of users want? We might be able to get another three or four years of huge sales out of AZ for very little investment."

I thought this over. "It's definitely worth considering. Let's talk about it with everybody else."

George M. Tracy
Consultant

As a team works on its issues, it often occurs that there are opportunities for what we call "low-hanging fruit." These are near-term gains—not the big, strategic, long-term gains that are a year or two or three down the road, but they are significant nevertheless. It's the kind of thing where people will look around and say, "This is a real opportunity. Why aren't we doing this now?" And so, the team—the Core Team, with overall responsibility for the total mission—will assign two or three people to what we call a "fast-break team"—as in, "Hey, we've got the ball in an open court; let's get a quick score." And those managers will make it happen.

That's what Sterling Grove and Pat Tyler became engaged in, a fast break. If they could develop Grasshopper quick enough for BigBox to buy it, it would be a significant near-term gain.

Typically, these fast breaks will get a lot of notice. And as the gains come in and begin to add up, that's often a turning point in the acceptance of the change we're trying to bring about.

Diane Sullivan
Manufacturing Manager–Logandale Plant

The big "ah-ha!" for everybody with respect to supply chain was that the marketing forecast was generally right, but at the same time very wrong. In total dollar amounts, it was, so to speak, on the money much of the time. Yet in terms of predicting the actual orders of specific models, it was usually wildly inaccurate.

What had made the forecast totally unwieldy was the proliferation in recent years of different configurations of AZ that Marketing had concocted so as to give the sales force something "new" to talk about in front of various customers. At Logandale, we would just finish a run of 10 thousand AZ-150/B4A2s in the color red, exactly what the forecast had called for, when the computer screens would fill up with actual customer orders for AZ-150/D5P18s in the color orange. Those letters and numbers after the slash meant a completely different configuration with different parts, even though it was a model AZ-150. And if we didn't have the parts for the unexpected rush of D5P18s in orange or couldn't get them quick enough . . . ? Well, then all kinds of things happened in the dead of night.

After the workshop, I actually brought the Supply Chain Team to Logandale for a meeting, so they could see what we were having to deal with. When a SKU is just an item in a catalog or a drawing on a CADD screen, it's relatively easy to deal with. But when you see bins of parts, some brimming over and some empty, and an assembly line change-over to make a new model and stacks of work-in-process, you get a better sense of what the reality is.

Yet aside from a greater appreciation of the challenge forced upon those of us who had to build the product, there were no immediate offers of help. I don't know what exactly I expected, but I thought people would try to come up with solutions. Instead, Adam Bernstein (who genuinely annoyed me several times) and the others retreated to their old position: "Gee, we're sorry this is such a pain, but there's not much we can do about it. You'll just have to grin and bear it as best you can."

To which I said, "No, sorry, there have to be solutions. It's up to all of us to figure them out and put them into action."

Adam really made me mad when at one point he talked about how this would kind of go away on its own in a few years. He said, "Look, if it's mainly a matter of too many SKUs. That should fix itself over time. AZ will eventually be phased out as we introduce SOS, which will have fewer options in the early going. Life should get easier!"

I didn't buy that. Neither did George Tracy. I brought up the issue in a meeting of the Core Team—the team made up of all the Advocate Team leaders. Adam was there, and everything was in the open.

At the next Supply Chain meeting, George was there and he said in no uncertain terms, "In order for you folks to achieve the strategic targets that Rick Riggins has set for this company, Essential has to have a first-rate, world-class supply chain management system. Nothing less will do."

"I'm not saying we couldn't benefit from a better system," Adam argued, "but I just don't see what else we can do! I mean, the SKUs are in the AZ catalog!"

"Well, then reprint the catalog!" I argued back. "Get rid of the low volume SKUs!"

"Diane . . . ! Our customers have come to expect a wide variety of choices! It's not as simple as just reprinting a catalog!"

"Hold on a minute," said George. "Just because the SKUs are in the catalog, does that mean you have to have finished goods sitting in a warehouse?"

Adam and I looked at each other.

"After all, what is the purpose of having finished goods in stock?" asked George.

"We keep finished goods in stock so that we can ship quickly," I answered.

"Exactly," said George. "The issue is not really too many SKUs in the catalog, but how can you produce a specific SKU quickly enough to meet the customer's expectation for delivery?"

I got it immediately. "You're talking about an assemble-to-order system."

"Would that work for us?" asked Adam.

"It would mean less finished goods in stock, but potentially more flexibility and faster turnaround," I said. "Look, I'm not opposed to assemble-to-order, but it opens up all kinds of issues. Just from a manufacturing standpoint, the subassemblies are what take the most time. How can we build each order from scratch when the subassemblies are different for each model?"

"Why couldn't you have a ready supply of subassemblies for each of the AZ models?" suggested George. "Then, when a firm order comes in, you finish it with whatever features, color options, or whatever else the individual customer wants?"

"Wow," said Adam. "That would definitely be cool. Assuming it worked."

"I would love to do that," I said. "But we'd have to modify the order entry system. We'd still have to do some tweaking of the SKUs to eliminate redundancy. And we'd need Engineering to create more commonality between the various feature and option designs."

"Well," said Adam, "isn't that what this team is about? Let's go!"

18

George M. Tracy
Consultant

Think of a funnel. Now, what does a funnel do? It collects a fluid in a reservoir with tapered sides that has a small opening at the bottom. The fluid, as it flows toward the small opening, becomes concentrated so that it exits the funnel as a single, directed stream that is aimed at a specific target.

That's a simple analogy illustrating what happens in this process we call Enterprise Medicine. We collect from company management all kinds of input—facts, data, ideas, strategies, plans, and so forth—as well as the energy of the managers themselves. It all goes into the top of the process funnel. Over time, as all of the input moves down the tapered sides of the funnel, it becomes channeled into a single concentrated stream aimed where the company president intends it to go.

Well, you say, isn't that nice! Isn't that wonderful!

By contrast, let's ask ourselves, what typically happens when an organization—particularly a large one—attempts to change and focus its resources in a new direction? The process often resembles not a funnel but a sieve. At first, all of the input and energy starts to go in the same general direction, but as time goes on, most of it escapes through the holes in the sieve and whatever does come out the bottom is a weak dribble, rather than a forceful stream. Most of us who have worked any length of time in corporate organizations know that this is the case.

The reason the change process is a sieve rather than a funnel in most organizations is that as time goes on, individual managers are allowed to escape from it. Everybody goes in, but one by one, some managers decide, hey, well, this is too hard, I'm going to do it my own way. Or, this doesn't favor my agenda, so I'm not going to contribute to the main stream. Or, for the sake of expediency, I'm just going to go in this other direction. So the process ends with a mess, rather than everything going where it's intended.

For Enterprise Medicine to work, the company president or CEO has to stand firm and support those of us managing the process so that the sides of the funnel retain their integrity and there are no leaks. At the same time, there has to be reasonable pressure.

In a physical funnel, air pressure and gravity combine to push and pull the fluid toward the narrow opening. In our process, the pressure is provided by the monthly meetings. There are a number of distinct levels that are recognizable as we progress through the funnel.

First, there is what we call the "alignment of paradigms"—in other words, making the different models for supply chain, for market strategy, for product development, and so on work together as a conceptual whole. A lot of consultants and senior managers do that and then assume the job is finished, but that's really just the first step—which is not to say it's a piece of cake.

The next level down the funnel is the progress of the individual teams. Each of the teams is working on the issues that it's charged with handling and is reporting the discoveries and accomplishments at the monthly meetings on a formal basis, as well as with various managers on an informal, day-to-day basis.

As time goes on, a couple of things are happening. One is that the garbage is being thrown out. The sacred cows, the bureaucratic rituals, the misconceptions, the superstitions, the myths about the marketplace, the excess baggage that builds up within an organization as years go by— all of this is being identified for what it truly is and is being discarded. So there is less to deal with. Finally, managers are able to deal with what really matters.

The other thing that is happening is that the managers are being pushed closer and closer together in the funnel. The holdouts find they can no longer sit in isolation and pretend to cooperate. They have to work together and contribute. Of course, the better managers want this anyway. So you have more people working diligently to improve the things that are really important to the business.

That stage of activity in the funnel happens during what we call the "team knitting." The threads of the various efforts being made become woven together. The managers create their own network. You're not a manufacturing manager or a sales manager or whatever the function; you're a manager of the total business enterprise with special expertise in manufacturing or sales. Your value is not measured in terms of excellence within your professional specialty; your value is gauged by your ability to contribute as a team player to the success of the total business. That's an important shift in outlook.

The knitting together of the teams typically happens a few months into the process, and it can take as long as six to ten months for full synergy of this to come about. But it gets easier and faster, not harder and slower, as time goes on. Because, as I said, everybody is dealing with the really important things, not all the nonsense everybody used to think was important. Instead of investing time and energy in rigging the numbers and protecting the turf, they're actually working together for real performance.

Near the bottom of the funnel, we get to the strategy selection. Management decides, "We're going to do this; we're not going to do that." And then there is the buy-in of corporate management. Lastly, it's time to make it happen. That's the concentrated stream exiting the funnel. It's going out and implementing and coordinating all the efforts that are part of executing the strategic plan.

Now, though, rather than trying to do it all with a dozen different agendas, as you have before the change in culture, you're doing it with one agenda and a clear focus.

Jake Foster
Senior Vice President–Operations

If I'd had to hazard a guess, I'd say that within a few weeks after Dellwood, as many as half the managers in the company still didn't believe we were serious. They were going through the motions, but still assumed Enterprise Medicine would fade away as most other programs had over the years, yet as the date of the first monthly meeting approached, an awareness began to spread through the offices that this might be for real. Those who had piddled away the month were now caught in a last-minute crash to pull their parts together. You could almost hear a buzz throughout the building, an overtone to everything else going on day to day.

One logistical problem surfaced. We didn't have a conference room big enough to comfortably accommodate everyone who would be in the meeting at the same time. The advocate teams would present sequentially, but in attendance throughout the meeting would be the Senior Team and the Core Team of leaders, plus George and several associates. We needed a space that could accommodate twenty or more people at a time, and none of the conference rooms in the main building at headquarters were big enough. Luckily there was a vacant floor in the building next to Essential's, and we took out a short-term lease on part of that space. This became a sort of process headquarters, and we held all the monthly meetings and many of the team meetings here with the intent of eventually moving them into the main building.

The date arrived. And I have to say candidly that some of the presentations at that first monthly meeting were disappointing. The supply chain people, for instance, were bogged down in this "not much we can do" attitude. Granted, they had some tough issues, and Diane Sullivan had a number of day-to-day distractions (because of the supply chain!). But the attitude was clearly unacceptable. Rick, George, and I gave them some gentle prodding and insisted they keep trying.

The other teams' presentations ranged from underwhelming to encouraging, but the Vendor Management Team was abysmal. In a month, they had talked to one vendor, and to no clear purpose. And it had taken all of them to do it. Wendy Orman tried to make this sound like an accomplishment, like perhaps after a year of talking to other vendors they might have some recommendations. She had also missed one of the Core Team meetings, and she had offered some very lame explanations to the associate of George's group when he questioned Wendy on a few matters.

Rick was diplomatic during the meeting, but afterward in private he flatly told Wendy, "Don't come here next month with this kind of effort."

George promised to pay close attention to her, as she had indeed become a project. Wendy had all but begged for the leadership spot on the team, so we gave it to her. Obviously, it wasn't working out.

A day after the meeting, Bill Albrecht and Heidi Jordan came to me separately and asked to be taken off the Vendor Management Team. Bill thought the whole thing was a complete waste of his time. Heidi was more tactful, but her sentiment was much the same. When I asked them what the problem was, both mentioned Wendy Orman. I told them to stay with it, that we would likely be making appropriate changes very soon.

George Tracy had warned us that weak managers did indeed have reason to fear the process—because it left them no place to hide. Wendy had managed Purchasing for a long time. I thought she was more or less competent in terms of managing the function, but now I was having my doubts. She was well-liked by people in her own department and by many of her peers. Her name had not come up very often, either positively or negatively. However, there was a lot under the surface that we didn't know about.

In any case, the disappointments of Vendor Management and, to a lesser degree, Supply Chain were minor episodes in the scope of that first monthly review meeting. The bombshell was delivered by the Market Strategy Team. Linda Wong, Xavier Estaban, and Nick Corrigan delivered a blockbuster presentation. But the concussion nearly killed Rick Riggins.

Linda Wong
Marketing Director

Rick had to have some idea what was coming. At the workshop—and even prior to that—he acknowledged the skepticism about SOS. The first time the Market Strategy Team got together after Dellwood, we agreed that one of the very top priorities was to get an unbiased, unvarnished assessment of the market prospects for SOS. It was a crash project, but necessary, given the timing of what was going on internally within Essential and externally in the marketplace.

Already in the pipeline was some research to be conducted by an outside firm. That was budgeted as a normal part of the upcoming SOS launch. With a bit of arm-twisting (yes, I know it's funny to think of me twisting arms, but . . . trust me, I can do it), we got that moved up and were able to get some very preliminary results for the monthly review meeting, even though the final report would not be available for a number of weeks.

We did not rely solely on that, however. With the help of George and his people, we put together a short questionnaire, and everybody on the team began calling a combination of customers and end-users in every channel except retail. The results were not exhaustive, they were more on the level of a straw poll, yet striking enough to be ominous. We would not have the final, conclusive data for months, but in the end we didn't need it. We had the most important facts quite early, and they were drop-dead ugly.

I copied and forwarded e-mail to the appropriate people as the evidence came in, including Rick Riggins since he was both company president and senior sponsor for the Market Strategy Team. On the day of the monthly review, I stood in front of senior management and the Core Team and said, "Based on the data collected to date, the chances of a successful, marketwide launch of SOS are not good."

Then I gave them the facts we had collected.

"First of all, on the surface, there is interest among most end-users in at least some of the capabilities that SOS promises. Sixty percent of those questioned expressed mild to strong interest in one or more of the new capabilities.

"However, the more people know about SOS, the less interested they become. For instance, we researched a series of price points. At the price range that we expect SOS to have for it to be profitable, which is thirty percent higher than current AZ products, the level of interest dropped below fifteen percent. Furthermore, when we specified that SOS would not work in combination with many Z-standard applications, the level dropped to below seven percent.

"Even worse, among a group of end-users labeled 'experienced' (meaning they had had direct involvement with Z products for three years or more), the numbers started lower and ended lower. Experienced users expressed only a thirty percent interest in SOS, and this dropped below five percent once price and compatibility issues were brought into the equation."

I happened to look at Frank Harlan when I said the five percent number. I thought it was undeliberate, but maybe, subconsciously, it wasn't. I remembered the cold eye he'd given me a month before at Dellwood. Now, he was rigid with hate that he was trying to conceal.

I was killing his child. In his view. His unborn child, if you want the maximum emotional punch. Five years he'd been carrying it. I did feel for him, I really did. Briefly.

Rick Riggins
President

You can sit there and say, "Those knuckleheads! Didn't they know what they were getting into? Didn't they do their homework?"

Well, we *did* do the homework. We'd done the market research, years before. We'd done the technical studies. The trouble was that so much had changed since then.

Five years before, what we term the "performance" segment of the market was the hot rocket. It was like the stock market of the late 1990s; everybody thought it would just keep going up. SOS, which is a performance product, looked like a sure thing.

When the performance segment peaked about two years ago, we convinced ourselves that, hey, once we get SOS out there, it'll come back again! As we began to build the market chessboard during the workshop, laying out all the channels against the products and plugging in the hard data, putting everything together into one, comprehensive picture—well, the high end was clearly much smaller than what we had projected. It had even declined in actual numbers, and there was no guarantee it would grow again in the foreseeable future.

Now, this research coming in—admittedly on the fly, but it was far better intelligence than we'd had—was confirming my worst business nightmare. Well, perhaps that's overstating it. It was only two or three bad dreams rolled into one.

We'd spent 50 million, mostly of Borcon's money, betting on SOS, and it was turning out to be a very bad wager. Meanwhile, as we were spending the 50 mil, thinking that we would leapfrog everybody, our competitors had been working to catch up and pass us in the Z standard. Reliable had increased the functionality of their Z products by quite a good measure, while keeping the price about the same, and they were leading the way to Z3. Spectrum was nowhere close to us (or Reliable) on the sophisticated, performance end of the market, which was the AZ–300 and 400 series. But Spectrum had taken share in the low end and was poised to grab more, stealing from the AZ cash cow that I had counted on to keep us profitable until SOS rose to "dominance."

Finally, there was Nusult, a company that had scared everyone because it had come out of nowhere in just a few years. Nusult wasn't interested in the low end of the market, but they had a model that would run the socks off an AZ-400. Again, our counterpunch to them was going to be SOS. Or so we thought. There were now strong indications (that really hadn't surfaced until lately) Nusult was working on its own SOS equivalent, as well as a Z3 line.

Until we got people to volunteer what they knew, go find the facts, bring everything together in one place, and talk openly without weighing the comments politically, without fear of repercussions, we'd been missing the true picture. We'd been deluding ourselves.

I did not regret the decision to pursue SOS. Maybe it was never the best thing we could have done, but SOS wasn't a bad call at the time we made it. What I regretted was the way we had cruised along, assuming everything would work out in the end. I regretted the way we had ignored the many caution lights—the cost-overruns, the launch delays, the comments from the field sales force, most of which never reached my ears. Most of all, I regretted the time it had taken to get to this point.

If we had been able to bring SOS to market quickly, we might have pulled it off. SOS might have indeed become the standard, if we could had done it quickly, made it simple, versatile, and inexpensive. Instead, SOS was complex, pricey, inflexible, and slow to arrive. But this was not about SOS. This was about us.

You want to know what was the most wrenching revelation? It was that so many of what we considered to be core values of the company— made in the USA, being on the cutting edge, being state of the art, great engineering design, overbuilding the product for quality, offering the Cadillac of the industry, marketing a huge range of choices to the customer, brand loyalty (i.e., they'll buy it because Essential makes it)—just didn't seem to bloody well matter to the vast majority of customers.

We were on this great technical crusade developing SOS . . . and almost nobody cared. We'd put great time and care into designing the end-caps and the overall display strategy at BigBox . . . and yet most people just looked at the price tag, walked up the aisle, and bought cheapo, made-everywhere-*but*-the-USA knockoffs from Spectrum.

I'll tell you, I wanted to go to BigBox, and the first person I saw reach for something from Spectrum, grab the person by the shoulders and shout, "How can you *do* this to us!" And of course that person would have looked at me and said, "What, you've never heard that the customer is always right?"

George M. Tracy
Consultant

We had slated the market strategy discussion for last on the agenda because we knew it would take the longest. By midafternoon, I glanced at Rick Riggins, and he almost looked ill. Everyone else around the room appeared quite subdued as well.

So I suggested we take a half-hour break to let people catch their breath and check phone messages and e-mail. As Rick was leaving the room, I caught up with him.

"How are you doing?" I asked, out of earshot of everyone else.

"I'm okay," he said. "It's just . . . ugly. Not at all the way I thought things would be."

"Harsh facts are friendly," I told him. "Remember that."

He just looked away.

"We'll get there," I said. "I promise you."

Rick Riggins
President

I hurried toward my office in the main building. A couple of people tried to talk to me. I brushed them off and kept going. I needed ten minutes to myself. Even though I'm often accused of walking at the speed of a jogger, I couldn't out-pace Frank Harlan. He came from behind, nipping at my heels.

"Rick! Rick, we have to talk!"

"What, Frank?"

"You have to stop this! You have to put an end to it now! It's gone too far! They are attempting to waste years of development and millions of dollars!"

"*They?* I thought Engineering spent the lion's share of the money."

"SOS is a great achievement! How can you judge it on the basis of . . . *comments* from people who know nothing about it!"

I stopped and wheeled around. "What do you want me to do, Frank, ignore them? We've ignored far too much from the market for far too long."

"But you cannot create great products or great strategies by committee!"

"True," I said. "And that's not what we're doing. We're having an open communications forum to learn facts and determine options, after which *I* will make the final decisions in concert with you and the rest of senior management."

This calmed him momentarily.

"Oh . . . so, we'll be going ahead with SOS?" he asked.

"I'll tell you when I tell everyone else. Now, go back to the review meeting. I appreciate your thoughts, but if you've got things to say, that's what the review meeting is for."

The truth was, I didn't know what I was going to do about SOS or anything else. When I reached my office, I shut the door and dropped into the chair behind my desk. I just sat there staring out the window.

I would have given anything to have done what we were doing now a few years earlier. But that wish was useless. The only fortunate part of it was that we had not yet built any SOS units beyond prototypes and samples, so we didn't have additional millions sunk into finished goods inventory. Yet, without SOS as a clear winner, the company's future—and mine, everybody's—was clouded.

I had sold Borcon Corporate on the idea that SOS was the key to our future growth. What was I going to tell Corporate now? My credibility was on the line. It was a personal dilemma. I could turn tyrant and coerce everybody into keeping their mouths shut, go ahead with the SOS launch, in spite of everything we had learned, and maybe fake it until I got another job—at the risk of ruining the company. For me, that was unacceptable. I couldn't bring myself to do that. On the other hand, if I scaled back the SOS launch, Corporate could very well come to me and say, "You're only building 5,000 units? You're never going to get the growth you've promised with that kind of volume! Riggins, we want your resignation!"

Then it was like someone else spoke to me, though I was alone in my office:

You can't go backward. Keep the faith. Lean forward and charge.

Vince Springer

Senior Vice President–Marketing and Sales

Rick took a really long while to return—odd because he's a stickler for keeping to schedule—and George finally restarted the meeting so as to keep things moving. Anyway, when Rick came back, Frank Harlan was delivering one of his more inspired diatribes. The great part was that nobody was browbeaten. Half the people in the room spoke up, countering Frank's flimsy arguments about why SOS should be positioned as the mainstay of our business. In the end, Frank just ran out of steam and shut up.

Then Rick took the floor.

"Let's sum up a few of the things we can conclude at this point," he said. "First, it's looking as though the best-case scenario for SOS is to play a role as a high-end and, hopefully, high-margin niche product. It is not going to be the new, world-beating, market-dominating standard we wanted. Frank Harlan's engineers did a fantastic job, but SOS from a business standpoint is not going to guarantee our future.

"At the same time, AZ won't save us either. Not in its current form. So the AZ versus SOS argument is irrelevant. They're both inadequate."

I silently nodded when he said that. What he was saying was right.

"Well, we've got our work cut out for us. Because the challenge remains the same."

Then Rick reiterated the same goals he set forth at Dellwood.

"We've got to put our heads together and figure out how to get there!" Rick said. "Now, in light of everything we've learned, our next order of business is to identify the best opportunities that we can capitalize upon the fastest."

And that's what we spent the rest of the day discussing.

You know, I do believe that was the day I—Mr. Practical—got religion and actually got on board. Oh, I would continue to have certain doubts and concerns for a long time. That afternoon, though, was when I felt Rick Riggins showed true leadership. He faced the facts. He got the rest of us to do the same. And he pushed us hard, using his famous tenacity the right way—to bring forward the best opportunities . . . and also, I think, the best in ourselves.

19

Sterling Grove
Director–Engineering and Design

Frank Harlan was (by various accounts) an egomaniac, a control freak, . . . and a great engineer. He was not a great manager. He was kind of like a movie director who demands total control. I don't mean he was hands-on. He expected staff to do the actual work. But he wanted to direct every movement, every detail. Sometimes that resulted in a masterpiece . . . like SOS. And sometimes that resulted in a business failure . . . like SOS.

After the team review meeting, Frank would barely talk to me. I had been one of the ones who had spoken to the facts (and not in support of him, though I'd tried to be diplomatic). In any case, he would barely talk to me or anybody else. He retreated to his office—for weeks—and sat in there with the door shut. The rumor was that he was in there playing *Doom* on his computer. I'm sure he wasn't, but he also wasn't doing anything to support the mission that Rick Riggins had given us to accomplish.

As for me, I wasn't exactly hurt by the inattention. I had for years been a member of Frank's inner circle, but that was becoming a token of negative status. Things were changing much faster than I ever thought they would.

Among other things, I went on working with Pat Tyler and various people on the Grasshopper model. One fine day, I was seated at a CADD workstation on one side of my office and examining some of the Grasshopper files. I was adding a comment to one of the drawings so that I could turn everything over to the cost engineers, when a shadow darkened the screen and I realized someone was standing at my shoulder. I turned in my chair and right behind me stood Frank.

"What are you doing?" he asked.

"Oh, you mean this? I'm just working on the Grasshopper design."

"The what?"

"The store brand of AZ we're going to produce for BigBox."

He grunted. I started to tell him about what Pat and I had come up with, but from the look in Frank's eyes, I could tell he was not interested and, for certain, he wasn't pleased.

"If you can tear yourself away," he said, "I have a few things to talk to you about."

"Sure, no problem," I said.

I saved my work, and Frank closed the door to my office.

Then he pulled up a chair, looked straight at me, and said, "I've been doing a lot of thinking, and I've come to the conclusion that we can save SOS."

I was dumbstruck. I sputtered and stammered and couldn't say anything for a couple of seconds—and Frank didn't say anything either. He was reading my reaction, and I believe he had been expecting me to stand up and cheer or something. He was, of course, disappointed.

"Well, ah, Frank . . . what do you mean by that?" I asked.

"I think we can again make SOS the cornerstone of the company's future. It'll take some work, but I think we can overturn this silly strategy-by-committee decision to relegate SOS to being a secondary product."

"I'm sorry, I don't quite understand," I said. "The Senior Team and the Core Team have agreed—"

Frank winced. "That's what I'm talking about! All this *team* stuff! It's all just a lot of second-guessing and downright bullshit!" He paused then, sat back in his chair. "Okay, okay, I take that back. Part of it was useful. For one thing, it was good to identify some of the issues that SOS will face in the marketplace. I grant you we didn't have all those issues covered. We do need to work on those. But the conclusions they reached are just plain wrong! I am utterly convinced of that. To throw SOS into the corner and deem it to be merely a high-end niche product is absolutely stupid! After all the time and resources we've put into it? It's crazy! The more I've thought about it, the more obvious it is to me that *they just don't get it.*"

I virtually had to bite my tongue. I wanted to say, *Frank, you are the one who just doesn't get it.* But I couldn't bring myself to say that.

"So," Frank continued, "here's what we're going to do. First of all, put this piece of junk for BigBox on the backburner."

"Wait, Frank. You . . . you don't understand. We've made really great progress—"

"I don't care." With a fling of his hand, he waved it off to some Never-Never-Land for stupid ideas. "It's junk."

I was feeling numb.

"Now . . ." He had brought a thin manila file with him, and he picked this up from the corner of the desk where he had laid it and handed it to me. Inside was just a few sheets of paper. "Here is a list of your new priorities. I want you to pull together the best engineers we've got and go back to work on SOS. I want you personally to take the position of lead engineer, and I want Tony to back you up. For item number two on the list, I think Sanji would be a good choice. We've got to get the cost down; I do grant that the marketing idiots were right about that point. And we've got to fix the compatibility issues with respect to the Z standard."

I had been looking over the list as he spoke, and it almost made me nauseous.

"Frank . . . it can't be done," I said.

"Don't tell me that."

"But we went through this two years ago! We can't fix the compatibility issues, it's just too expensive! We made the decision then that the SOS design would start from a clean sheet of paper."

"Yes, but I am reversing that decision," he said.

I looked at Frank and wondered if he might be cracking up. Or, if he wasn't cracking up, I wondered if perhaps I was about to.

"Whether you revisit that decision or not," I said, "it doesn't change certain facts. We can't meet both of the objectives you just stated. We can't reduce the cost of SOS and increase the backward compatibility. The two are diametrically opposed to each other. It just can't be done."

"Then find a way!" he told me. "Because there has to be one. Okay, yes, maybe it will require a stroke or two of genius, but I think if you and the others go at it night and day, we can do it."

The energy just drained out of me. "Frank, in all honesty, we could spend six months or a year or *six* years on this and get absolutely nowhere."

"For your sake, that had better not be the case," he said flatly. "Because I am not giving up SOS without a fight. We are going to do an end run around their stupid convoy to oblivion and we are going to torpedo them with our hard work and brilliance. We will counter every one of their arguments with a technical triumph."

What could I possibly have said? Nothing was going to change his mind.

"And you can do it," he said. "Because the logic is clear. Once you get the cost out, then the added expense of compatibility becomes more affordable. You just have to do more with less."

Right, I thought, no problem. Piece of cake. Yet, I have to admit my mind was slowing turning to what Frank was charging me to do. Already, I was mentally gathering up some of the ideas that we had discussed and discarded so many months before.

"Now," Frank concluded, "I want this to be your top priority, of course. I want to meet with you tomorrow morning in my office at seven A.M. to discuss who you've got working on SOS and how much progress they've made. And we're going to continue having those meetings at seven o'clock every morning until we've got the solutions. Make any excuses you need to with respect to other projects; I'll back you up totally. For obvious reasons, we'll need to observe total secrecy, so make that clear to everyone who's brought in. I'm counting on you, Sterling. And I do very much appreciate your loyalty. That fact will be reflected in many ways in the future."

"Thank you," I mumbled. "But what happens if, say, we do somehow come up with a stroke of genius? The company is already moving in other directions."

"That's why we have to move fast. Once we have the solutions, we're going to march straight to Rick Riggins' office, and we're going to convince him beyond the shadow of a doubt that SOS is the winner that we know it's going to be."

Rick Riggins
President

Twice a year, Borcon hosts a day-long meeting for all the corporate business unit executives of my level and higher. It's called Leadership Council, or LC, but off the record it's often called Show-and-Tell. Because that's kind of what you do there—you're supposed to present to the corporation at large a detailed summary of how your business unit is performing, whether you're on plan (and of course you damn well better be), and what are the best things that are happening within your business. The last is supposed to be a kind of best-practice sharing of ideas from business unit to business unit, but in reality it usually is just an opportunity to score points with Brandon Claymore.

One of the two meetings is always held someplace nice—Hilton Head, Vail, Big Sur, or similar. But the other meeting of the year is always in Dallas at Borcon headquarters. When it's held in Dallas, at the end of the day, Brandon Claymore has everybody come out to the ranch for barbeque. About a week or so after the monthly team reviews came time for Leadership Council. This one was in Dallas, and 'que was on the menu.

As I say, we call these things Show-and-Tell, but they can turn into Show-and-Tell Hell. Everybody is seated around the outside of a U-shaped table. Brandon Claymore always sits at the bottom-center of the U, with the business unit executives lining both extending legs. You're told to prepare to present for roughly forty-five minutes, but you don't know when you're going to have to present and you don't know for how long. It's casual. Sort of. You present when Brandon calls upon you. You go to the top of the U, put on a wireless microphone, and the floor is yours until Brandon says it isn't. It's a think-on-your-feet kind of experience. Because Brandon will often interrupt you to ask for detail or to make you address a related area of what you're talking about or grill you thoroughly if he doesn't like what he's hearing.

Generally, the longer you can talk without Brandon interrupting you, the better you're doing. Occasionally, he will interrupt to give you praise or constructive input, but that's not often. So if you make it the whole forty-five minutes with only a few intrusions by Brandon, that means you've done a great job and he approves of the way you're running your business. If you get to the end and Brandon applauds—which means, of course, everyone else applauds—that's a real triumph. When Essential won the BigBox account, I not only got applause from Brandon and the other executives, I got a standing ovation.

I had been preparing for LC since right after we held the workshop at Dellwood, and I'd spoken with Nancy Quinn about what I was going to say. Nancy, of course, had introduced George Tracy to me, and I'd been keeping her informed of what we were doing. She was very much an ally at this point. When I told Nancy that I wanted to talk about the teams we'd formed and about Enterprise Medicine, she was all for it. She even suggested I move that up in my presentation so that I talked about it before I got to all the bad news, like Essential's past six-months' performance.

Then came the conclusions about SOS. Of course, I had to tell Nancy. But she was in Europe, helping Brandon negotiate this megadeal. Or that was the general rumor; the particulars were ultra top secret. Anyway, she was out of the country and not terribly available; I guess they were negotiating day and night on this thing. I sent her e-mails about the change in strategy surrounding SOS, and I got back some brief replies but worded such that I thought she was being very supportive—although she added we would have to talk about all this in depth once she got back to Dallas.

Still, I have to say I was kind of nervous about including SOS in the LC presentation. Yet it had to be in there. I couldn't just forget to mention it. So I spent many hours playing wordsmith, rewriting and editing my presentation to try to show the revelations about SOS in the best possible light.

Finally, it occurred to me. Everything we were doing with George Tracy and the teams and even with respect to SOS was ultimately very positive. Why should I soft-pedal it? We were doing the right things, damn it. We were going to save the company and ultimately make it highly profitable. I really believed that. Why should I shrink from what I genuinely believed? So I finished the final draft in that spirit.

Off to Dallas I went.

Half the trick to dealing with Brandon Claymore is not allowing him to intimidate you. My turn to present came midafternoon. The head of the avionics division had gone before me, and he'd been up there for well over an hour being grilled by Brandon and the corporate staff. Midway through, he had abandoned his prepared presentation and winged it. But he had done a good job of defending himself and his actions with respect to his business unit, and while there was no applause when he was finally allowed to sit down, there were a number of approving nods and smiles from his peers. I wasn't expecting any standing ovation, but I thought I'd have no problem doing as well, if not better.

Jake Foster
Senior Vice President–Operations

I noticed the change in Rick as soon as he got back from Dallas. Something had happened. When I saw him in his office the next morning, I went in and asked him, "How'd it go at Leadership Council?"

He kind of shrugged and said, "Not well."

When I pressed him to tell me more, he made it clear he didn't want to go into detail. What he did say was that they were highly pissed off about the change of direction with respect to SOS.

"We may have to make a show of rolling out SOS as planned," he told me.

I said, "A show? What do you mean by that? I thought we were in agreement."

"We may not be able to do everything we've been talking about."

"But, Rick . . . what kind of message is that going to send to the rest of the company?"

"*They* don't care about messages," he said. "Brandon doesn't care about what we tell our managers. Brandon cares about growth. About cutting costs. About a return to profit."

"Well, who doesn't? And if Brandon cares about growth and profits, then he ought to back us on the new directions we're taking."

"He isn't, Jake. He isn't. Believe me, I tried. I really tried."

"Did he specifically say we had to roll out SOS?"

"He said he wants a payoff on the SOS investment. Other than that, he wasn't terribly clear about anything."

I muttered some kind of expletive. Rick picked up a file on his desk and smacked it down again, like he was swatting a bug, and said, "That's the way it is."

Then he turned his back on me for a moment. When he faced me again, I could see the frustration on his face. He began to ramble about getting together with Vince and with Frank. I told him Frank was out of town but that we could probably get together tomorrow.

"Then today," he said, "I want to meet with you and Jane Grimm. We have to get to work right away on cutting costs. I think maybe one of the first things we'll have to cut is George Tracy."

My mouth dropped open. "You can't be serious, Rick. We can't go backward. We can't pretend that Dellwood and the rest of the progress we've been making never happened."

He didn't respond to that. All he said was, "The only good thing is that I think Nancy Quinn is still in our camp."

But I didn't know what he meant by that, and I felt I couldn't press him for any more detail, not at that moment.

Rick Riggins
President

When Brandon called on me at Leadership Council, I took the microphone and said, "Let me open by saying that it's been an exciting couple of months for us at Essential. How exciting? Well, in the next few minutes, I'm going to describe for you a process that we are in the midst of going through that is going to remake the management culture of our organization and will transform our business. You see, not long ago, my management team and I took a long, hard look at our business . . . and, frankly, we didn't like a lot of the things we discovered. There were realities that, to be honest, we had not acknowledged, and that we needed to address. I'm going to go over those with you, and describe for you some of the exciting new directions we're headed in that will put us on a path for growth."

So I began. But about ten minutes into my presentation, as I was explaining the facts that caused us to rethink having SOS be the centerpiece of our growth strategy, I happened to look at Brandon. He was looking right back at me, and his face was a red mask of rage. And he exploded.

"Do you mean to stand there and tell me that after all this time, after all the money we've poured into SOS, you're going to throw up your hands and walk away?"

"Brandon, if you put all the facts together and look at them as a whole, it's clear that we're doing the right thing. I mean, if we keep on going down the path we were on, we could ruin Essential's business."

"Then why the hell did you start down that path in the first place? For years, you've been standing up there and telling us that SOS was absolutely going to be the salvation of the civilization. Or at least that's what you implied!"

"At the time, that's what I believed. But now it's clear—"

"Yes, now you're going off on completely new flights of fancy, is that it? Now you're going to 'change the culture.' Sounds like an even bigger waste of time and money than this SOS boondoggle you sold us on. Tell me, which of those touchy-feely management psychology books did you get this crap from?"

From that point, I would occasionally attempt to stammer some kind of defense, but it did no good. Brandon just ranted on and on, to the extent that my face, my whole body became numb. He began loud and got louder. Every single word from Brandon's mouth went off in my ears like a firecracker.

My last words in front of the group were, "Brandon, if you'll just give me a chance—"

"You've had your chance. Sit down!" he yelled. "I don't want to waste these other people's time on you."

So I sat there for the rest of the day hardly able to concentrate enough to hear what anyone else said. Mostly no one would look at me. It was as if I didn't exist. I had never in my years of coming to these things ever seen him treat anyone as harshly as he'd treated me. I knew it was over. In my mind, I began to word the sentences of my resignation letter.

At the end of the afternoon, everybody stood and got ready to go back to their hotels to change into casual clothes for Brandon's barbeque. But I had already determined I wasn't going. I would stay in my hotel room that night and finish my resignation letter, then see him in the morning and get it over with. What was the point of going out to Brandon's ranch and pretending to have a good time?

As I was trying to slink away unobserved, though, Nancy Quinn grabbed my arm and pulled me into her office. She closed the door and we talked for a couple of hours. Then we went out to the ranch. Everyone had eaten dinner by then, but we put in an appearance and saved some face. Brandon never once looked in my direction.

Nancy Quinn

Executive Vice President–Borcon Corporation

Brandon Claymore is your basic self-made billionaire. He started with a cement company his father had run. Through his own shrewdness, his taking control, his no-nonsense style, his ability to master both details and the larger picture, his ability to close a deal, he built this empire . . . or, I should say, this *family* of businesses that is the Borcon Corporation today.

I've known Brandon more than twenty years, and I've reported directly to him in one capacity or another for nearly ten. The way that he blew up in Rick Riggins' face at Leadership Council is actually rather rare these days. Brandon does have a temper. He's not proud of it, he works to control it. But the temper is there, and all the veterans have experienced it at one point or another. Mainly, he blows up when he's frustrated—and with Borcon's stock price taking the dive that it did . . . well, he was not pleased with the way Borcon was headed. Brandon puts a lot of pressure on himself, and in turn on us.

What happened to Rick at Leadership Council was somewhat his own fault, on several levels—his previous overselling of SOS being one of them. But I admit I shared some of the blame. Rick had contacted me right after he and his managers had that meeting in which they reconsidered their commitment to SOS. Naturally, I was very upset. This was a huge miscalculation and I had signed off on it. Two senior managers, not one, had blown it.

Unfortunately, during that period, I was in the midst of several major undertakings. I told Rick to come up with a solution to the SOS debacle before I brought it to Brandon's attention. I intended to talk to Rick face-to-face, but each time we scheduled a meeting, I had to cancel. Events related to a deal that Brandon and I were trying to put together required me to go to Europe, and by the time I got back Leadership Council was just a few days off. In the meantime, Rick had written a long, detailed explanation of the reasons for rethinking the SOS commitment. I read that and I admit it made sense, but I wanted to know more before I went to explain it to Brandon.

I'll be honest with you. The deal we were trying to put together was so complex and so important that this thing with SOS got put on the backburner. So when Rick presented at Leadership Council that

Essential was going to retreat from SOS, he must have assumed I had briefed Brandon, when in fact Brandon was hearing about it for the very first time. That's why Brandon lost it the way he did.

As soon as Leadership Council ended, I grabbed Rick by the arm and we closeted ourselves in my office. Bear in mind, it did not reflect well on me that one of my top managers had been publicly flogged.

Rick was trying to put on a brave face, but he was devastated. It took me a long time just to get him to turn off the speech that he was going to hand Brandon his resignation. In effect, I said, "Look, Rick, resigning isn't going to help you, isn't going to help me, help the company, or help Brandon Claymore. If Brandon wants you fired, so be it; he'll probably be generous about the terms, knowing him the way I do. And I don't think he will fire you, not yet anyway. When he blows up, it's actually better than if he seethes about it, let me tell you. It's when he seethes quietly that you'd really better look out. So don't resign. If you bug out on your own, it's not going to accomplish anything."

Finally, we got down to the real issues of what was happening inside Essential. We talked about SOS, but I have to say Rick couldn't make his case to my satisfaction, not even as well as he had in his letter. Maybe he was so demoralized by what had happened that afternoon that he was distracted, I don't know.

In any event, time grew short. I knew we had to at least put in an appearance at the barbeque, and it was getting late. At last I told him in so many words, "Rick, it does appear that there is some strategic confusion within your company. If indeed there has been a mistake of this magnitude, let me tell you that you and your company cannot afford to make it twice. Go back to Grandville and review everything. See if there isn't some way to salvage the investment made in SOS. And, above all, you have got to start showing sales and operations improvements as soon as possible."

Then we got in my car and drove to the ranch. Brandon was strutting about in full-Texan: the boots, the ten-gallon hat, the big silver belt buckle, the works. I made sure he saw us, but I also made sure we didn't approach him. Brandon stayed clear and avoided us, and I knew that was ultimately to our advantage.

Brandon hates himself when he loses control. The rough-tough cowboy thing is far more myth than reality. He thinks that image gives him an edge, but it really is just an image. He has his insecurities just like the rest of us. He is far more sensitive than most people would ever expect.

One time I was on the receiving end of his temper—not quite to the degree that Rick got it, but nearly. And I have to say, I deserved it. I thought it was over for me. The next day, though, Brandon walked into my office and sat down. He didn't apologize, but somehow I knew he regretted some of the things he'd said. Anyway, he was quite charming—he can charm the fangs off a rattlesnake when he wants to—and in the end we understood each other. And I worked all the harder to deliver results that would please him.

Let me tell you, when you do get it right, Brandon will make you feel like you're on the top of the world. That's the great thing about him. When you do deliver, nobody is more appreciative or more generous with compliments and credit as well as the material rewards than Brandon Claymore. That's a big reason why I've worked for him all these years—and why I most likely always will.

20

George M. Tracy
Consultant

My wife used to ask me why I often can't tell her where I'll be two or three weeks in advance. I always explain to her it's because I have clients who don't know in advance when they're going to need me.

In the middle of a week when I thought I was going to be in the office for a few days—my *own* office—I got a call from Jake Foster. He sounded unsettled. He explained the conversation he'd had with Rick after Rick's return from Dallas and said, "I'm sorry to do this to you George, but if you don't talk to Rick, all the progress we've made may come to a screeching halt."

So I thanked Jake for letting me know, called Rick right away, and after a conversation with him, we agreed that I would rearrange my schedule and be in Grandville the next morning.

When I arrived at Essential, the receptionist called Rick's office and told me to go right up. To get to the elevators, I had to walk past the offices of Marketing and Sales, which were on the first floor. Halfway down the hallway between me and the elevators, I saw Vince Springer.

Vince was talking with a somewhat younger guy, a manager I recognized from the workshop. Took me a few seconds, but I finally placed him; it was Pat Tyler, one of the marketing managers. He and Vince were facing each other and didn't see me coming because they were locked in conversation. Or perhaps I shouldn't call it "conversation"; Vince was doing almost all the talking.

I was too far away for most of it, but as I got close to them, I distinctly heard Vince say to Pat, ". . . because that was really stupid on your part."

"Yeah . . . okay," Pat mumbled.

And then they both noticed me at the same moment. Vince wheeled about and, instantly cheerful, said, "Hey, George, old buddy! How's it going?"

"Not bad. How about with you?"

"Great! Hey, are you supposed to be here this week?"

"Oh, I was just driving by, thought I'd stop in for a cup of coffee," I joked. "No, Rick and I have a meeting this morning."

Vince didn't press for detail. He was already walking the other way, waving, chuckling, and smiling as he backed off. "Catch you later then!"

"You bet," I said. And then I continued toward the elevator, and as I did so Pat sort of fell into step with me.

"How've you been, Pat?"

He shrugged. "Okay, I guess."

To keep it light, I slapped a grin on my face and asked, "So, what happened just now? Did you get mugged?"

He stopped in his tracks, looked at me, and said, "Well, ah . . . now that you mention it, yeah, I did."

I spotted an empty conference room just across the hall. I put a hand on Pat's shoulder and said, "Come in here and tell me about it."

"Won't you be late for Mr. Riggins?"

"Nah! He can wait."

Patrick Tyler
Product Manager

Everything had been going really well. At least I thought so. Then I began to notice little things that were not so great. People began hedging, waffling on things they'd said or promised.

Once we got back from Washington, Sterling Grove had at first told me Engineering could have the design for Grasshopper—the BigBox AZ product—worked out in a very short time, maybe even just a few days or certainly no more than a few weeks. A couple days later, I called to touch bases with him, he said he wasn't sure when he could have the Grasshopper design. It was like, "Huh?" I asked Sterling what the problem was, and he became really distant and vague. All he would tell me was that he'd run into "complications."

I didn't know what to make of this, so I talked to Linda Wong. She's one of the team leaders, as is Sterling, so I thought maybe she could find out more.

But Linda came back a day later and said, "I don't know what to tell you. Something's happened, but nobody's talking. It's like the wall of silence is back." Then she said something that was totally as if Dellwood had never happened. She said, "Just do your end so that nobody can come back and blame us."

"How am I supposed to do that?" I asked her.

"We've done marketing plans without cooperation from Engineering before this."

"Yeah, but then things come back to haunt us."

"Just be conservative in your assumptions," she told me. I guess I looked annoyed, so she added, "I'll see what else I can find out."

I decided to do the same. I gave it one more shot and went upstairs to see Sterling.

"Can't you give me more to go on?" I asked him.

He was defensive at first, then finally said, "I'm sorry we just don't have time."

"How come?" I asked him. "I thought Grasshopper was top priority."

"Not anymore. Frank Harlan put us on something else. It's top secret. Nobody's allowed to talk about it."

"Top secret? What could possibly be so 'top secret' that the rest of us can't know about it?"

"Yeah, I agree, but . . ." At last, Sterling said, "All right, some how, some way, I'll get you what you need."

Two days later, he showed up in Marketing with pretty much the finished design for Grasshopper. He'd had a cost engineer work on it too, and I had what I needed. It must have been double top secret to do what he did.

Anyway, I'm in the open office part of the floor—in a cubicle—and the whole time we were talking, Sterling was keeping his voice low and his head down.

"What are you so nervous about?" I finally asked him.

"Nothing," he said. "But keep this quiet. I don't want this getting back to Frank Harlan."

He was like almost whispering when he said that. It didn't make any sense.

Now, this morning, we had this meeting. Nick Corrigan was there, as was Linda Wong, and a few other people. Well, Vince Springer joined us. It was a good meeting on the whole. Everyone seemed pleased that Grasshopper was moving forward, not as quickly as possible, but relatively so. Anyway, I had the price points for Grasshopper worked out. Nick was delighted when he saw them. The prices I'd worked out would still give us decent margins both for us and for BigBox, and yet would be very competitive against our own AZ and against competing brands.

Vince Springer didn't say very much during the meeting. Just a few comments. Afterward, once Nick and Linda and the others had moved on, he stopped me outside the conference room. I actually thought at first he was going to compliment me.

Instead, he just about buttonholed me and said, "What the hell are you doing pricing the Grasshopper brand so low?"

I tried to explain, but Vince clearly couldn't get beyond his worries about what this was going to do to AZ sales. And to drive that point home, that's when he made the comment about how "stupid" it had been on my part not to have run those price points by him before the meeting. And that's when George happened to walk past.

I told all of this to George. I concluded saying, "I didn't know he wanted to see anything in advance. I thought showing him and everybody else the prices in the meeting would be good enough. Wasn't that what the purpose of the meeting was?"

George shook his head and said to me, "Vince is trying to get you to be biased toward AZ. He wanted you to know privately what his own priorities are, so you will factor those in the next time without being directly told. That's why you got mugged."

Then, as he stood up, he gave me a pat on the shoulder and said, "But don't worry. We'll take care of it."

"How?"

He thought a moment and said, "While I'm talking to Rick Riggins, see if you can find a roll of masking tape."

George M. Tracy
Consultant

You're in a meeting with a number of people and everything seems to be going beautifully. Then there is a break or the meeting ends, you go out in the hallway, and suddenly you're accosted by someone who was in the meeting who now nails you for something you said. Typically, the someone is your boss, or in any case someone with more authority or organizational leverage than you have. This sort of private coercion is what we refer to as a "hallway mugging."

Hallway muggings are a common symptom of organizational dysfunction. They happen because people don't have the confidence to voice their reservations about an idea publicly. They, the muggers, feel they have to pay lip service to the idea under discussion in the meeting, so they exert their authority later, quietly, in the hallway.

There is a fairly easy way to put an end to hallway muggings, and I fully intended to use that method. But I didn't want to keep Rick waiting any longer.

Sterling Grove
Director–Engineering and Design

I came back from lunch, and as I walked to the elevators, I saw Pat Tyler lying flat on the carpet. Kneeling right next to him was George Tracy. I broke into a run, thinking, "Oh my God, something's happened to Pat."

As I ran up to them, though, Pat had a big grin on his face. George had a roll of masking tape, which he was using to outline the shape of Pat's body on the carpet.

A minute later—and by then there were probably a dozen people standing around—George finished, and Pat stood up, leaving the taped outline of his body, just like you'd see on TV when the police investigate a crime scene.

"What's all this?" I asked.

"You'll see," said George.

Just then Rick Riggins walked up with a sheet from a flip chart, which he and George proceeded to post on the wall using more of the masking tape. Written on the paper with marker were these words:

Important Notice!
Pat Tyler Received a Hallway Mugging
By Vince Springer
Today at Approx. 10:15 A.M.
If You Feel You've Been Mugged,
Please Report it Immediately
By Calling Rick Riggins' Office at Ext. 420!

Everybody who read it began to chuckle. I was about to move on, but Vince Springer came around the corner.

"What's all this about?" Vince asked.

Then he read the notice, looked at the body outline, and immediately began to blush. A big smile slowly spread across his red face, and he said, "Okay! Okay! Call off the hounds! I confess!" He held out his two wrists, like a guilty suspect. "Go ahead, slap the cuffs on."

Rick Riggins came over, put an arm around his shoulders, and said, "No, that won't be necessary. But we are going to leave this here for a day or so because we want everybody to get the point. Meanwhile, I would like you and Pat to schedule another meeting with the others as soon as you can to talk out the problem you had. That'll be your community service in lieu of jail time."

"Seriously," George told everybody, "we want everybody to remember that the rules have changed. We want to encourage everybody to speak openly. You can say anything to anyone—within the bounds of decency, legality, and all that—as long as you say it publicly, honestly, and you have reasons or facts to support what you say. No more lip service in meetings. No more bodies in the hallway. No more skeletons in the closet."

21

Rick Riggins
President

We talked for nearly an hour, but in the end there was really nothing to decide because the situation was crystal clear.

I felt I had lost face in Dallas, lost credibility at a time when it was most needed. Indeed, I probably had. I explained all of that to George, and he pointed out that nothing important had changed with respect to the facts of the company's business.

"You're not going to resign," he said. "You've already decided that. And if Brandon Claymore intended to fire you anytime soon, you'd surely have heard the word by now."

"True."

"So if you're staying, the only logical choice is to press onward. If you try to reverse the changes that are underway, what will that accomplish?"

I had to agree. Knowing what we now knew, to go back and refocus on SOS just to win some short-term appeasement from Brandon and Borcon Corporate was ridiculous. It would even be unethical.

"Rick, the main thing that Claymore wants from you is that you make this company successful. It's really that simple. Prestige, political points—they're meaningless compared to making the business profitable and getting it to grow. What you and the rest of management have started will achieve that better and faster than anything else you can do."

Again, I had to agree, and I felt embarrassed. What had happened at Leadership Council was the result of misunderstanding, poor communication, bad timing, and Claymore's own frustration—in short, nothing of major consequence to larger issues we faced.

I felt badly, too, that George had needed to rush to the scene, that I hadn't been more stalwart. I remembered what he had said in the beginning, when we first decided to embark on this course: *Rick, you've got to be a rock. You've got to be the bookend that keeps everything upright and in place.*

Commitment is always more than one decision. When you truly commit you decide over and over and over again with every test put before you. Well, on that day, I decided yet again that I—that we—had to press onward. We had to see this through.

George and I together called Nancy Quinn. We spent an hour and a half on the phone with her. By the end of the call, she wasn't wild with enthusiasm, but she gave us the green light to keep going with the initiatives we'd begun. She was going to be traveling again soon, but she promised that before she left she would make peace with Brandon Claymore and persuade him of the need for patience. Then, upon her return, she would come to Grandville, and we would give her a detailed briefing on how we were doing.

I felt just a bit light-headed after the call, I was so relieved. We had time now. But we would have to show results and do it quickly.

Jake Foster
Senior Vice President–Operations

Coming back from lunch with a group of people, I walked past the body outline on the carpet and read the poster. Everybody laughed. But I think everybody did a mental check to determine whether any of us had committed any similar "crimes" lately. I know I did the check. Even though I fully supported what we were doing, I never presumed that I was above the law, so to speak, or that I couldn't, in my zeal for improvement, have cut a corner or two.

In any case, all of us went back to our offices. I hadn't been in mine more than a few minutes when Sterling Grove rapped on my door.

"I was wondering if I could talk to you."

"Sure, come in," I said. From the expression on his face, I could tell something was wrong.

"First of all," said Sterling, "I hope you're not going to blame me for anything I'm about to tell you. I mean, I hope you won't be pissed off that I didn't talk to you sooner."

"I can't promise anything until I hear what it is, Sterling."

"Okay, but I just want you to know in advance that I really support what you and George and Rick and most everybody else is trying to do. I was walking by that thing downstairs, the mugging notice, and it convinced me that I had to step forward."

"All right, but could you cut to the chase, please?"

"Frank Harlan has put me and most of my engineering staff back to working on SOS. He's totally ignoring the changes in direction the rest of the company is working on."

I did a double back flip out of my swivel chair. Well, no, I didn't, of course. But I felt like I did. That's how shocked I was.

I'd been making an effort to keep tabs on Frank and the engineers, but I'd been stretched thin the past few weeks. I grilled Sterling forward and backward until I felt he had told me everything he knew about what was going on. Then I thanked him, shook his hand, said I would deal with the situation, and sent him back to Engineering.

I gave Sterling Grove enough time to return to his office, then went to Engineering to see for myself. Trying not to attract attention, I wandered the floor peering discreetly over shoulders to see what was on the workstation screens. One young engineer glanced up and froze when he recognized me with a deer-in-the-headlight look on his face.

"Hi, I'm Jake Foster," I said, stepping into his cubicle. "I'm not sure we've met."

As we shook hands, he said his name was John something.

"So, John, what are you working on?"

"Oh, just . . . you know . . . routine stuff."

"Say, isn't that an SOS schematic on your computer screen there?"

"Um . . . yeah."

"Didn't you know we're de-emphasizing SOS in a major way? How come you're working on that?"

"Well, ah, that's what I was assigned to work on."

"Tell me, how many engineers do you think are working on SOS right now?"

"Gee, I really wouldn't know. A lot, I guess."

"Let's find out," I said. "Pardon me."

Then to his shock and amazement, I moved aside some papers,

climbed on top of his desk, and stood up so that I could see the whole department and they could see me.

"May I have your attention!" I called out. "Could everybody please stand up and come out of your offices!"

Engineers with puzzled and bemused expressions appeared from one end of the floor to the other, standing in their cubicles and in the aisles outside of their offices.

"This will just take a few seconds," I said. "How many of you have worked on SOS today or in the past few days?"

A forest of arms and hands went into the air. I didn't bother to count them.

"How many of you are spending a significant amount of your time on SOS—say, twenty percent of your time or more?"

Almost the same number of hands stayed in the air.

"Thank you!" I told them. "That's all I need to know."

With a steadying hand from John, I hopped down from the desk and headed for Frank Harlan's office in the far corner. Every eye was on me.

"Should we just keep going on SOS?" somebody asked.

"I think many if not all of you will be receiving new assignments shortly," I said.

At this, a small cheer went up among those within earshot. Obviously, they perceived this renewed, secret push to fix SOS to be as futile as Sterling did.

Frank Harlan, who had witnessed the desktop survey from his office door, was glaring at me as I approached. His anger faded to fear, though, as he saw how mad I was striding toward him.

I shut his door behind me as I entered and said, "I want an explanation."

"Jake, this is *my* department!"

"No, this is not *your* department. This is *the company's* department. And I want to know why this department is disregarding the business priorities that the company president and the Senior Management Team and the rest of company management have established."

To tell you the truth, I wanted to fire Frank Harlan on the spot. But even though he reported to me, I didn't have the authority to terminate him on my own. I would need Rick Riggins and Pam Cantrell of Human Resources, and possibly even the blessing of Borcon Corporate, to do that.

He tried indignantly to lay a guilt trip on me at first. Claimed that I had been overly dramatic. That he had intended to tell me about SOS within the next few days, as soon as he had firm evidence that the problems were fixable. That the renewed work on SOS was intense but short-term, and there was no need to inform anyone outside of Engineering. That he was within his authority . . . blah, blah, blah. I refused to budge.

"Tomorrow morning at seven A.M.," I concluded, "I want to see you in my office for a complete, detailed review of staff assignments."

On my way out, I heard three or four of the engineers humming a song. They were in their cubicles working, but they were humming something. It was a familiar tune, but I couldn't place it at first. Back in my own office, the name of the tune suddenly came to me. It was from the movie *The Wizard of Oz:* "Ding dong, the witch is dead . . ."

CURE

22

Jake Foster
Senior Vice President–Operations

Not long after putting down the SOS rebellion, I concluded that I had to go to Rick Riggins and Pam Cantrell and tell them, "We need to terminate Frank Harlan."

"Are you sure?" Pam asked me. "By all accounts, he's a brilliant guy."

"I don't care if he's Albert Einstein squared," I said. "He has become a major obstacle to everything we're trying to do, and I don't think he's fixable. We need to terminate him."

It still took months to get rid of Frank—months of pure aggravation to my life—but ultimately he accepted the severance package offered by Borcon Corporate. He left with little fanfare. I personally helped him carry the several boxes of personal items he took from his office and load them into the trunk of his Mercedes. He had no parting words, wouldn't even look at me, just got behind the wheel and drove away.

No doubt about it, firing people is the worst part of being a manager. Even though I genuinely hated Frank Harlan by the time he left—he was arrogant, self-righteous, unyielding, devious—I felt no joy in watching him go. All I felt was relief that he was gone.

After Frank's departure, the atmosphere in Engineering was noticeably different. Took me a while to identify what that something was, but then it hit me. People were talking to each other. Of course, people talked to each other before, but it was always hushed, serious. Now it was open. The talk was lively. One afternoon, I was in Engineering and I heard something that I realized I had not previously heard on that floor: Somebody laughed out loud. In all the months of meetings with Frank and his department, I never heard anybody laugh. Not once.

However, the obvious question that arose after Frank got the boot (which Rick, Pam, and I began asking even before he was out the door) was, who should replace him? I considered promoting Sterling Grove, but I didn't feel he was quite ready. I wanted to watch him in action for a while. And, aside from Sterling, nobody else within the department stood out as any kind of leader. That unfortunately was one of the legacies of Harlan's reign. The natural leaders and the independent thinkers, knowing they couldn't win against Frank, had all left years before.

Pam Cantrell began a search for the new head of Engineering, both inside Borcon and outside at large. Since we hadn't waited for a successor before terminating Frank, I took over in the interim. I didn't plan to leave the position unfilled for more than a few months (though in fact it lasted longer), but in the meantime, my one personal goal was to smash the silly notion in that department that engineers could only be understood by other engineers. In every meeting we had, I made sure they understood they were in a business, not an ivory tower. If an engineer tried to impress or obfuscate with technical gibberish, I'd keep him in the room, drilling him until he explained the issue to my satisfaction in terms any good business manager could understand. The *business* value had to align with the engineering value. With few exceptions, the engineers eventually got the point: You're here to serve the business and its customers, not the other way around.

Personnel issues went well beyond the head of Engineering. There was Wendy Orman, our purchasing manager. Even before the second month review meeting, we removed her as leader of the Vendor Management Team. Had to. Her no-brainer approach to the supplier issues made it a no-brainer for us to yank her. That's not to say it was easy. She naturally thought she deserved a second chance; I felt we couldn't afford to take the chance, the issues being as critical as they were. We made Bill Albrecht leader of the team and gave Wendy her second chance with the status of a regular member.

She blew it. At every interaction, she either sulked or obstructed. Mostly it was the latter. Finally, George and Bill brought it to the Senior Team's attention, and we collectively made the decision to remove her from the team.

This action definitely sent a message—to her, and once word got around, as it quickly did, to a few other managers who were playing passive-aggressive sorts of games. As the weeks went by, it became more and more obvious to everybody who were the best players, the managers who were really going to change the company and create the future. Wendy Orman was clearly not one of them; she wasn't even in the room. She was on her way out.

I personally sat down with her to tell her the facts of life. At the end of the discussion, the last thing she said to me was, "Well! I'm just going to have to talk to my husband about this."

I kind of said, "Huh?"

But Wendy turned on her heel and left without further explanation. So I went to Pam Cantrell and told her what Wendy had told me.

Pam, in a hushed voice, said, "Didn't you know? Her husband is an attorney. Even worse, he specializes in employee discrimination lawsuits."

A couple of tumblers on the combination to Wendy Orman clicked with that revelation. There had been all those complaints over the years, yet nobody had been able to make her respond. It was more than just bureaucratic apathy; Wendy apparently thought she was untouchable. Indeed, Pam Cantrell was genuinely nervous about dealing with her.

Driving home that evening, I passed Logandale. I thought about that evening some months before when they were faking the shipment of an order because of a parts snafu. Thought about all those clueless people scrambling through the night to somehow make everything okay in the end. And I thought about Wendy Orman, home in bed sleeping soundly, with no cares or worries as to whether any order reached any customer. I imagined Wendy dreaming that night of her bonus check, the one she would get for all the money she had "saved" the Essential Corporation, and the party she would throw for the people in her department to celebrate their accomplishments.

We got lucky with Wendy Orman. Gloriously, wonderfully lucky. She quit. About a month after my heart-to-heart chat with her, she announced she'd accepted another job as purchasing manager at a medical center in a neighboring county. Gave us a mere two weeks notice; I said, "That's all right, we'll get by."

In the end, she bilked us for all kinds of things we would ordinarily never have given to an employee who quit for another job. We even paid for her going-away party, at which I'm sure I was burned in effigy. But the best part was that in the months following she hired key members of her department away from us. Excellent! My feeling was, let her raid to her heart's content. She probably thought she was getting revenge.

The Purchasing Department was one of those situations in which the closer you look, the more screwed up things you find. Like the filing system, which Wendy herself had designed and which was absolutely byzantine in complexity. You basically just had to know where things were in order to find them. There were any number of inefficiencies hidden beneath the relentless pursuit of low price.

The kicker? In many cases Essential was in fact not getting rock-bottom prices from suppliers. For instance, Wendy was disinclined to consider longer-term contracts (which often would allow deeper discounts) because that would mean fewer bids per year, which was the basis for her annual bonus.

It was so bad I decided Larry Oletta, her boss and the director of materials planning, bore some of the responsibility. I know Wendy was difficult to manage, but Larry had been totally uninvolved. For a variety of reasons, not just his nonmanagement of Wendy, I made it a goal to move him out as well. We simply could not afford people like Wendy and Larry, and it had nothing to do with their salaries.

I did discover a good surprise in Purchasing: Beth Somers. She had been there long enough to understand Wendy's filing system but not long enough that she had become a clone of the department's one-dimensional values. She was bright, well-organized, and learned quickly. I made her interim department head, and within a month, Beth had redone the whole filing system so that it made sense, and she was actively seeking input from other managers to find out what their needs were. I told Pam Cantrell to call off the search for a new purchasing manager, and we made Beth's appointment permanent.

Adam Bernstein
Marketing Manager

You know how I truly began to comprehend operational flexibility? I began to get it while commuting to and from the office. You see, every day I drive Memorial Parkway. I've taken that route for years, and let me tell you, it is a pain. The local joke is that it's called the Parkway because while driving it you feel like your car is parked. But the only real alternative to get from one side of town to the other is Allied Avenue through downtown Grandville, and that's even worse.

The civil authorities have never been able to figure out how to make Memorial Parkway function as an efficient conduit of traffic during most hours of the day and evening. Memorial is limited access, but there is a stretch of three miles with a multitude of intersections. Within that stretch is a big shopping mall, the campus of a community college, and a minor league ballpark that's home of the Grandville Grizzlies.

Over the years, the highway people have tried timing the lights different ways, but no combination of fixed settings works well. There is too much variation in traffic. For instance, when the college is changing classes, because most of the kids commute, that screws up everything for half an hour or so at odd times throughout the day—except during winter, spring, or summer breaks, when you'll sit forever at certain traffic lights for no apparent reason. If the Grizzlies are in town and you happen to be driving through when the fans are coming or going to the ballpark, it's going to take you an extra half hour, minimum.

And then there is the railroad crossing. Between the shopping mall and the college are the railroad tracks. You just never know when a freight train is going to come through. Grandville, more than a century ago, got on the map because it was a railroad town. Today, as the chamber of commerce might boast, that heritage continues! Trains of a hundred cars or more cross Memorial Parkway at random times of the day . . . as the drivers of hundreds of automobiles and tractor-trailers sit and watch.

Here's the thing: At times, I can make it from one end of Memorial Parkway to the other in twenty-five minutes. In a minivan. At other times, I could be in a Ferrari, and it would take more than an hour. And even if you put me in the biggest sport-utility vehicle on the planet, it won't go over a freight train. You just never know how long it's going to take.

See, if I knew in advance that a freight train was coming, I would take Allied Avenue, which is forty-five to fifty minutes even during rush hour. So it's a roll of the dice. Do I get onto Memorial Parkway and hope there is no freight train, no ball game, no college kids, and no sale at the mall? Or do I just resign myself to inch along from light to light on Allied? Or, an even better question, how can the problem be fixed so that the variables do not interfere with an efficient, predictable flow?

On a particularly jammed morning on Memorial, I watched five drivers deliberately go through a red light at a major intersection, I presume due to sheer frustration with the system. The next morning more drivers tried the same thing, and eventually there was a terrible accident. The day after that, there were traffic cops at certain lights, which reduced the law breaking, but if anything made the traffic situation even worse. The cops didn't communicate with each other, and none of them could see far enough in any direction to pick the optimum time for changing his light—so this was yet another variable thrown into the mix.

Anyway, it began to dawn on me in the months while we were dealing with the supply chain stuff at work that Memorial Parkway is a rather similar problem. Think about it. Two systems. One is a highway system. The other is a supply chain system. One has vehicles en route to destinations. The other has inventory en route to customers. By analogy, the intersections and traffic lights would represent stages of processing in a supply chain.

Let's stick with the highway system for a moment. How can we make that system perform so that any given vehicle can have an efficient, predictable path to any desired destination? Well, it's useless to fuss with the current paradigm; that's been done and not much more can be achieved. When the traffic lights are timed for "average" conditions, the results are still unsatisfactory.

Of course, capacity is expensive to build and maintain, and adding more is often very disruptive. The government could build a highway parallel to Memorial or expand Memorial to ten lanes, but that would cost many, many millions. Essential could build another plant next to Logandale, but that too would be prohibitively expensive. So the inclination is to maximize the productivity of the existing capacity. The government tries to make all traffic on the north side of town flow via the Parkway. Essential tries to make all inventory flow through Kenosha and Logandale.

When we load up the system with inventory (or cars) it seems like we're getting great productivity. Resources are being utilized to the maximum! Everyone is busy! Memorial Parkway is jammed! Is that what we want? No, because maximum utilization of resources does not create maximum efficiency. It creates gridlock.

What you want is optimum flow. Maximum flow might cause accidents—quality problems—so you don't want that. You want to enable the quickest speed that does not result in calamity, balanced against other factors like cost and demand.

Ideally, you want vehicles to flow through intersections with minimal delays and to arrive at destinations at fairly predictable times. Same with products and services going to customers. They can arrive earlier than expected, which is usually a pleasant surprise, but when they arrive significantly later than expected, dinner is cold, customers are grumpy, etc.

What prevents optimum flow? One big enemy consists of factors that are difficult to predict. Like freight trains. A cracked master cylinder on an old machine at Logandale, to use a story Diane Sullivan told us. A four-car pileup at the intersection of Memorial and Giant Mall Boulevard half an hour before the Grizzlies play. A QC inspector rejecting a parts delivery at the same time as a buildup of customer orders. You know these things are going to happen from time to time, but you can't predict exactly when. The problem is the uncertainty.

Early in the process, Diane Sullivan was complaining that the marketing forecast was always wrong. Well, it's the uncertainty factor! We're pretty sure a certain volume of orders will come over time. We know which way the tide is flowing, but we don't know exactly when the individual waves and little ripples of demand will occur.

How do you deal with uncertainty? In part, with information. If there were sensors at certain points along Memorial Parkway and the streets and boulevards feeding into it, you could count cars entering the system, so to speak, and get a computer to project what the traffic would be like ten minutes later at the worst intersections. Likewise, sensors on the railroad tracks would tell you when the crossing would be blocked and for how long. If Essential's sales force had good software that would transmit order data to the network, then Materials and Manufacturing could learn almost in real time when demand was picking up or dropping off.

But good information is not enough, even if it's timely. You need flexibility. Instead of having fixed settings on the traffic lights for average traffic, suppose they would automatically adjust according to conditions? And the highway network would adjust not only one light, but all of them as necessary in order to optimize flow in all directions. Train coming? Have electronic messaging along the side of the highway: "Freight Train Due! Take Allied Avenue To West Side."

The greater the flexibility, the less you have to worry about uncertainty. If Essential had a variety of routes within the supply chain, and we had a system that could quickly assess the best one to use, we wouldn't have to worry as much about the many variables that could cause a long delay and could cost us revenue. How could we get that flexibility without building another Logandale? For one thing, suppliers. Yes, making more use of suppliers might add to costs, at least superficially on a per unit basis. But the gains in flexibility translate into cheap capacity, relative to what Essential would have to expend to add plant and equipment. Why not use it?

Mind-set. The inclination had always been to stuff as much through Logandale as could possibly be stuffed and to go outside only as a last resort. And I do mean stuff the system. The great fear was that we would lose share by not having enough during times of high demand. So Mike Zarelli and Larry Oletta would cram the inventory through, and if it sat in a warehouse for a year or more, so be it. Salespeople didn't care. Marketing didn't care. At least the product would be there if someone ordered it. If we didn't sell it now, we'd sell it later. Then we began adding all those SKUs—and the system couldn't handle it anymore. We had added all kinds of choices, but nobody thought about the need for flexibility, for handling smaller lot sizes quickly.

What we learned as an organization was to move away from stuffing inventory into a channel and toward flexibility. We needed agility. We needed to be able to adapt almost on the fly when necessary.

As the months went by, we began to plan for this new flexibility. We moved to statistical forecasting. We completely threw out the old model of pushing inventory into the factory, into a warehouse, and then into the marketplace. We went to a pull model that adjusted inventory to actual demand, sort of like having sensors built into the highway. With Charlie Packer's help we made sure the sales force couldn't run red lights without being noticed—manipulate the system to give one order preference over another. We did everything we could to create a master production schedule that was stable, yet adjustable according to changing needs.

Ultimately, some of the best work Supply Chain did came by working with the other teams. We worked with Product Development to encourage common subassemblies that would work across all product lines, making these subassemblies relatively more predictable to forecast and reducing uncertainty. We worked with Market Strategy on the data aspects. Sales Effectiveness worked closely with us on software that would link salespeople's laptops to databases in Marketing and Operations. And after Wendy Orman left, we coordinated everything Supply Chain was doing with Vendor Management. The object of it was the same: Reduce uncertainty, increase flexibility. What we gave the company, in turn, was a supply chain that offered a big advantage in cost and performance.

As long as I work at Essential and live on the other side of town, I'll probably always be creeping along in traffic twice a day on Memorial Parkway. What I talked about earlier—the sensors, the roadside message boards, the computer-optimized traffic lights, and so on—that's not exactly Buck Rogers stuff anymore. It could be done. But it won't be. There is no political will to make it happen. Simply getting an overpass across the railroad tracks could take decades. Every motorist on Memorial Parkway thinks that's just the way it is. Well, that used to be my attitude toward supply chain. That's what all of us thought. We never realized what we could really do.

Jake Foster
Senior Vice President–Operations

Honestly, you could feel the momentum building month by month with every review meeting. Just from an operations perspective, we were making tremendous progress, moving toward flexible manufacturing with an assemble-to-order system based on actual demand. Even in a relatively short time, we had moved away from building to forecast and instead were scaling everything to the idea of replenishing inventory—as in, you ship a hundred AZ-150s, you build a hundred to replace them in the available supply stock, rather than building a thousand at a time just because those metrics make Logandale look more efficient. We were working on achieving a steady flow of subassemblies—that we were getting Engineering to standardize as much as possible—that could then be customized to suit incoming demand. It would be a while before we would achieve that, but we were headed there. Hey, if you're an operations geek like me, this was exciting stuff.

And this kind of thing was going on everywhere within Essential. As formidable as the established MO of Essential had once seemed, it was crumbling. People were getting behind the change, either because they genuinely believed in it or because they were afraid of being left out. I greatly preferred the former motive, but the latter was acceptable as long as the person wasn't faking it. Anyway, the number of people George termed "projects" was dwindling. Those who were unfixable were gone or would eventually be going. Unfortunately, Mike Zarelli was looking like he might be one of those who was unfixable.

Mike had dropped the ball. He had been given the assignment of finding global sources of production that would at least put Essential on a par with the likes of Spectrum. He just didn't get it done. He was "too busy." His contacts were slow getting back to him. He'd have it in a few weeks. Linda Wong, as composed a person as you'd ever want to know, nearly lost her temper with him. It was clear to everyone in the meeting with Linda that Mike just wasn't interested in delivering.

I had a talk with him. "Mike, this isn't like you. I mean, hey, you're a can-do guy by your own admission! You're supposed to have this global stuff sorted out by now. What's going on?"

He tried to give me the old excuses at first. Then he claimed that the global sourcing stuff didn't make sense to him. He didn't want to say it, but we were nuts. If the goal was greater flexibility, how could we achieve that if the supply chain stretched all the way to the other side of the world? On the surface, it wasn't a bad argument. But I explained to him, "Mike, we haven't made the final decisions yet, but from what I can see we're not talking about finished products, we're talking mainly about subassemblies, which have high predictability in demand, and certain high-volume parts. And we'd be getting them for such relatively low cost, we can afford higher inventory to guarantee a ready supply."

He grunted.

"What's the matter, Mike?"

"Nothing."

"No, come on."

"You want the honest truth?"

"Yes."

"I don't want to do it."

"Do what?"

"I don't want to move production overseas. It's the wrong thing to do. I'm sorry, that's just the way I feel."

I started to say something and he cut me off.

"That's *my* plant, you know. *My* plant. I was there when Logandale was being built. I spent the best years of my career managing Logandale. You got any idea how many hours I spent there, fixing this, tweaking that, getting that place to run *perfectly*? Going in weekends, holidays, middle of the night when there was a problem. And now . . . what was it for? You're going to kill the place and you want me to be the executioner."

I blinked. "Whoa, Mike, nobody is talking about shutting down Logandale!"

"Yeah, that's what you say now. I mean, that's what I'd say if I were in your position."

There was a hint of dampness at the corners of his eyes. This was more emotion than I'd ever seen from the guy. He straightened up in his chair then.

"I'm sorry. I'm out of line, saying these things."

"No," I said, "I asked you what was going on with you and you told me."

"I know it's just a stinkin' factory. But it used to be *my* stinkin' factory."

"Mike, in my career I've had to lay off exactly four thousand three hundred eighty-nine people. One night when I was working late I went back through the press releases and added up the numbers. I've had to permanently close two facilities. I've been yelled at, called obscenities, gotten threatening phone calls. I hated every minute of it, but you know, if you're a manager, then to one degree or another it comes with the territory.

"I don't know what's going to happen to Logandale. Will it still be running five years from now? Twenty years from now? Who knows? Whatever we ultimately decide we need to do, the years *you* spent there were meaningful and had value. The years of everybody else who worked there were meaningful and had value. You built good products, and you provided for yourselves and your families. But as you say, it's just a stinkin' factory, not the Great Pyramid.

"The one thing I know is clear is that if this company doesn't find a way to compete against price, Spectrum is going to run us out of the low end of the market. That pushes us out of the retail segments and leaves us with the AZ-300 and 400 series, and maybe SOS if it can get even a toehold in the marketplace. We'll be relegated to a niche, and whatever we can hang onto probably won't justify keeping even half the people in this company."

"I know that," he said. "In my head, I know that."

"Mike, if you want an early retirement, I'll talk to Pam and Rick and see what I can do. Whatever happens will be off your shoulders. But we sure could use your help getting things turned around."

I left him then to think about it.

Within two days, Mike was sending out the first of many well-documented reports on manufacturing options. Two weeks later, he had dusted off his passport and was on his way to Asia to meet people. Personally, I gained new respect for him.

Nick Corrigan
Director–Retail Sales

Vince Springer was right about Grasshopper, the product that was intended to become BigBox brand of AZ. He had fought it from the beginning, and sure enough it turned out to be a significant threat to our main AZ product line. What he did not foresee, what none of us could foresee was that Grasshopper was a threat not just because of price. Grasshopper turned out to be better than the low-end AZ models in almost every way.

It was scary. All those years, we'd been running the business on the assumption that for all practical purposes there was nothing more that could be done with AZ. That the design was bulletproof. That in order to make the company's sales grow, we would have to add features and complexity. We would have to develop and invest in new technologies. These assumptions, of course, were what led to the SOS debacle.

Yet, in a relatively short period of time—weeks to months, depending on when you start the clock—Sterling Grove and a handful of engineers had overturned those assumptions. And they did it with a little bit of legwork, some inspired technical work, and—the key really—management support.

Grasshopper was going to be cheaper to manufacture than AZ, yet it would have equal or better functionality than the AZ-130 and 150. It would offer everything that 80 percent of all BigBox customers wanted from this type of product and as high as 60 percent of all other users (even the "professional" segment) wanted. We would make decent margins on Grasshopper even if we manufactured it at Logandale. But Jake Foster had put together a fast-break team headed by Mike Zarelli to find high-quality, lower-cost manufacturing alternatives in Asia or Latin America. So we knew we could do even better in terms of margins once those arrangements were set up. There was even a realistic chance that we could beat Spectrum on every count—price, design, and quality.

Obviously, this put us in one hell of a jam.

Sterling Grove
Director—Engineering and Design

You see, over the years, a lot of us had had ideas about how to improve AZ. None of these ideas were revolutionary, but many of them were good ideas. Some were even suggested in meetings and memos and so on. Most of the time, though, the ideas never got beyond the suggestion phase. What kept the lid on was that the same question always arose:

"Is it really worth my personal effort to get, first, the rest of Engineering and, second, the rest of the company to think about a minor improvement?"

It was hard to argue that any one of them would have significantly increased the profitability of the AZ product line. So the potential gain was dicey. Yet we all knew that rocking the boat was frowned upon, and it was hard to justify the risk in terms of one's career.

Therefore, the basic AZ design didn't change for a period of many years. In all honesty, it's not necessarily a wise move to go tinkering with a proven design. All I'm saying is that when Grasshopper came about, there were all these ideas that people had filed away, and this was the opportunity to put them to work.

So we not only knew exactly what the product functionality should be from a marketing standpoint, we had all this pent-up inspiration to let us save a penny or two, to make this feature a little more reliable, and overall to give this old product a fresh design.

It got even better, too. I took the Grasshopper design to Logandale to have them make some prototypes for me. Yes, I could have gone to the Hangar, and in terms of policy that was what I should have done, but I went to Logandale because I wanted the everyday production people to have a hand in this. Logandale was still in the midst of sorting out their supply chain issues, so I can't say the timing was ideal. But to Diane Sullivan's credit, she worked the prototypes into the schedule. From that, we got an unexpected gain from the production people who came back with about two dozen suggestions on how to improve the manufacturability of Grasshopper, most of which we were able to incorporate into the design.

The sum of all this was that we had in Grasshopper what was probably as close to an ideal product as we had ever come up with. And we had done it in a matter of months, not years.

23

Jake Foster
Senior Vice President–Operations

Yes, the Grasshopper design was looking good. And somehow, I just knew Vince Springer was going to hate it.

Sterling and the Product Development Team presented the Grasshopper prototypes at one of the monthly advocate team meetings. These meetings were turning out to be a great way to get action and move forward because they represented a good cross-section of company management. Typically, all the team leaders were there, plus senior management, George and often some of his associates, and anyone else who needed or wanted to be there.

Partway into the Grasshopper demonstration, as the prototypes were handily outperforming the AZ-130 and even the AZ-150 benchmarks, I glanced at Vince Springer. He was biting his fingernails. I could almost read his mind: Grasshopper wasn't just good; it was *too* good.

We got into open discussion, and Vince at first paid lip service to Sterling and the Product Development Team, saying what an excellent effort they had made. In the next breath, though, he made an attempt to bring the whole process to a screeching halt.

"I hope you don't expect a decision on this today," said Vince.

"Why not?" Rick asked.

"Well, we really need more time to think about it."

Rick shook his head. "Come on, Vince!"

"Seriously, have we truly considered all the ramifications? We can't do that without a full program of testing and without a trial-marketing program, and we really ought to do focus-group research. We need more time."

Listening to him, Nick Corrigan was just about writhing in agony. "Vince, we don't have more time! BigBox is going to lock us out and bring in either Reliable or Spectrum if we don't get a hard offer to them sometime in the next week or so! It's taken everything I have to keep them patient this long! This is a huge opportunity and I need to close the sale now!"

"I would rather have us lose the opportunity," said Vince, "than go forward with what may turn out to be a huge mistake."

"What are you talking about?" Rick asked him. "There is almost no way that BigBox isn't going to love this thing."

"Look, everybody's done a great job, and I don't want to offend anyone—"

"Please, Vince, *please* offend us!" I begged.

"Why the hell do we want to give this to BigBox!?" he blurted. "I thought that Grasshopper was supposed to be a discount version of the AZ-130. If you give BigBox a better version of what we've got on the shelf, then we're killing our sales of AZ. Months ago, when this whole thing first surfaced, that was my original concern. Now, my fear has turned into a nightmare!"

I wanted to applaud. "Excellent! I'm glad you brought that up. Because if you hadn't, I was going to. You're absolutely right. We're going to shoot ourselves in the foot if we make Grasshopper the BigBox store brand."

"Well, then, what are we going to do about it?" Vince asked.

"We're going to work out the conflicts," I said.

"Excuse me," said Linda Wong, "but I think the solution is simple."

"You've got the floor," said Rick.

"Grasshopper should not be our discount AZ product," she said. "Grasshopper should be our premium AZ product."

"Go on."

"It's easy. We slap a BigBox logo onto an AZ-130 and send it with Nick to close the sale on the store brand. Shortly thereafter, we then do away with both the AZ-130 and the AZ-150, and we replace them with Grasshopper, since it outperforms both. Grasshopper has cost us almost nothing to develop, yet we can sell it for a premium price, relative to the AZ-130 we're offering BigBox. And as a bonus we also save some money by consolidating two models into one."

Around the room, heads began to nod approval.

"I like it," said Rick.

"Works for me," said Vince, "because everybody wins. BigBox gets a store brand that's every bit as good as our standard base model—because it *is* our standard base model. Yet we still hang onto the high ground. Which also benefits BigBox and us, since Grasshopper will sell at a higher margin. And the buyer gets a choice of lower price or better performance. It's great!"

Of course there had to be a naysayer.

"Isn't this whole thing just a tempest in a teapot?" asked Vivian Lebeque. "After all, it's still a reality that AZ is going to go into decline when Z3 enters the picture. In fact, aren't we going to look a little ridiculous in the marketplace, bringing out an improved AZ when everyone else is moving on?"

"Are you saying we shouldn't do it?" Rick asked.

"Well . . . no, I suppose not," said Vivian. "But there are going to be some smirks on the faces of our competitors."

"Fine," said Rick. "Let 'em smirk. Maybe they'll underestimate us. If we're lucky, maybe this will force them to reduce prices on their own Z products earlier than they otherwise would."

"I have to admit," said Vince, "that I am glad it was our own people who came up with Grasshopper. And I am very glad that Reliable or Spectrum did not come up with something like it three or four years ago. They'd have caught us napping. It would not have been pretty."

"Yes, well, let's not dwell on that," said Rick. "Instead, let's be sure we crunch the numbers to be sure that Linda's idea adds up. Barring some problem with the math, Nick should get his butt to BigBox with a re-painted AZ-130 and sell this."

Nick Corrigan was a happy man at the end of that meeting.

The best thing though? The fact that the company, faced with a thorny issue, could get it out there, resolve it quickly, and move forward. We had turned on a dime, based on a single meeting, and we were moving in a new direction. Six months before this, that outcome would have been unlikely. With every passing week, I could almost feel the company pulling together, becoming stronger and more agile.

Nick Corrigan
Director–Retail Sales

When my sales team and I walked into BigBox with the AZ-130 to propose as their store brand, I was as confident as I'd ever been going in to make a sale. Right off the bat, though, they started messing with us.

As soon as we were done with the presentation, they hit us with, "Why are you showing us your base standard unit? We want your premium standard unit, the AZ-150, as the BigBox brand."

So we danced around that one for a while. Finally, I said, "Look, for the 150, I'm going to have to get approval from my boss"—meaning Vince Springer—"and from the company president."

I went out to my car, called Vince, but actually we'd already worked it out in advance. We knew there was a good possibility that they were going to do this, and we were ready to give them the 150. We knew that with Grasshopper we could still outperform the store brand and, if necessary, underprice it in other channels.

But we didn't want to make it look like it was easy for us. Vince and I talked for a while, I told him how it was going. Then I called my wife, to see how her day was shaping up. We talked about what to get Billy for his birthday. Next, I checked my stock quotes. Anyhow, I kept them waiting inside for forty-five minutes.

I went back to the meeting room inside the BigBox offices, walked in kind of bent over with my arm twisted behind my back, and said, "Okay, I got good news for you. You can have the 150."

What ingrates they are. They were like, "Okay, now what else can we get from you?"

They started haggling over quantities and prices. We went back and forth for the better part of an hour. Finally, it was clear to me that they were not going to give an inch, in effect forcing us to supply the product under terms that made it very iffy whether Essential would ever make any real money from the arrangement.

So we walked out. I sent everybody else on the Essential team out of the room, and then I said to the BigBox people, "Look, if you don't want to play ball with us, then I'm going to go to Giant and QualityMart, and I'm going to offer one or both of them the 150 as a store brand."

And I wasn't bluffing. I had talked to Rick Riggins and the Market Strategy Team, and we had agreed before the meeting with BigBox that we were not going to close a sale just to close a sale, just to get revenue.

Furthermore, I had already talked to Giant and I had feelers out to QualityMart. I was more than ready to pitch to them if need be.

The BigBox people were pissed. It was like, "How dare you!" But I could tell they were scared, too.

We got three miles down the highway when my cell phone rang. It was BigBox's chief buyer for our category: "Hey, why don't you come back. I think we can work something out."

When we went back in the second time, I thought to myself, *Press the attack and take no prisoners.* We finally hammered out some numbers that satisfied both sides.

Then I said, in so many words, "Okay, now let's talk about the upfront money BigBox is going to pay us as a commitment to make the store brand happen for you."

We had never asked them for a large upfront payment before this. Most of the time, it had been as if we were financing their inventory.

Man, what a day that was. I was exhausted by the time we left. But so were they. BigBox is a tough customer—as tough as they come in retail. Hey, I respect that in many ways, but at Essential we had determined that we could not let them mop the floor with us any longer. We just couldn't afford it, even for the sake of not losing market share. Better to walk away, if it came to that, and save capacity and capital for serving a more profitable channel.

On the way back, I called Grandville and got both Vince and Rick on the line to tell them the news.

"Three million up front," I told them, "and we get half of it in ten days, the balance in sixty."

Rick Riggins was one happy camper. Because that three mil, while it wasn't all that significant in absolute terms, was coming at a time when the company needed the cash as a shot in the arm.

Up to then, that was one of the best sales I'd ever closed. It wasn't just the dollars involved. It was that I now felt like more than just a salesman. I felt like an owner of the company. A partner.

Jake Foster
Senior Vice President–Operations

To make a supply chain work, you've got to do the math, and the math is hard. The more we delved into it, the more it became clear that as a company we had never really worked out the math. Yet mathematics wasn't the main reason why the system was screwed up, and fixing the math wasn't about to fix the system.

There were all these various, but related problems. There were the turf wars. The arguments over the unreliability of the marketing forecast. Salespeople manipulating the system to ensure that their particular customers were taken care of. Production people manipulating the system to ensure that their own asses were covered. And on and on.

At first, Diane Sullivan and the Supply Chain Team did make some headway, and Charlie Packer was a big help in closing some of the systemic loopholes that allowed the manipulation to take place. But then there was kind of a whiplash effect. As I spoke with Diane Sullivan, she kept insisting that she wasn't getting enough cooperation, especially at the lower levels of the organization.

Well, after probing, it turned out to be the craziest thing. Everyone hated the situation, but a great many were afraid to fix the problems. Why? Because then they would lose control. The old way of doing things was screwed up, but everyone had a measure of control over the system. Nobody wanted to give that up.

"What if I have a bad month?" was the sentiment. "I won't be able to spin the dial and cover myself." It always seemed to be "what if I have a bad month," never "what if we have a good month." Of course the notion of control people had was largely illusion.

It took a lot of hand-holding—not to mention some gentle nudging and pushing, because we were not going to back off—to get everyone to believe that they would really be better off with a good system that they couldn't manipulate rather than a snafued system that they could mess with.

Gradually, yes, the situation improved. We changed the performance standards to put heavier weight upon customer satisfaction numbers and on-time delivery statistics. That took off some of the pressure, yet put pressure where it mattered. Diane and the team made progress in seemingly little ways, like working with Engineering to eliminate redundancy in part numbers. And longer term, they worked on standardizing parts—and later still on eliminating parts. In years past, in the name of technical perfection, Engineering had ignored or resisted those kinds of things.

It would be quite a while before we could declare the fight won. But I think the surest sign to indicate we were headed in the right direction was during meetings when I noticed that the sales and marketing people were actually taking manufacturing people's side of an argument—and vice versa. Like, "We [sales/marketing] need to give Logandale a quicker heads up on the AZ-300/B orders because /B options are a bitch to find on short notice." And the manufacturing people telling each other, "Screw the batch sizes, it doesn't matter if we save the three cents; Charlie's people say Southeast Supply gave us a special order and that opportunity is more important than being cheap."

Hey, what do you know? People were finally realizing that they really did work for the same company and that they damn well ought to support the same goals.

George M. Tracy
Consultant

Each team undertakes a journey. Along the path of that journey are five stages of development, and they pretty much need to be done in sequence. It's like driving from Kansas City to San Francisco; you've got to go through Kansas, Colorado, Utah, and Nevada before you can get to California.

The first stage deals with the team's mission and charter. We're bringing together a number of diverse individuals involved with different functions and disciplines, and the charter is a means of getting them to focus on what their team's undertaking is about.

"Focus" is an important word here. If you're making your way through Kansas, it doesn't mean you can't be thinking about your route through the Rocky Mountains just because you can't see them yet. But you don't want to think about the Rockies so much that you find yourself driving through Oklahoma. Likewise with the teams; they can and should be thinking about destinations ahead, but highest priority goes to finishing the stage they are in at a particular time.

As I say, there are five stages through which a team progresses. The first three are often completed during the workshop, although the slower-developing teams may be refining some of these stages over the several months that follow the workshop. The first revolves around the team charter, and when the team has successfully completed that stage, its members all can say, "We understand the issues, the scope of our work, and we're ready to move forward."

In the second stage, the team scopes out what type and size of opportunity their work should target; they quantify what is to be gained once the opportunity is achieved. There are typically three ranges of targets—low, medium, and high—that the team determines. In effect, the team is saying, "With the low target, we're almost certain we'll gain such an amount, even if things don't work out as well as planned. The medium target is what we'll probably achieve. With the high target the numbers are a stretch, but if everything falls into place we can make them."

The third stage is to come up with a work plan. The work plan has to consider the milestones along the way to completing the team's work, acknowledge the obstacles that will likely lie along the way, and generally deal with who's going to do each part of the overall task and identify any additional resources they will need. Once the team has completed the third stage, everyone can say, "We have a route mapped out for where we want to get to, we know the objectives along the way, we have figured out how we're going to work together, and we recognize at least some of the difficulties we're probably going to encounter."

Then following the workshop the team goes to it. They work at it week after week, month after month until—in stage four—there is substantive progress. And as the team reaches objectives and overcomes obstacles, everybody is able to say, "Look at the real gains we've made. We've dealt with the issues we identified back in stage one when we created our charter, and we have come a long way toward making real an opportunity that was just an idea not so long ago."

The fifth stage? This is arguably the most important of all, especially in terms of long-term, ongoing gains benefiting the organization. But that comes in due time.

24

Charlie Packer
Regional Manager–Field Sales

My brain has a pretty good, built-in bullshit detector. When I hear b.s., it's like a little siren goes off inside my head. It's been fairly reliable over the years, and has kept me from believing things that would have hurt me in the long run. When I first heard about George Tracy and senior management bringing all of us to the big meeting at the Dellwood, it triggered the b.s. detector. After the second day, though, it wasn't going off as often as I thought it might. If the workshop had been structured so that Rick and the senior managers and the consultants did all the talking to the rest of us, then I think, yes, the detector would have been going off every other sentence. Instead, I came away with the feeling that maybe this was for real. Maybe we could change things. Maybe.

Then, once I was back in the field for a few days, I began to think, well, the revival has left town. That's the end of that. E-mails from Tom Wright and Vince Springer were no different than before, and the b.s. detector started going off again. I figured it was back to same-old, same-old. It easily could have gone that way. So many times management will bring everybody into the tent for these evangelical programs. We hear the preaching, we sing the songs together, and then a few months later we're all back to our sinful ways.

I'll tell you, I never felt good about the crap I used to pull. You know, rerouting the trucks, juggling orders on the computer to get priority for

my customers, all that stuff. Yes, it did make me feel clever, and I liked it
when my customers were appreciative that I could pull a rabbit out of the
hat for them. But I never convinced myself that it was the right way to
do things. It was strictly survival. Because, hell, the vast majority of the
sales force did the same things as I did. I was perhaps just a little more creative than the rest, that's all.

After I moved into management, the larger picture became clearer to
me. I began to see how truly stupid all these little games were. But they
were necessary because of the games that were being played at the top, in
Grandville and in Dallas.

I thought for sure that the Dellwood get-together would go the way
of so many others. Then, to my amazement, a miracle happened. There
was follow-through. All right, it wasn't a miracle. It was just that people
were actually doing what they said they were going to do and not just
going through the motions. They were really going after results, and they
were not taking no for an answer.

In fact, I got caught on the wrong end of that. Diane Sullivan and
Adam Bernstein, the two leaders of the Supply Chain Team that I was on,
had asked me to be part of a subteam—a fast-break team, as George
called it—to look into ways to make the order entry and tracking system
more tamper-proof. On the theory that it takes a thief to catch a thief, I
was supposed to work with the computer people and with Eric Tillwell,
who headed production scheduling.

Well, Eric and I were supposed to have a meeting in Grandville with
Gordon Villers and some of his computer nerds. Something came up.
Something *sales* related. So I canceled. Figured I could just blow it off.
Tom Wright wasn't barking at me to go to it, and I didn't figure Vince
Springer would care. Back to games as usual.

Almost as soon as I backed out, I got a call from Eric. I explained that
this other thing had come up. If the fast-break team wanted to resched-
ule for the following month, maybe I could be there. Eric wasn't pleased,
I could tell, but so what?

The "so what" was that I got a call from George Tracy, asking why I
was, in effect, neglecting my duties on the fast-break team. I explained
again that something had come up, etc. And I knew George was a consultant; I didn't have to listen to him. If he didn't like it, so what?

Twenty minutes after I talked to George, I got another call.

"Charlie, this is Rick Riggins calling."

Oh! What can I do for you, Mr. Riggins?

"I think you should clear your schedule to be at that fast-break team meeting."

If you think it's that important, Mr. Riggins. No problem, I'll be there.

That only happened once. It wasn't just that I got the message from on high. It was that after the first few meetings, I actually *wanted* to be part of the process. Why? Because my bullshit detector quit going off. We really began to fix the problems. This was *not* a waste of time.

From years of experience, I knew where all the holes in the fence were. I knew how they needed to tighten up the system, yet that was not the biggest value my presence added. From years of experience, I also knew all the reasons those holes had been poked in the fence to begin with. If all we'd done, as a fast-break team, was tighten up the system and made it more restrictive, we would have failed. People would have worked all the harder to poke new holes in the system and come up with even more devious work-arounds—and if they didn't succeed, customers would have left and business would have suffered. We needed to make the system more flexible and more communicative, and I pounded the table long and hard to make that happen.

Did it indeed happen? Not overnight. Not even a few months. As we patched the holes, things for a while even got worse rather than better. Because as we made it more difficult for people to play games, a number of them got hostile. They were pissed off at us because we were taking away their edge. Their power. Some of my own salespeople threw tantrums. The production people, I'm told, just about got death threats.

But guess what. When you have a system that's reliable, that gives you useful and accurate information with realistic delivery dates and inventory levels, there is far less need to play games. You don't need to play the games, because you're not having the problems that make you invent the games in the first place. Fewer problems, fewer games . . . hey, guess what, my salespeople now have more time to sell! The good ones—and it becomes increasingly apparent who they are—are calling on new customers! Our production people have more flexibility to deal with the unforeseen and respond to opportunities! Gee, what do you know! We're bringing in more sales at lower cost! Everybody's more efficient! And the better we get, the more we can do.

What we'd had before was a downward spiral. What we created was an upward spiral.

George M. Tracy
Consultant

Some companies I work with, the majority in fact, are not in the condition that Essential was in. They're not hobbling about on crutches, to return to the medical analogy. They're not bedridden or on the verge of collapse. These companies can walk just fine. They can walk, but they can't run. When they need to run the 100-meter dash or go out for the marathon or just plain hustle to catch the train that's leaving the station—when they have to push themselves beyond the norm because of competition or whatever—that's when they find they're not in the shape they thought they were.

There is a state beyond mere health, beyond being okay. Call it athletic. Consider the companies that consistently outperform and outmaneuver their competition to be the corporate athletes, if you will.

Essential was ridding itself of the dysfunctional behaviors caused by insecurity and fear, and was soon approaching a state of health. Which was good, but the market requires more than just okay performance. You have to outperform over time. You have to become an athlete.

I mentioned that there is a fifth stage in the process, one that is of the highest potency. That fifth stage is the point in the process at which the athleticism develops. It's when the teams achieve what we call cross-team knitting. That is, the teams and their managers begin to network. All of the various initiatives become woven together. Teams start discussing knitting during the workshop; however, the real progress on knitting begins during this fifth stage.

By now, the teams are beyond just fixing problems and resolving issues. Now, there is mutual trust and respect. The incompetent and the dysfunctional managers with self-centered political agendas are being identified, isolated, and removed if they can't adapt. That clears the lanes for the healthy managers, the best managers in the organization, to make the moves and really get things done.

Ideas are flowing. Decisions are being made quickly. Managers can speak their minds without fear of retaliation because their comments might bend some executive's nose out of shape or contrast with some senior manager's personal agenda. Now, there is a collective vigor. Positive action builds on positive action, a sort of chain reaction of good consequences.

Jack Welch of General Electric coined the phrase *boundaryless.* When a company becomes boundaryless, its people can go in any direction, do anything appropriate to achieve success. They feel like nothing is impossible. This is what happens when the teams begin to interact and work together—often in completely new and unexpected directions.

It's a wonderful thing for everybody.

Xavier Estaban
Director–International Sales

The reality that I had accepted (and resented) for many years was that the company's so-called "international sales" would always be seen as a secondary category. When Essential management talked about sales and markets, they really saw in their minds' eyes customers in the United States and perhaps Canada. It had been this way for decades—long before I was working for Essential. For forever. International sales were an extra. An add on. The company would develop and market something for North American needs, and if it happened to have applications on other continents, then so much the better. But they would never start out thinking of the world as the market, with North America being only one valuable segment, albeit the most attractive. It is perhaps a subtle distinction, but an important one.

Slowly over the years, I had been able to get Vince Springer and to a lesser extent the Marketing Department to think of Europe as also being an important market. Lately, I had been working to raise their esteem for places such as Latin America and Asia. Yet the very fact that the company had three national sales directors and only one international sales director (yours truly) showed, I think, a definite bias. My own job title implied that world markets would always be segregated within the organizational mentality from national/American markets. I probably sound like a complainer, which I feel I am not. Still, I must admit I grew tired of my sphere of responsibility being treated like a third world country.

I do grant that it can be complicated getting products across borders. Those realities, too, I deal with every day. And, yes, there is sometimes higher risk and lower efficiency participating in the markets of certain nations around the world. Yet one need only observe that the expansion of global commerce has been underway for many decades now. Does anyone really think that trend will reverse itself? What are the long-term prospects for a company like Essential if it does not aggressively pursue opportunities on a global scale?

Toward SOS, my opinion generally had been neutral to slightly negative. In many markets worldwide, there was not much penetration of AZ, nothing approaching the level in North America, which meant with SOS we would not have to fight the compatibility issues. On the other hand, the high price of SOS meant we were not likely to sell a lot of units either. It was rather unexciting no matter how one looked at it.

Grasshopper was a different story. From the first mention of it, I was mildly interested because BigBox had a few stores in Europe and Japan. These stores did not stock AZ, but instead bought from Spectrum. Perhaps with a discount version of AZ, we could gain a toehold.

I was there when Sterling Grove showed the prototypes to the rest of the company. I had made a point of attending for that reason. I suddenly began to see new possibilities that went far beyond just selling to BigBox. So I put together my own team (myself and two other people) to look into the potential—which turned out to be considerable. By the time of the next Core Team meeting the following month, my little team and I had our facts together, and I got us a spot on the agenda.

The key to it all, as I told everyone when I presented, was the global sourcing of production to reduce costs. If we could get the cost down, then guess what? We could go head-to-head with Spectrum in any number of national and regional markets around the globe. We not only had a better-performing product, but soon we would be able to underprice them.

You see, Spectrum was the only real global player in the industry. Nusult had a small European presence, but didn't have the resources to expand. And Reliable seemed to have deliberately chosen to stay close to home, to focus strictly on North American customers and markets. Do you see where I'm driving? If we could outmarket Spectrum, we stood a chance to become the number one Z-standard provider worldwide.

Adam Bernstein
Marketing Manager

To which I said, "The number one Z-standard provider worldwide? Why would we ever want to be that, Xavier?"

As these Core Team meetings have evolved, they've become less and less formal—even as, shall we say, the intellectual discipline has become more rigorous. You'll hear somebody say something, and if it doesn't make sense, people will challenge it. And I don't just mean the senior managers.

"Striving to be number one worldwide in the Z standard right now," I said, "is kind of like striving to be number one in typewriters when word processors and PCs are about to enter the market."

Rick Riggins actually ribbed Xavier a little bit, saying, "You haven't been having secret meetings with Vince Springer have you? Because we all know Vince's stand on AZ."

Vince, with a smile on his face, put up his right hand and said, "I swear! This is their own thinking. You can't give me either the blame or the credit."

Xavier Estaban is a Hispanic American with an Ivy League education. Went to Yale on a scholarship, I believe. He's not very tall, but he fills the room with a certain presence. He has a polished, urbane demeanor and quiet seriousness that just cannot be dismissed. Xavier stood there solidly while these comments were made.

"Seriously," said Rick, "can you give me one good reason why we would want to be first in the Z standard when we know that standard is going to fall by the wayside?"

"I can give you not only one," said Xavier, "I can give you three compelling reasons for doing what my team and I propose."

And as he proceeded to explain over the next ten minutes or so, I several times felt the hair on the back of my neck stand up. What Xavier outlined was a multiyear strategy offering hundreds of millions in additional sales that made perfect sense for us. It went far beyond just the Grasshopper product itself, and it was clear that if we executed this quickly and well, we stood a chance of enhancing the market positions of all of our products, present and future. Furthermore, we could significantly weaken one competitor and relegate the other two to being also-rans in the market for possibly many years to come.

All of this sprung from a product that a few months before few in the company had wanted to see us make, that the head of Engineering had tried to kill, a product that was almost the opposite of what we had once thought of as ideal for us. Yet here we were, in a forum that in spirit was more like a New England town hall meeting than a classic business presentation, thinking in a whole different way.

We were no longer managers defined by the carefully chosen words of HR job descriptions and neat little boxes on a chart. We truly were becoming entrepreneurs, seizing the moment to take the first steps toward a global opportunity.

25

Nancy Quinn

Executive Vice President–Borcon Corporation

Was it the month after Essential had the workshop? Or was it the month after Leadership Council? Without the figures in front of me, I can't remember. Just as well. Their numbers were ugly. That I distinctly recall.

I flew to Grandville to see for myself what was going on. Brandon and I were still trying to put together the European deal, so I didn't have a lot of time—but I made time for this.

Rick Riggins kept trying to tell me that the past month, whatever month it was, marked the low tide. He insisted that progress was being made.

Uh-huh, I said in so many words, prove it.

He introduced me to any number of team leaders and coleaders and so on. And they talked about what was happening, and a great deal of it did sound sensible and promising.

However, as I was leaving, I said bluntly to Rick, "Look, I'm sticking my neck out for you. If this isn't the low tide, you'll be floating on it next time I come back."

Well, I put it a little nicer than that . . . but not much.

Had Essential been having its troubles a year or two before this, I'm not sure I would have had the patience—and I'm not sure Brandon Claymore would have permitted me to have the patience. Fortunately (and I realize the irony as I say this), a disaster was just revealing itself at the time.

With no prior warning that anything was wrong, our MRN Division had a financial meltdown. Lucky for me, MRN was not one of my responsibilities. I say "lucky" in retrospect. MRN had been our star business for the previous three or four years. I'd have given my eyeteeth for MRN because MRN's growth and profitability had been unbelievable! And in the end, that was exactly what they were. Unbelievable.

I suppose the good part, if you want to look for one, was that it really woke Brandon up. The division president had been delivering exactly what Brandon had been demanding: ever increasing growth along with ever declining costs. Only he hadn't been entirely forthcoming about how he was doing it. Eventually, when the math didn't work, he and the division CFO came to some kind of understanding, and behind closed doors, they all but invented their own numbers. Whatever numbers Brandon wanted, that's what they gave him, along with whatever rationale that made the numbers seem plausible.

Integrity. There is no substitute for it. And I'll say this about Brandon: He has always been a straight shooter—straight from the hip, quite often, but straight nevertheless. He was devastated that this man, this division president, whom he trusted so much, could have done this to him and to the business—and that he, Brandon, could have induced so much pressure that the deception was deemed necessary for success. That is, for what appeared to be success.

The European deal, into which I had personally put so much time, fell through. We had been struggling in any case to make the deal work, but the weight of MRN was too much. It clinched the collapse. Cash and other resources that we had counted on to pull the deal off were suddenly sucked away to cover the shortfalls at MRN.

I was furious at the MRN people. I talked to Brandon a number of times about MRN and repeatedly we came to the same questions. How could they not have known it would end this way? How could we not have known that they were straying so far off the path and so close to the edge? It defied all logic. All common sense. Clearly, the human capacity for self-deception is remarkable.

It was against the backdrop of the MRN meltdown that Essential came forward with an unmistakable turnaround. At first, nobody at Corporate paid much attention. Our attentions were consumed by the mess at MRN. As I recall, I was simply relieved that Essential seemed to be stabilizing. Then, as months went by, it became clear that Essential was doing more than stemming its losses; performance was definitely on an upswing.

Actually, I was a little concerned that Essential might be another MRN in the making. Rick Riggins had been on the outs with Brandon, so was Rick now stretching reality to fit expectations? I went to Grandville several times and spent a fair amount of time there. With the European deal gone, I had the time. And Rick welcomed me. He wanted me to see what was really going on.

He was proud of so many little things now. In years before, he had always featured the big-deal stuff in his reports and presentations. The "big wow" kinds of things, like winning BigBox. Like new technology that would make everything else obsolete. New programs that would bring in huge gains. Now he seemed more focused on smaller, incremental improvements. For instance, we were going over a report, and Rick made sure I noticed how much product returns had declined.

"Well, that's good," I said, "but what's happened? Have you improved manufacturing quality or what?"

"Not so much the manufacturing quality," he said, "but the quality of a lot of things throughout the business."

Like the quality of the sales organization, as he went on to point out. They were culling from the ranks the weaker salespeople, and one of the ways they were doing it was by examining returns from customers. The better salespeople had far fewer product returns, especially at the beginning of a new accounting period. Now, those games were being stopped, and the less capable salespeople, who played them the most, were being moved out. Hence, lower returns; hence, a much better inventory picture; hence, an improvement in overall efficiency, including manufacturing efficiency; hence, cost savings—and so on and so on.

That was just one "little" example. Rick kept stressing that most of the improvements we were seeing were what he called "low-hanging fruit." That these gains, while significant, would begin to fade, and the major future gains would come from strategic initiatives that his managers were putting together.

Naturally, I was intrigued. Essential had already booked a three percent increase in sales (and this at a time of the year when sales should have decreased) and a four percent improvement in gross income. Not bad, as far as those went. Now Rick was talking about keeping the momentum going, about cross-team knitting that was taking place and about racing to capture opportunities that had been invisible to them just a few months prior.

As we drilled down into the details, I found that this was not wishful thinking. There was a solid basis of facts that formed the road they were taking. And I learned this not by talking just to Rick Riggins, but by talking to any number of other managers at Essential.

This was what made Essential so striking in contrast to MRN. The main cause of the MRN implosion had been that over time fewer and fewer people knew the complete truth of the division's situation. Pressure had caused people to hide the facts to preserve their own status. Eventually, even the division president and the division CFO—who thought they were in control, who thought that they were the puppet masters—even they didn't know what was going on.

What Essential was doing was exactly the opposite. The company was turning itself around by keeping integrity paramount. More and more people, not fewer and fewer, had access to the facts and could see the big picture. Through openness, they knew what was really going on. By knowing what was really going on, they felt more secure. Feeling secure, they had greater confidence to take more risks, both personally and on behalf of the business. And again because of the openness, the risks taken would be smarter risks. Therefore, the odds of winning were higher, and with winning would come the reinforcement to make the integrity, the openness, and the confidence self-sustaining.

I spoke with Rick about this over dinner one evening. He agreed with me but added, "I hate to say this, but in all honesty, if we hadn't done something to end the dysfunctional politics and create a healthy organization, Essential could easily have been another MRN."

I found that chilling.

Yet it gave me an idea, and over coffee I asked Rick, "How would you feel about making a presentation to the rest of Borcon on what Essential is doing?"

"I've already done that," he said.

"When?"

"Leadership Council."

I blushed. "Yes, that's true," I said, "but I don't think anybody really listened."

"You think they will now?"

"Yes. Partly because of MRN," I told him, "but also simply because the directions you're now taking are interesting enough that I think the whole corporation would benefit from knowing about them."

"When would you want me to do this?"

"How about at the next LC? Only my thought was that it wouldn't just be you presenting. It might be more convincing if Brandon and the others heard the story from the teams and the managers as well as from you."

"Yeah, that's worth a thought," he said. "But . . . isn't the next LC supposed to be in Hawaii? That would be very expensive in travel costs and time to fly everybody across the Pacific."

"Well," I said, "this is between us. The formal announcement won't be out for a few days, but we've decided Hawaii is out. It's been such a lackluster year anyway, and with the MRN disappointment, the feeling is that a Leadership Council in paradise sends the wrong message. Brandon wants to hold LC in Dallas again, but I'm thinking of perhaps talking him into flying the Borcon executives here, to Grandville."

Rick was surprised. "I don't know what to say," he told me. "I'm not opposed to it. In fact, it would be a huge honor for everyone here. Still, I feel I need to talk to my managers first. I don't want to commit them to something if they're not totally confident they can deliver a good presentation."

"That's fine," I said. "And anyway, I have to talk to Brandon."

So we left it there. When I got back to Dallas, I broached the subject with Brandon. As you can imagine, I had to do this delicately. Given that he had blown up at Rick during the last LC and his current sensitivity over the MRN mess, I had to phrase it carefully so there was no implication that Brandon would be eating crow by taking everyone to Grandville. Yet I was forthright as well. It was time for real change, and Brandon recognized this.

It took a couple of broachings, but Brandon seemed to consider the idea seriously. Then he asked me, "Look, is this really going to be worth it, bringing the executive leadership of the whole corporation to listen to a bunch of middle managers?"

"Yes," I said simply. "I believe it will be."

"Why? What is so special about what they've done?"

"Well," I said, "I asked the same question of George Tracy."

"Who?"

"The consultant Rick Riggins has been working with. You've met him, Brandon."

He grunted in that charming manner of his. "I meet lots of consultants. The only thing I remember about most of them are the bills they send."

"Anyway, I asked this George Tracy what was so special about what he brought to the game, and he said that he wasn't selling anything special. Or exotic. He wasn't selling magic bullets or gimmicks. Mostly, what he had to offer was a return to common sense."

"You mean we've got to pay for that, too?"

"Apparently, yes, we do. He quoted Voltaire—"

"Who?"

"A Frenchman who died a long time ago."

"I don't remember dead Frenchmen any better than I remember consultants."

"To refresh your memory, one of the things the dead Frenchman said was this: 'Common sense is not so common.'"

Brandon frowned and let out a sigh. "I have to agree. Especially in view of what those idiots at MRN have done to us."

"Common sense disappears when politics, power, and fear determine decisions."

"Your George said that? Or was it the dead Frenchman?"

"No, *I* am saying that."

He was quiet for a moment. "All right," Brandon said. "It's my fault."

"To get back to common sense, you've got to eliminate the fear, share the power, and shake up the politics. It's simple medicine, but it's not easy to swallow."

Brandon got up, went to one of his windows, and thought a while as he stared in the general direction of his ranch, somewhere on the horizon. He grunted once more, then said, "Oh, what the hell. It won't hurt anyone to hear that kind of thing. Go ahead and set it up. Bear in mind, though, it's your credibility at risk if this isn't worth our time."

"Oh, Bran, you're such a sweetheart," I told him.

Then indeed I did set it up. Rick got back to me, saying, yes, they wanted to do the presentation. And I never feared that it wouldn't be worth my fellow executives' time. Fears that they might not appreciate the value of what they saw and heard? Yes, it's true, I had a few of those. Some of them would never get it. As the dead Frenchman said . . .

Adam Bernstein
Marketing Manager

He's not as tall as I thought he would be. You hear things about the guy, and somehow I always imagined Brandon Claymore would be, you know, as big as Texas. But he's only five foot seven or thereabouts. Not that it matters. It just surprised me. You can't tell from the pictures in the annual report.

We were again at Dellwood. By "we," I mean all of the Core Team Leaders, the Essential Senior Management Team, as well as Mr. Claymore and the Borcon Corporate executive leadership. Yes, all of the Borcon business-unit top managers, plus selected members of Mr. Claymore's staff. And George Tracy and a few of his associates were there as well, although they stayed mainly in the background, kind of as moral support.

It was seven months after our workshop at Dellwood and about six months since Borcon's last Leadership Council. This time, we were not here to change Essential's management culture or solve the company's problems. We were well along the track of accomplishing both of those. This time, we had taken over the Dellwood to present our strategic plan to Borcon Corporate.

And by now it was indeed our plan. Most of the managers who had been at Dellwood the first time had a hand in creating this plan we were about to present. This was a work of the best—the best people offering their best ideas and best efforts. Yet it was homegrown. It was 100 percent ours. George Tracy and his people had helped point us in the right directions, but this was *our* plan, no question.

As for presenting it, there were some nerves to deal with. This was a heavy group, if you know what I mean. To make it worse, the story had got around about what had happened to Rick at the last Leadership Council. My fear was that Brandon would start yelling. Even after all our hard work, maybe it wouldn't be good enough. On the other hand, this was the chance to show what we were capable of.

Rick Riggins
President

This presentation had been Nancy Quinn's idea. She thought we could handle it, and she wanted to show us off. But I never would have agreed to it unless I had total confidence that we could stand up to this group. I've heard rumors that some people said I wanted to get back at Brandon for the beating I'd taken at the last Leadership Council. That's ridiculous. This wasn't getting back at anybody. This was simply revealing the kind of organization we had become.

Of course, when we rehearsed the night before, it was only sensible for me to tell everyone how to handle Brandon. I said to them, "If Brandon asks you a question, tell him the truth. Give him the facts. That's easy because this plan we've put together is based on the facts. We've considered the alternatives to what we're proposing. We know the logic behind the choices we've made. So if Brandon or anyone else wants to argue with you, argue back. Brandon loves a good argument—and he respects the people who can prove their points against him."

Linda Wong
Marketing Director

We were meeting in the Dellwood's Kodiak Room, which is named after a large Alaskan grizzly bear. To my knowledge, there are no bears of any sort in the woods around Grandville. Whether there were carnivores here before me in the room, however, I wasn't sure.

That morning, I had overheard two of the business unit executives talking in the lobby, joking that this didn't look like Hawaii or Hilton Head or Aspen or Cannes or any of the usual "fun" spots that were the locale of past Leadership Councils. I'm pretty sure they knew I was standing nearby and could hear them, yet they continued to run down Grandville and the Dellwood using words and tones that made it clear they thought all of this was beneath them.

Remember, the change that had taken place, the elimination of politics-as-usual, had been within Essential, not Borcon Corporate. At headquarters in Dallas, politics was still very alive and very much a factor, based on everything I had heard. I expected for the most part a polite reception to our presentation. Any backstabbing would occur later, behind the scenes. Yet I wouldn't have put it past some of those execs to try to nail us in front of Brandon Claymore, to ask questions or raise issues that would make us look dumb and make themselves look smart.

The seating was arranged in a broad U-shape of tables and chairs, in several rows. The business-unit execs were seated around the outside of the U, with Brandon Claymore dead center in the middle. At the top left of the U was a podium and rows of seats for all of us from Essential. There was a large projection screen offset to the right where everyone could see it. Each speaker worked from the podium or could walk around in the center of everybody using a wireless mike. It was like theater-in-the-round with the Essential team as the chorus.

26

Rick Riggins

President

Excerpt from presentation remarks

Good morning. Less than a year ago, Essential Corporation embarked on a company-wide effort to examine the fundamental assumptions of our business and the ways in which we had been managing it. What we discovered about our markets, our customers, our operations, and ourselves as managers was very enlightening—and quite sobering. We discovered many strengths, but we also discovered a number of erroneous beliefs that we took as truths. We took a close, hard look at where we had been, where we should go, and what we need to do to get there.

What you are about to hear and see is the future strategy for our business over the next three to five years. The strategy we've developed received contributions from every Essential manager making the presentation today and many others besides. This strategy is homegrown, created mostly by our own hard work. It is practical, grounded in reality, yet it seeks achievable results that exceed Borcon's expectations for its businesses. The goals we have set for the business will, once achieved, confirm Essential as far and away the leader of our industry . . . with sustainable growth in revenue and net income, and return on invested capital that any management in our type of business would be proud to deliver.

Already we have harvested low-hanging fruit identified early in this process of change. These include the following:

- Thanks to a number of supply-chain improvements, an overall inventory reduction of thirty-three percent.
- An increase in inventory turns from six to eight, with target stretched even higher, even ten or twelve turns.
- A company-wide reduction of expenses equivalent to three percent of sales.
- Furthermore, we have also been able to help our field sales force work more efficiently, giving them more time in front of customers, which has translated into an increase in sales revenue from this group in the past quarter, despite very similar market conditions in the same quarter last year. Our intent, as you'll hear later, is to double the time the sales force spends actually selling to customers. So we think this increase will stick and that it is only the beginning of more good things to come.
- Finally, we have introduced a store-brand of AZ at BigBox with favorable terms for Essential (an achievement in itself) that mean a significant near-term increase in revenue and net income. And we have done this in a way that fits perfectly with our long-term global marketing strategy

Those are highlights of what we might call the "hard" results of near-term improvements. What I can't leave out are the "soft" results—the improvements to our management organization. For instance . . .

- Essential today has improved communication and cooperation throughout the entire company.
- Managers who have participated in the process of creating the strategic plan have greatly increased understanding of the overall goals of the business. They understand more than their own specialized functions, and this has resulted in much better policy and decision making.
- A year ago, in all honesty, we had trouble facing harsh realities when they surfaced. Now, we view harsh facts as friendly. They present in many instances opportunities for improvement.

Looking back at Essential's past, we can clearly see that the original growth of the company was rooted in, what was then, advanced technology. As a result, we became a company that was engineering driven. But as time went on, we needed more than that to survive and grow.

Even as parts of the organization continued to view technology and engineering design as being the primary drivers of success, Essential became sales driven. As you can imagine, this generated a number of conflicts and a misalignment of efforts.

Our original intention last year when we began this process to create the new strategic plan was to become market driven. Being market driven is what the stronger companies in our industry and many of the best companies around the world have sought to become. Now, however, in recent months we've come to see that we have the opportunity to become something even better. Our goal is to become market *driving*.

We intend to press forward with a market dominance strategy, maneuvering within the global marketplace to contain all other competitors to market niches. In the past, we once thought this could be achieved primary by way of cutting-edge technology. We're less arrogant in our assumptions these days. We now know that dominance in our business comes by superior fulfillment of the needs of customers and end-users. Specifically, our goal is to dominate within five years all growth segments of the world market.

Our means for accomplishing this are to improve continuously along three critical criteria, what we call the Three Bests:

- The Best Innovation in Products and Services.
- The Best Customer Relationships—and along with that the best understanding of the end-users.
- And to offer the Best Values in growth category products and services that we bring to market, with respect to quality, price, design, and whatever is foremost in the choices of end-users.

So there is no misunderstanding, let me assure you that Essential is not the best in any of these three today. But we will be the best five years from now, and we will use measurable data to confirm this as we progress toward those goals.

By achieving the Three Bests, we anticipate major performance improvements over current levels:

- At minimum, a doubling of sales revenue in five years.
- A tripling of operating income within three years and significant percentage increases thereafter.
- Increases in ROIC that will put us in the top ten percent of all companies in North America.

Are we dreaming? Listen to each of our managers as they tell you how we will do it.

Linda Wong
Marketing Director

Excerpt from presentation remarks

When we take a look at the market chessboard, we see a near-term problem glaring right at us. It's Z3. Longer-term, we've got great stuff coming through the pipeline. But the company has to get through the next year or two on good financial footing until these new offerings are ready. The only way to do that is to deal with the Z3 hole.

Now, as we all know, Essential is in this predicament because of SOS. We risked our money and our future on SOS, and that risk didn't pay off. Yes, SOS may well earn back its development cost and turn a profit, but that's years away. We need to make money now. It's no use to keep flogging ourselves because of that mistake. That's the past. Yet the question remains, how are we going to deal with this reality?

We need a Z3 offering. We don't have time or money to develop one from scratch. The only real alternative is to buy a solution. How do we do that? *Can* we do it?

Well, Reliable isn't going to help us. Reliable has already spotted our weakness, and they are moving fast to exploit it. Their Z3 models are already on the market. They're a good competitor. We have to be better.

As for Spectrum, they've always been a step behind in technology and a step or two ahead in terms of production cost and distribution. They're good at knockoffs. They don't spend much on R&D, but they wait until the market clearly makes up its mind about something new. Then they rush their own version of it into the scene. Judging from past offerings, we probably wouldn't want to put our name on their version of Z3, even if we could get them to go along.

But then there is Nusult, which has become a major player in the past few years, albeit a distant fourth in terms of sales. Market intelligence told us a while back that Nusult had a very good Z3 design. Yet we also know that Nusult doesn't have the marketing muscle—in terms of sales force, promotion dollars, and so on—to maximize the potential of the product, unless they want to grind it out against Reliable and Spectrum for a number of years to come.

Given our position, we were willing to bet that they might want to make things happen quicker and so might be open to some kind of deal. A few months ago, we made some quiet overtures toward licensing their Z3 design. Nusult was mildly receptive, but once they came back with numbers, the price was too high. We'd make a very thin profit, given the price points we'd be up against, and if Spectrum became aggressive on price, we'd probably lose money due to the overhead in royalties we'd be paying to Nusult.

So we had to become creative. My team and I noticed during discussions that the Nusult people were discreetly pumping and probing us about our plans for SOS. As it turned out, Nusult had an SOS development program, but it was way behind ours. They simply didn't have our resources, being a much smaller company. Long story short, we pitched a deal to them: What if we give you our SOS and you give us your Z3?

They couldn't believe their ears. It sounded to Nusult as though we were giving away the store. In fact, they couldn't move fast enough to close the deal. Within weeks, we had hammered out a cross-licensing agreement, giving us Z3 for a small royalty per unit in exchange for the use of our SOS patents.

Because of this, we're going to be able to fill the Z3 gap quickly. Our first Z3 offerings will be available before the end of this quarter, and the sales force is already taking advance orders.

Jake Foster
Senior Vice President–Operations

You could tell SOS was still a raw wound with Brandon Claymore. When Linda Wong brought up SOS, Brandon set his jaw and ground his teeth.

Once she got to the cross-licensing deal with Nusult, Brandon couldn't take it anymore and just about came out of his seat.

"Now hold on," he said. "I've got to stop you right there. Do you know how much money this corporation has poured into developing SOS?"

"Yes," said Linda. "A little over fifty million dollars."

"Well, I am glad you are aware of that. Yet, knowing that, you think—and apparently all the senior managers in your company think—that's okay to just give this SOS technology to a competitor?"

Tiny Linda (she's only five foot one) walked straight toward the Texan, which took just a bit of courage, given how agitated Brandon had become.

"Mr. Claymore," she said, "we are not *giving away* anything. We still own all the key patents on SOS. Nusult is merely licensing them. Furthermore, we are going into this with our eyes wide open. This is not a win-win proposition. This is win-lose. No matter how the market action plays out, Essential wins and Nusult loses."

"How do you figure that?"

"With Nusult's Z3, we get a premium product we can bring to market right now and sell it to a customer base that is five to six times larger than the near-term customer base for SOS. In return, Nusult gets a superior technology that is wonderful to behold and that, in the light of reality, is likely to remain a niche product that only an advanced minority will ever embrace."

"Are you not forgetting," said Brandon, "that Nusult doesn't have a fifty-million-dollar goose egg sitting on its books? Without that financial drag, don't you see, they can go out and price SOS much more aggressively than we can! How could you fail to understand that?"

She didn't flinch. "We *do* understand that—and much more. If Nusult goes to market with aggressive pricing on SOS, we'll be cheering them on. More power to them. Because at the same time, we'll be making more money with their Z3 than they'll be making with our SOS. Here . . . let me show you."

She went to the laptop that was running the slides for the presentation and brought up a spreadsheet with numbers on how several different scenarios of Z3 versus SOS market penetration might play out. Every variation projected that Z3 over the next few years would make more money than SOS.

"If you're stuck on making back the fifty million put into developing SOS," she concluded, "you can see that we're going to earn that amount faster with Z3 than we will with SOS. And remember that Z3 is just one part of the company's total strategy."

But Brandon wasn't finished with her. "Suppose you're wrong," he said. "Suppose Nusult knows something you don't. After all, why else would they have gone for this arrangement?"

"Nusult went for the cross-licensing agreement because they think the way that we did in the past. They still believe a new technology will always win over an older one. Maybe that will turn out to be true in the long run. But the question of who *makes the most money*, that's a different issue. In terms of which company makes money at the greatest rate, Essential is the winner."

"You haven't answered my question," said Brandon. "Again, suppose Nusult knows something you haven't counted on. You've just handed Nusult the ball. What if they run hard with it and score touchdown after touchdown."

"Fine. Let them. We'll still win. If they want to put their marketing dollars into SOS, that's great. Because if Nusult does persuade a significant percentage of the market to switch from Z standard to SOS, we can turn around at any time and go in big. With the cash flow from Z3 and the other sources, we can outmarket them. No matter what happens, we are going to eat Nusult alive."

Brandon Claymore blinked.

Xavier Estaban

Director–International Sales

Excerpt from presentation remarks

I'd like to introduce my new business partner, Mike Zarelli. Mike, please stand up so they know who you are. Six months ago, Mike and I barely knew each other. We both worked for the same company (at least in theory), but we almost never interacted with each other. Mike was in Operations, managing Manufacturing; I was in International Sales. We had very few occasions to talk to one another. There was in those days an invisible wall between our functions—and indeed between all functions within the company.

Just a few months ago, that changed. The whole company changed. The walls cracked and crumbled. And now I know Mike well enough to be able to tell you from personal experience that he snores. Not only does he snore, but he snores louder than anyone I've ever heard in my whole life. How do I know this? Because I slept in the seat next to him on the flight to Singapore. Well, at least I tried to sleep.

Yes, in the past few months, Mike and I have not only been to Singapore, we've also been to Shanghai, China, and to Monterrey, Mexico—together. Separately, Mike has been to Dublin, Ireland, and a number of cities throughout the United States and Canada. I have been to Osaka, Japan, and to Warsaw, Poland—and in the line of the same mission. Why are we doing all this globe-trotting? Because Mike and I are masterminding the launch of a new, and yet old, product code-named Grasshopper, a product that is the cornerstone of a global marketing strategy.

Why all the excitement over Grasshopper? After all, Grasshopper was conceived as a discount store brand of AZ for retail giant, BigBox. As it happened, our friends in Engineering did a better than expected job of designing Grasshopper, such that it could outperform our basic AZ designs. Fine, but as we all know, the Z standard is going to fade from the marketplace. It will soon be replaced by Z3 and by other, more sophisticated products like the Firefly design now in development and—who knows?—possibly even SOS at some point. Yes, this is the most likely scenario that will play out over the next few years . . . in North America.

What is going to happen on other continents around the globe? Well, overseas it is just as likely that Z will remain the prevalent standard for many years to come. Why? Do Europeans and Asians and South Americans and Africans and Australians prefer to be behind the times? No, of course not. Yet Z will leave those markets much more stubbornly because of one big reason. Because of Spectrum.

In North America, Reliable and Essential are the market leaders, with Spectrum taking third place. In most countries around the rest of the world, the ranking is reversed. Spectrum dominates.

Spectrum has always thought globally about its markets. It's not an American company, and though headquartered in London, it's debatable whether Spectrum has any specific national bias. This competitor of ours has succeeded not in spite of the fact it doesn't make great products, but because of it.

Some years ago, Spectrum recognized that Z-based products would become not only standardized but would achieve such parity as to effectively render them commodities. Our company, Essential, came to the same conclusion—though a bit later than Spectrum did. Our reaction was to invest in SOS. Spectrum pursued a very different strategy; they simply accepted that Z would become a commodity and aggressively developed the strengths that would serve them best in a commodity type of market.

What works best in a commodity market? Well, first and foremost, you want low costs. You want high volume. You don't necessarily want to offer great products or excellent service because almost by definition this narrows the market to those willing to pay extra for the greatness or the excellence. You instead are constantly seeking the sweet spot that allows you to offer good quality and performance at the cheapest cost to the broadest possible customer base. There is no romance in this, but that's the reality.

Those are the things Spectrum went after. Those and one more. You want the market, if at all possible, to have a preference for your brand. This has given Spectrum a bit of trouble, because Essential's AZ series really is considered the gold standard—the one that if all other factors were equal, most customers would prefer. Spectrum has found this hard to fight, even by offering their own Z products at lower prices.

So what has Spectrum done? In country after country around the globe, Spectrum has worked diligently to stack the odds in its favor by working closely with bureaucrats and politicians to write the Z standard into laws, codes, specifications, and policies. All in the interest of public safety, of course. Well, I say that with tongue in cheek.

That is why Z will not disappear anytime soon. Spectrum has codified Z. As Essential, Reliable, and Nusult push the envelope with expensive technical advances, Spectrum retains a huge safety zone that girdles the globe and ensures a continuing market for its products—until such time as Spectrum has its own low-cost version of Z3, at which point it no doubt will revisit the bureaucrats and politicians and have the codes and specifications updated.

It's no secret that this has been going on. Our main North American competitor, Reliable, has moaned and groaned about Spectrum for many years—and at one point tried to sponsor a campaign to penalize Spectrum in the United States because of Spectrum's political advantages overseas. The campaign failed, so Reliable has thrown up its hands, all but abandoned markets outside North America, assuming it was impossible to beat Spectrum outside our own continent. The situation for Essential is not much better. Because of our own national biases and our reluctance to explore global supply chain solutions, our costs ruled out any chance at real competitiveness overseas. Meanwhile, we've been preoccupied with BigBox and SOS and any number of other issues—as Spectrum has been out there conquering the rest of the world market . . . and ruling it.

Had it not been for this company's actions six months ago, we would certainly have lost the game. I am convinced of that beyond any doubt. This company would have patched over the problems, would have pushed ahead with SOS, would have promised the moon and the stars to BigBox as we had repeatedly—and within a year or two, we would have been flat on our backs. Now that candidness is not only allowed but encouraged, I can say that my only hope this time last year was that my own early retirement would precede the company's demise. Because the way we were running our company last year, *there was no way Spectrum could lose!*

Spectrum may still win in the end. We shouldn't discount them or underestimate them. Yes, we've changed our management culture. The very fact that I am here today speaking to you and able to say the things I've just said proves that we indeed have changed the culture. Yet none of us should declare victory. What we *do* have now, as a result of the actions we've taken, is a real chance. To be blunt, I think we can turn the tables on the s.o.b.'s.

Why? I think it's obvious. Thanks to Spectrum, there is a codified worldwide demand for Z-based products. And thanks to Grasshopper, we now have a version of AZ, the perceived gold standard of the industry, that outperforms all of their Z offerings. And thanks to Mike Zarelli and his colleagues and the fact that this company no longer considers offshore production a taboo, we can make this superior product cheap enough to compete with theirs. In many markets, we should even be able to underprice them. A year ago, this situation was unthinkable. Today, it's actually happening.

We suspect that Spectrum either never considered or they ruled out the possibility that we could roll out a superior version of Z. They have been banking all this time on the premise that since nobody else was putting development money into Z, why should they? We further suspect, based on past behavior, that Spectrum's strategy is to wait until the market shows a definite preference for either Z3 or SOS. Then they will charge in and do a knockoff of the best designs, or they may attempt to buy one of us—Essential, Reliable, or Nusult—using the cash flow from global sales of Z. I think they're going to be *very* surprised when we start milking their cash cow.

Mike and I—and the rest of the team as well—have been tight-lipped about what's coming. In getting the various bids and proposals for global sourcing, we started the negotiations by showing vendors only the older design for AZ—not Grasshopper. And in general, we're very careful about who gets to see the complete Grasshopper design. We doubt that Spectrum has any inkling that this is coming. Still, we can't afford to be arrogant.

After Grasshopper goes to market, assuming we maintain the element of surprise, our guess is that it will take three to six months for Spectrum to truly understand what's hit them. After that, they'll probably move very quickly. Our estimate is that Spectrum will be able to reengineer their own Z products to match Grasshopper in about twelve months. Remember, they don't have a very good technical capability, and they may not be able to match us anytime soon. But if they are able to knock off Grasshopper, then we've got a window of opportunity that's only a year, two years tops.

What are we going to do after that? I turn the microphone over to Vivian Lebeque to tell you about Firefly.

Thank you.

Vivian Lebeque
Product Manager

Excerpt from presentation remarks

Let's review the big picture.

Through our cross-licensing arrangement with Nusult, we've covered the Z3 gap. This should counter anything that Reliable has to offer beyond standard Z products. Because we'll be selling basically the same

Z3 and SOS products and because Nusult has a much smaller sales and marketing footprint than we do, it's highly unlikely Nusult will gain share or otherwise outperform us.

Through Grasshopper and our corresponding move to make this applicable not only to BigBox but also to world customers, we counter Spectrum. And we hit Spectrum in overseas markets that they thought they owned and that we could never dominate. Meanwhile, Spectrum has nothing to counter Grasshopper; we also suspect they're behind the curve on Z3 and have nothing with respect to SOS.

So what is Spectrum going to do? Probably cut prices—at least until, as Xavier explained, they can scramble to copy Grasshopper. If they do cut prices, that's fine with us because our production and distribution costs will be equivalent or maybe even lower, and we'll have a superior product. We can match their price or come close, and they should lose share to us. Meanwhile, their profit margins on Z get very thin, limiting their resources and their influence.

Xavier said that a year ago, because of the way we were running our business, Spectrum couldn't lose. Now, because of the way we're running the business, *Spectrum can't win.* Same for Reliable and Nusult.

But can Essential win? We know at this point we're not going to lose this fight. We know we're going to be a contender. The question now is, can we deliver the knockout punch to win?

To do that, we need something more than Grasshopper, SOS, and a competitor's version of Z3. Fortunately, we do have that something. If we didn't, we'd have to invent it. Within the next twelve to eighteen months, however, and possibly sooner, we're going to have a product that is compatible with all versions of Z—even with Z3—and yet extends functionality in a range of new directions. We call this product Firefly. . . .

Brandon Claymore
Chairman of the Board and CEO–Borcon Corporation

It always annoyed me they code-named their products after bugs. I mean, it's just a personal thing, but you know . . . Grasshopper? Firefly? I kept wondering when they were going to come out with the Termite or the Fruit Fly.

I suppose I may have an aversion to insects. Or maybe an aversion to things too cute. However, I have never taken issue with their choices. If I said anything about hating bugs, I'm sure it would cost us money one way or another to have all the silly names changed. Anyway, I'm really not that much of an autocrat. And let me say in my own defense that I've been working hard in recent years to be an autocrat only when absolutely necessary.

I thought the Grasshopper world strategy was very, very good. The whole thing showed that they were thinking in new ways. *Really* thinking. And they were getting value from what they already had—an older product that they tinkered with so it would now run the socks off everything else in the category. And spotting the way their competitor was locking in a market for themselves and turning that into an opportunity. Magnificent! And the way they were working together with each other, the different functions, to make it happen fast. That was great! I was saving my praise for the end, but I liked it. You looked at the numbers they presented and the logic, and there was almost no way we couldn't make real money off this.

Then this Vivian woman gets up and starts singing her song about Lightning Bug or Firefly or whatever. And I thought to myself, *oh shit, here we go again.*

I said, "Let me stop you right there. How do you know you're not creating another SOS?"

"For one thing," she said, "the investment in Firefly's development hasn't cost anywhere near what SOS cost."

"Well, that's a relief. So you're saying that when this flops, when this Firefly self-incinerates somewhere down the road, it won't be as *huge* a loss."

"We don't expect *any* loss. We expect that Firefly will be a big winner, possibly the biggest in the company's history."

"Of course you think that, or you wouldn't be recommending this thing," I told her. "But my thoughts run along the lines of once burned, twice careful."

"Mr. Claymore—"

"Brandon," I countered. "If you're qualified to be in one of these presentations, you're qualified to call me by my first name."

"Brandon, SOS was a mistake. On the other hand, if we retreat from all future opportunities, we surely will incur more risk to the business than we would by doing nothing in the name of being careful."

"Yes, I do agree," I said. "I also agree that this particular business of yours, ours, does require and benefit from a technological edge. But how much of an edge do you really need? What is it going to cost you? How much is the customer willing to pay for?"

"Absolutely. We've considered those issues."

"Suppose you've miscalculated. Suppose the research is flawed. Suppose the customers you're so certain will love this thing do indeed love it, but don't buy it. Because after all, how many times has that happened? You produce a million of this whiz-bang thing, and then when you get in front of the customer it's too expensive or the market goes flat or what have you. What are you going to do then?"

"We'll do what makes sense. We'll cut our losses, which won't be excessive, because we won't have a million of these sitting around."

"You're sure of that?"

"We—all of us—now have access to all the numbers and facts that we need. We have access to each other. Nobody is locked out. Nobody is insulated. If the situation goes against us, we can change direction very quickly."

"You believe that?"

"Yes. It's for real. Six months ago it wasn't, but now it is. The fact that I'm standing here in front of you is proof of that. So is the fact that we're about to challenge the world market with a product—I'm talking about Grasshopper—that didn't exist two quarters ago. Do you realize, Brandon, that Firefly was once politically incorrect in this company? And that was not very long ago. Today I can honestly tell you that there is nothing in this company related to the running of the business that is politically incorrect. Whatever needs to be said *is* said. Differences of opinion are encouraged. We run the business on the basis of the facts, and the facts tell us that we have a likely winner. If we don't, then we have a development team and process in place now that can produce other winners to replace it. Would you like to know more about that?"

"Yes, I would," I told her. "Very much I would."

I began to relax then. Vivian went on to demonstrate that she and the others had thought through the significant possible outcomes, from failure through runaway success. At times, I interrupted and asked questions, and at various points other managers of the company chimed in with support or comments—to the extent that as the morning wore on, the event became less of a formal business presentation and more like an extended conversation around a dinner table. I preferred it that way. In my experience, formal presentations can hide as much truth as they reveal. Better to have an open discussion.

After Vivian, one of their engineering managers, a fellow named Silver-something . . . no, his name was Sterling, I believe, got up and described the company's development process and how this would become the engine of growth for the future. I was encouraged to hear him say that the service side of the business was being examined and pursued with far greater vigor than in the past. However, I was skeptical that they could come up with a major new offering every few years. If they could, fine; but it seemed to me that a continuing stream of incremental improvements—small steps rather than giant leaps—would be the more practical way to achieve the desired result. But in any case, that was not what was most important.

If you just took what they had actually done, the individual changes in themselves were not all that earth-shattering. They had axed a turkey—SOS. They had come up with a couple of new products codenamed after bugs. They had come up with a disciplined development process for creating new products and services. They had solved some supply chain issues and had moved to a global outlook in terms of production. They were putting in place a much improved information and reporting system. They had reorganized the sales force and done a number of little things to make it more productive. And so on and so forth. Well . . . it *was* a rather impressive list taken in sum.

Yet the great part was how it all worked together. It was more than a list of improvements, it was a multifaceted total solution. There was a low-cost design concept . . . that augmented a supply chain makeover meaning cost and delivery advantages . . . that offered synergies for a global marketing strategy . . . enhanced by an increasingly productive sales force . . . that would propel ongoing innovation in products and services! Imagine!

And there would be an initiative manager, soon to be named, who would report directly to the Senior Team and coordinate what was going on. Every action proposed had clear objectives and was aligned with Essential's total strategy. Furthermore, the objectives and financial targets were linked to Borcon Corporate's P&L and five-year targets. All ducks were in-line! Let me tell you, this was way more disciplined and clearsighted than anything the other Borcon units were doing.

To my right and to my left sat the executives of the Corporation's other businesses. It had been a bit of a gamble—well, really a gamble on the part of Nancy Quinn—to bring the Leadership Council to Essential. But the gamble had paid off. I had gotten their attention. Every so often, if there wasn't an outright comment from one of the business unit presidents, I would notice an appreciative nod of the head, or one of them trying to catch the eye of a staffer when one of the Essential managers said something of larger significance. Just think, what could this corporation become if all of its businesses could come around the way Essential had?

I have invested my life in this entity known as the Borcon Corporation. For what? For money? For greater and greater levels of wealth? Not really. It's more than the money. It's always more than the money, as nearly everyone at the top will tell you. It's the challenge. It's the great game of it all. It's the love of winning.

At the end of the day, I began the applause and as the others around me joined in I got to my feet. We all stood and applauded the Essential managers. Later, in due time, there would be more tangible rewards, but for now this ovation carried an abundance of meaning. I looked from face to face. Rick Riggins, a man redeemed. That new fellow, Jake Foster. Next to him, Vince Springer—and I saw him turn to Jake and shake hands. Linda Wong, the marketing head, with a beaming smile. Xavier Estaban—what a fine surprise he turned out to be. And the engineer, Sterling. And all the others. You could see the same thing on every face. They knew what they had done, knew who they were.

They were winners.

Epilogue

Rick Riggins
President

How often does any plan work out exactly as expected? As it happened, we missed something. There was a significant flaw in the market research we were applying. Turned out we had not been giving sufficient weight to the experience levels of the end-user. Those who had been using Z products for longer periods of time were less swayed by low price. Instead, they wanted specific combinations of options. Some, like the contractor/installers, wanted a simple way to program settings on the device once they were at the job site. So as the user base grew more knowledgeable, their choices became more sophisticated. A rock-bottom price often was not the most important thing. We didn't know any of that until a year or two after the strategic plan had been created.

There were other things. The entire industry went into a slump. It's pretty hard to strive for doubling your sales when the market just isn't buying. And Spectrum proved to be far more resilient on a global scale than we thought, especially in markets where a great many transactions happen under the table. We had to pull out of certain markets because we just couldn't get past the corruption.

But that was okay. We adapted. And we did it quickly without getting bogged down in turf wars. That's the great thing we gained by changing how we managed. We gained agility. Rather than drifting with the inertia of the past, we can bring everyone together, get agreement on the facts, and change course quickly. And we're doing this as a matter of everyday business.

It's been over three years since the presentation to Brandon Claymore and the Borcon executives. Despite setbacks, we are on an annual basis very close to making the targets we set. The industry began coming out of the slump nine months ago, and we now are outpacing everybody. You see, even healthy people occasionally get sick. But when you're healthy, you recover and get well faster. That's what's happened to Essential. Spectrum lost money last year, mainly because of their Z products unit, and may show a net loss for this year. Reliable went all of last year in the red. But Essential was never out of the black because we spotted the change in the market early, cut inventory and costs quickly, and moved aggressively with innovative services in areas unaffected by the slump. It was a great move. Yet the last thing I want this company to be is arrogant.

Looking back, it's not a matter of how good you are; it's a matter of how fast you're getting better. Success easily becomes a setup for future failure. This company's success with AZ almost led us to ruin. It led us to assumptions we never should have made. It gave us a sense of security. We thought we couldn't fail. Will that ever happen again? Hey, we're gaining share on everybody! We've never been this profitable!

You see? That's what I worry about.

Change is not about running the same old race faster; it's about finding better ways to run. It's about figuring out what kind of race you can win. If we can't win a sprint, maybe we can win a marathon. If we can't be competitive in either a marathon or a sprint, maybe we play football. Or whatever! No matter who you are, there is a game you can win.

How's everybody else doing? Well . . . we lost Jake Foster. Not to cancer. We lost him to Corporate. He's now working hand-in-hand with George Tracy to bring the kind of change Essential achieved to all the other business units. I understand his wife, Sandy, just about strangled him when he suggested the move to Dallas, but she's fine now. Grandville was a little . . . remote for her. Jake has become a contender for a vice president's position at Corporate.

Vince Springer was tapped to take over the MRN unit of Borcon. Vince is very much like someone who's seen the light. He was a reluctant convert who became zealous once the transformation took hold. There's no stopping him.

I moved Linda Wong into Vince's spot at the head of Sales and Marketing. Adam Bernstein is now head of Marketing. Most of the people who were on the original Core Team have moved up a level or two on the organization chart. One exception is Sterling Grove, who is where he has been, the head of Design Services, and when I talk to him, I hear no complaints. Not everybody wants positions of greater responsibility. Diane Sullivan is now running Engineering.

Mike Zarelli retired a few months ago. I see him on the lake fishing and occasionally on the golf course. Bill Albrecht is now Director of Production, which includes both Material Resources and Manufacturing. And Logandale is still very much in operation, though mainly as a final assembly plant for quick-turnaround, customized orders, which have become a significant source of income for us. The plant doesn't try to do soup-to-nuts manufacturing anymore. Most subassemblies come from Asia, and the high-volume, shrink-wrapped stuff is produced in Mexico, Ireland, or Kenosha, Wisconsin.

Frank Harlan tried to start his own company after the noncompete clause in his contract expired. He was going to start a company that would make a variant of SOS but couldn't find enough backers. Now he's an engineering consultant. Last word on Wendy Orman was that she was getting her law degree. As I said earlier, you've got to find the race you can win.

And me? I always perceived Essential as a stop along the way to taking over Brandon Claymore's office. I'm not lying when I say I don't want Brandon's job anymore—or anything else at Corporate. This has become a great business. Why would I want to leave it? We're having fun. I'm staying.

Acknowledgments

The Cure could not have been written without the experience and help of many people. First among all for the authors' thanks are the clients of GMT Consulting. Enterprise Medicine is not a theory; it is a practice based upon actual experience with management at more than 200 companies over many years. We thank you for the opportunity to work with you. Please consider this book a tribute to your vision, self-confidence, and courage to open up your businesses to the type of boundaryless honesty and accessibility so essential to the journey described in *The Cure*.

There are three specific individuals who deserve special thanks. One is Randy Larrimore, a Harvard MBA and former McKinsey consultant who grew into a group executive and CEO. He provided us with experiences in a wide diversity of businesses including Moen, Master Lock, Aristokraft, Titleist, FootJoy, Waterloo (Craftsman Toolboxes), and United Stationers. Randy is an executive who "got it" from the beginning, who understood the power of Enterprise Medicine practically from the first time we described it to him. He has been a valuable ally over the years, and we have learned tremendously through our association with Randy.

Another is Frank Feraco, a "sales guy" who grew into a highly intuitive and dynamic executive. In our many years of working with Frank, he invested his energy in the success of Kohler, Textron, Danaher, Emerson, Coleman, Sterling, and Porter-Cable/Delta. Everyone at GMT has appreciated his trust and confidence in our abilities. All of us have grown personally and professionally by virtue of our relationship with Frank.

Yet another is Mike Hoopis, a "manufacturing guy" when we first met him who has grown to become an enterprise leader. Working with Mike in Stiffel Lamp, PricePfister, Black & Decker, and WaterPik Technologies helped us learn about global strategy and about managing a supply chain, and we are very appreciative of his trust in us. It was by working with Mike that we came to develop Innovation University, a concept we use today in many clients.

To Mike, Frank, and Randy, our sincere thanks. We could not have developed and demonstrated the power of Enterprise Medicine without you.

In addition, the authors would like to thank the partners of GMT Consulting—Rick McAllister, Bob MacDonald, and Dave Webb—for reading and commenting upon the drafts of the manuscript, and for lending their expertise to the project. Of special note are the efforts of Bob MacDonald, who developed the business model for the fictional company and industry described in the novel, and whose insights were extremely valuable in enhancing the realism of the story.

Bob Cecil and Alan Komm, GMT associates, made significant contributions to the project and provided an excellent window into their consulting experiences in a wide variety of businesses and management functions; we thank them for sharing their experiences.

Our sincere appreciation goes to Matthew Holt, our editor at Wiley, who recognized the value of *The Cure* and believed in its potential, and to the many others who helped produce the book. Your efforts did not go unnoticed.

And finally, Dan Paul would like to express his gratitude to his parents—to his mother, Barbara, who encouraged in him the positive thinking to believe that Enterprise Medicine was possible; and to his father, Harold, who taught Dan his first lessons in business and provided him a role model for honesty, integrity, and the value of hard work.

Dan offers special thanks as well to his wife, Diane, and their two sons, Danny and David. Thank you for believing in the importance of his work over many years and the family sacrifices it required.

Jeff Cox would like to thank Peg Reidy, MD, and Ira Handler, MD, for their suggestions with respect to medical aspects of the story. He offers his love and appreciation to his wife, Sue, who gave him invaluable insight into the thinking and day-to-day experiences of a senior manager. And he gives his love as well to his children, Hannah and David, the reason he works so hard.

Our thanks to all of you.